INVENTING EUROPE

By the same author (forthcoming)

*RETHINKING IRISH HISTORY (with Patrick O'Mahony)

* *also to be published by Macmillan*

Inventing Europe

Idea, Identity, Reality

Gerard Delanty

Senior Researcher
Centre for European Social Research
University College Cork
Ireland

First published 1995 by
MACMILLAN PRESS LTD
Houndmills, Basingstoke, Hampshire RG21 2XS
and London
Companies and representatives
throughout the world

ISBN 0–333–62202–2 hardcover
ISBN 0–333–62203–0 paperback

A catalogue record for this book is available
from the British Library.

10   9   8   7   6   5   4   3   2   1
04 03 02 01 00 99 98 97 96 95

Typeset by 🅰 Tek Art, Croydon, Surrey

Printed in Great Britain by
Mackays of Chatham PLC
Chatham, Kent

Contents

Preface

The twentieth century, the most destructive century in human history, is now drawing to a close and as it does so it is timely that we reflect on one of its most enduring themes, the European idea. A critique on the idea of Europe is long overdue. While there are many books on nationalism, racism and fascism in the broader perspective of history, there is no systematic and critical study of the idea of Europe in relation to the politics of identity in the modern polity. The idea of Europe is a major aspect of modern political culture and is astonishingly under-researched. Most discussions on the idea of Europe tend to take a particularly unreflective nature without any regard being given to the wider historical context and the political consciousness accompanying it. There are several studies on the idea of the Orient as a European construction while the idea of Europe itself as an invention has never been scrutinised. The mystique of the nation has also been finally subjected to major intellectual critiques, yet nothing has been written to dispel the myth of Europe as a unifying and universalising project.

The present study emerged out of my research and teaching on national identity and political culture over the past five years. One of the most striking features of European identity is that the dynamics involved in its invention are not unlike the process by which regional identities were superseded by national identities in the nineteenth century. In particular, it also strikes me quite forcibly that, like nationality, it was also in adversity that the European idea emerged and was sustained more by conflict and division than by consensus and peace. Macro-identities, such as the European idea, the national idea or religious world-views, are more commonly divisive than unifying and are frequently products of enforced and violent homogenisation. We can quite well reflect on whether we need such 'identities'.

Given that European identity has become the burning political issue in recent times, it is a matter of some surprise that a book has not as yet addressed itself to this problem. With the collapse of the Cold War and the consensus that sustained it, our view of the European past and present has undergone a major revision. Berlin is no longer the symbol of a divided Europe but the capital of a united Germany. The war in Bosnia is another factor seriously undermining the prospect and possibility of a European identity. Europe itself is being put into question in Bosnia at the time of writing, 1993/4. A book written on the idea of Europe after the collapse of communism will inevitably be a very different one from before, now that many of the illusions afforded by the Cold War have melted away in the mood of uncertainty that is the hallmark of the present. The rise of xenophobic nationalism, neo-racism and the spectre of a 'Fortress Europe' suggest a reopening of the past that is not for the better. What is to be questioned is the idea of a European identity as a totalising project and the ethno-culturalism that accompanies it. I hope to be able to point to the need for a collective identity based on autonomy and responsibility rather than the chimera of a supra-statehood. A very basic problem, then, is can a European identity emerge as a collective identity capable of challenging both the cohesive force of nationalism and racism without becoming transfixed in either consumerism or the official culture of anonymous institutions? The search for new principles of European legitimacy is inextricably bound up with the attempt to create a space in which collective identities can be formed. It may quite well transpire that intractable disunity is the condition for a European identity.

I should like to emphasise that this book is written for social and political scientists and not for historians. Despite the heavily historical nature of the book, which I think is unavoidable, it attempts to offer a theoretically informed historical sociology of the idea of Europe. It is primarily intended for students of the social and political sciences looking for a critical analysis of problems of European identity in the broader perspective of history. In order to achieve this task I have drawn heavily on a wide variety of historical, social and political studies and do not, in a work of this schematic and interpretative nature, claim originality on all the issues discussed, nor can I claim the same degree of familiarity with the primary source material that the specialised researcher can. I have drawn on the existing historiography in order to illustrate a theoretically based argument with critical intent. Nevertheless, I do hope that the book will be of interest to the specialised historian for the theoretical perspectives and broader context it offers. The book has been written in the manner of a critical intervention in the contemporary debate on the meaning of Europe. It is intended to be provocative and critical as much as theoretical and informative. It is unlikely that a short book of this nature can achieve more than assisting in the formation of new terms of critical debate.

In so far as I am aware no systematic and critical study has been written on the European idea as a totalising re-appropriation of forces that lie deep in European history. The majority of studies on the idea of Europe tend to focus on the theme of European unity, which is generally taken to be the Europe of the European Union. These typically tend to be of an uncritical and even laudatory nature and often delivered in elegiac prose (Del Corral, 1959; Couloubaritsis, 1993). The best of these, such as the classic monographs by Hay (1957) and Fischer (1957), are informative but do nothing to offer an intellectual appraisal of a diffuse construct. Interpretative works, mostly written in the 1950s and 1960s, have been written by Barraclough

(1955, 1963), Beloff (1957), Chabod (1961), Curio (1958), Duroselle (1965), Foerster (1967), Gollwitzer (1964), Heather (1992), de Rougement (1966) and Voyenne (1964), to mention the more significant ones. Yet, even these suffer from a lack of contemporary relevance and often tend to be uncritical. The uncritical nature of reflections on Europe is also apparent in the otherwise important work by Compagnon and Seebacher (1993). The emphasis on Europe as a 'cultural challenge' is evident in Domenach (1990), Patocka (1983 and 1991) and Rijksbaron (1987). There is also a vast range of books and articles ostensibly about Europe, but which in reality have very little to say on it and in fact deal with other related issues, such as modernity, democracy, nationalism. Europe has also been written about as a philosophical ideal (Patocka, 1983; Heller and Fehler, 1988; Heller, 1991). There are also a number of books that deal with the question of the historical frontiers of Europe (Halecki, 1950; Toynbee, 1954; McNeil, 1974; Webb, 1952). The idea of Europe is of course a favourite theme of historians, who generally use it in an unreflective manner as a foil for what is in fact most commonly a group-history of the nation-state. This is what is usually called 'the making of Europe' (Bowle, 1952; Burns, 1947; Dawson, 1932; Hazard, 1990; Wolff, 1968). Invariably in these works Europe is some kind of self-positing spiritual entity that unfolds in history and never needs to be explained. Some noteworthy departures are Bartlett (1993), Scüzs (1988) and Seton-Watson (1989). As a strictly geographical concept there are studies by Cahnman (1952), Louis (1954) and Parker (1960). The idea of Europe frequently emerges in the context of studies on the idea of the Orient (Said, 1979) or in the context of Europe and Islam (Barker et al, 1985; Daniel, 1960, 1966; Djait, 1985; Kabanni, 1988; Lewis, 1993a). The Weberian theme of the 'uniqueness of the West' has also formed the basis of an important body of comparative historiography relevant to my theme (Anderson, 1974a, 1974b; Baechler, 1988; Chirot, 1985; McNeil, 1963; Mann, 1986, 1993; Meyer, 1989). Sociological studies on the idea of Europe are few (Morin, 1987; Münch, 1994; Weidenfeld, 1985; Rootes and Davis, 1994) though Europe as a theme is rapidly becoming a focus for sociological research (Bloomfield, 1993; Haller, 1990; Hamm, 1992). There have been hardly any studies on the idea of Europe as a basis of collective identity (Garcia, 1993; Nelson et al, 1992; Smith, 1992; Balibar, 1991a). The *Mitteleuropa* debate has posed the question of European identity from a different perspective (Hobsbawm, 1991c; Kundera, 1984; Schöpflin and Wood, 1989). Most critiques of Europe of the European Union generally take European identity for granted and concentrate on political institutions (Galtung, 1973). Eurocentricism has been the subject of few useful critical studies (Amin, 1989; Lambropoulos, 1993; Hall, 1992). A work of major significance on the historical foundations of

European identity is Bernal's *Black Athena* (1987). Other reflections tend to be of an impressionistic nature (Barzini, 1984; Enzenberger, 1989; Kramer, 1980, 1988; Nooteboom, 1993; Phillips, 1987). Some useful reappraisals of the idea of Europe can be found in special issues of the *History of European Ideas* (1980, 1), *Past and Present* (1992, 137), and *History Workshop Journal* (1992, 33).

I have drawn off a wide range of theoretical traditions, including the Annales School of comparative historiography with its notion of the *longue durée*, German historical sociology – particularly Max Weber's critique of 'Occidental rationalism' – and the British Marxist historians of whom I should like to single out Eric Hobsbawm (1983), who famously developed the concept of an 'invented tradition', which has inspired the title of this book. Mention must also be made of a work whose central theme no book on the idea of Europe can ignore: Theodor Adorno and Max Horkheimer's *Dialectic of Enlightenment* (1979). An indictment of an entire civilisation, this celebrated work of the 'Frankfurt School' of critical theory poses the question of the very possibility of a European identity in the wake of the Holocaust. Finally the writings of Michel Foucault and Jürgen Habermas have been central to my theoretical approach.

I hope that I shall at least succeed in systematising within an interpretative framework the existing disparate scholarship of the idea of Europe and that perhaps someday a critique of the discourse of Europeanism will be written as part of a critical theory of modernity.

Gerard Delanty
Hanover

Acknowledgements

The author of a book of this general and interpretative nature inevitably incurs debts of gratitude to many friends and colleagues whose advice and criticism of drafts in the various stages of its production have been crucial to its completion. Gudrun von Alten has seen the book through from beginning to end. I should like to thank Patrick O'Mahony for encouragement to write the book. Various drafts have been read by Peter Bennet, James Deutsch, Walter Lorenz, Christine McCall, J. P. O'Carroll, Patrick O'Mahony and Luisa Passerini. Drafts of individual chapters have been read by Isabelle Denhez, Phil O'Flynn, John Maguire, Senia Paseta, Tracey Skillington and Piet Strydom. Responsibility for errors of fact and judgement of course remains mine. I am also indebted to my editor Jo Campling, Mark Hamilton for technical assistance, several librarians and seminar participants in Germany, Ireland and Italy. I also wish to thank Annabelle Buckley and Anne Rafique for their editorial assistance. I am grateful to the Centre for European Social Research at University College Cork, Ireland, for support in completing this book.

1 The Ambivalence of Europe: A Theoretical Introduction

This book is about how every age reinvented the idea of Europe in the mirror of its own identity. I shall bring 'Europe' into focus as a cultural construction and argue that it cannot be regarded as a self-evident entity: it is an idea as much as a reality. Europe, I shall be arguing, is a contested concept and it was in adversity that it became a self-conscious idea. As the central and organising metaphor of a complex civilisation, the European idea expresses our culture's struggle with its contradictions and conflicts.

Much discussed in recent times is the question of 'European unity', yet little thought is actually given to the meaning of the term Europe and its relationship to problems in contemporary political identity. The discourse of Europe is ambivalent in that it is not always about unity and inclusion, but is also about exclusion and the construction of difference based on norms of exclusion. It embodies a great complex of ideas and ideals. Take unity for instance. For many Europeans unity is a cherished goal only so long as it is unattainable; or, indeed, as a strategy to enhance social exclusion or to strengthen the power of the centre over the periphery. Lying at the core of the idea of Europe is a fundamental ambivalence about the normative horizons of collective identity in the modern polity. This ambivalence is apparent in an unresolved tension between two models of collective identity: an exclusivist and formal notion of the polity, on the one side, and on the other, one based more on participation and solidarity. My concern in this book is to dispel the mystique of Europe in order to assess the extent to which the European idea can in fact be the basis of a collective identity unencumbered by the narrow normative horizons of national identity and the chauvinism of the 'Fortress Europe' project. The question of whether a multi-cultural society can evolve a collective identity that is not based on ethno-culturalism is as important as matters pertaining to economic and political integration. The limits and possibility of the European idea as a basis of collective identity is what this book is about. My tentative answer is that the idea of Europe can be the normative basis of collective identity only if it is focused on a new notion of citizenship.

My theme is that of Europe as an idea that has forever been in a process of invention and reinvention as determined by the pressure of new collective identities. What I wish to deconstruct is the Platonic-like vision of an immutable European ideal, the notion that the idea of Europe has always been linked to the pursuit of the values of freedom, democracy and autonomy. That there is such a thing as, what Karl Jaspers (1947) once called, a 'European spirit' or – as other writers earlier in the twentieth century such as T. S. Eliot (1946), Edmund Husserl and Paul Valery believed – the unity of an essentially European tradition is a pervasive assumption underlying contemporary visions of Europe. While not all will agree with T. S. Eliot (1978, p. 160), when he wrote in 1947, 'that a new unity can only grow on the old roots: the Christian faith, and the classical languages which Europeans inherit in common', there appears to be widespread consensus today that the cultural foundation of Europe is deeply rooted in Latin Christendom, humanist values and liberal democracy (Kundera, 1984). I hope to be able to show that these beliefs are ungrounded, or at best mystifying, and that if the idea of Europe is to be used as a normative concept, it is necessary to subject it to critical reflection. It is not possible to see European history as the progressive embodiment of a great unifying idea since ideas are themselves products of history. No coherent idea runs through European history from the earliest times to the present and the historical frontiers of Europe have themselves shifted several times. Yet something can be discerned in the great flux of history and it is not the unity of history but adversity: the European idea has been more the product of conflict than of consensus.

With respect to the notion of 'European unity' I shall be arguing that the critical and self-examining traditions in European culture have in fact rarely appealed to the idea of unity as their normative standpoint – the exception here being anti-fascist resistance. The idea of Europe has been more connected to the state tradition and elite cultures than with the politics of civil society. What is therefore important is that it be disengaged from the state tradition if it is to be used as a normative idea and a basis for rational collective identities in the modern polity. Without a social dimension the European idea will fall into the hands of the nationalists and bureaucrats. I am not then appealing to some kind of abstract cultural essence, an 'autonomy of the spirit' (Finkielkraut, 1985) or what Jan Patocka (1983, p. 23), following in the footsteps of Husserl, calls 'a concern with the soul around which the project of the life of Europe is crystallised' with its roots in Platonic metaphysics. Nor do I find adequate the view, expressed by President Vaclav Havel of the Czech Republic in a speech to the European Parliament in Strasbourg in 1994, that Europe needs 'a spiritual or moral dimension' which would be capable of articulating an identity and the recreation of charisma. Though broadly agreeing with Havel's plea for a non-technocratic European identity, I wish to take issue with those who regard the normative basis of collective identity as residing in the contents of culture or the project of modernity as the unfolding of the great promises of the Enlightenment, a notion that has been formulated by Gorbachev (1987, pp. 197/8): 'Europe "from the Atlantic to the Urals" is a cultural historical entity united by the common heritage of the Renaissance and the Enlightenment, of the great philosophical and social teachings of the nineteenth and twentieth centuries.'

To speak of Europe as an 'invention' is to stress the ways in which it has been constructed in a historical process; it is to emphasise that Europe is less the subject of history than its product and what we call Europe is, in fact, a historically fabricated reality of ever-changing forms and dynamics. Most of Europe is only retrospectively European and has been invented in the image of a distorted modernity. Moreover, the history of Europe is the history not only of its unifying ideas, but also of its divisions and frontiers, both internal and external. Since the idea of Europe is not a mysterious substance floating above the real world of society and history, I shall attempt to show how it is interpolated in concrete configurations of power and their geo-political complexes.

Defining Europe is then fraught with problems, for Europe is a protean idea and not something self-evident. It is erroneous to regard Europe as merely a region for the simple reason that it means different things to different people in different contexts. Europe does not exist any more naturally than do nations. It is like most of our political vocabulary, constituted by history and, at the same time, constitutive of that very history. European identity did not exist prior to its definition and codification. It is a doubtful construct anyway given the apparent irresolvable conflict of national cultures and oppositional collective identities. Unifying myths of integration should be viewed with scepticism unless they unambivalently accommodate diversity. In the present context what I wish to emphasise is that the idea of Europe was constructed with strategic goals in mind and the 'reality' that it designates is also used strategically. The sociological concept of a 'discourse' can help to explain this: Europe cannot be reduced to an idea, an identity or a reality since it itself is a structuring force. What is real is the discourse in which ideas and identities are formed and historical realities constituted.

In contextualising the idea of Europe, I intend to demonstrate that the idea of Europe is a historical projection, a universalising idea under the perpetual threat of fragmentation from forces within European society; it is essentially the unifying theme in a cultural framework of values as opposed to a mere political norm or the name for a geo-political region. It can be seen as the emblem and central organising metaphor of a complex civilisation. But Europe is more than a region and polity, it is also an idea and an identity. In the following chapters I shall outline the historical process in which the idea

of Europe was constituted as a cultural frame of reference for the formation
of identities and new geo-political realities. My aim is to trace the process
through which Europe became first a cultural idea and then a self-conscious
political identity. The linchpin of my critique is that in this transformation,
and in the cultural shifts accompanying it, the idea of Europe always remained
tied to ethno-cultural values which have had a reifying effect on collective
identities. It will also become apparent that the idea of Europe failed to
become a cohesive collective identity, for instead of a European identity configurations of national identities formed. Most discussions on the European
idea fail to distinguish between the idea of Europe and European identity as
a form of consciousness. The idea of Europe existed long before people actually began to identify with it and to see themselves as Europeans. What we
need to know more about is exactly how Europe became established as a
reality for knowledge – a cultural idea – and how it subsequently lent itself
to power.

Since the distinction between Europe as an idea, identity and reality is crucial to my argument, some further preliminary conceptual clarification is
required. It may be helpful to conceptualise this with the help of the metaphor
of the football game: the ball is Europe, the players the identity projects and
the pitch the geo-political reality on which the game, in this instance the discourse, is played. This analogy also underlines my contention that the idea
of Europe is never totally controlled by any of the players in the field; it occu-
pies the cultural-symbolic space which is competed for by collective identities. The European idea is quite simply a political football. But, to take the
metaphor further, it is not without its referees, for the social reproduction of
reality also involves a normative dimension; that is, it can be linked to a
moral dimension which has the power of critical self-reflection.

Though I am principally concerned with Europe as an idea, it is important
to see clearly the three levels of analysis that are involved in the theory of
the 'invention of Europe'. As an idea Europe is a kind of regulative idea for
identity-building processes. The idea of Europe is a cultural model of society, a focus for collective identities. Castoriadis (1987) has written about the
function of the 'imaginary' in the constitution of society. 'Social imaginary
significations' are part of every society and in particular, in the present context, the 'central imaginary'. The point at issue is the manner in which a society imagines itself in time and space with reference to a cultural model. This
is not unlike what Anderson (1984) has called an 'imaginary community' to
describe the national ideal. The idea of Europe should, however, be seen as
an even higher degree of abstraction than the national ideal. Following
Durkheim, I believe it can be seen as a collective or social representation
encompassing within it a heterogeneity of cultural forms (Moscovici, 1981,

1984). Social representations are not merely reproductions of reality, they are also prescriptive and serve as regulative ideas for the formation of collective identities.

However, when cultural ideas become part of political-identity building processes they can become ideologies. By ideology I mean an all-embracing and comprehensive system of thought, a programme for the future, and a political doctrine for the mobilisation of the masses. 'When a particular definition of reality comes attached to a concrete power interest, it may be called an ideology' (Berger and Luckmann, 1984, p. 141). Identities become pathological once they take on the character of a dominant ideology and the individual can no longer chose his or her identity. When this happens identities become life-lies: identities stabilise as objective forms of consciousness. In other words identities become vehicles for the reproduction of dominant ideologies. National identity, sexism, sectarianism and racism are examples of regressive forms of identification with authority: identities become reified and anchored in the state, gender, church and colour. Identities can also take on a pathological form when they are constructed against a category of otherness (Fabian, 1983; Gilman, 1985). Instead of identity being defined by a sense of belongingness and solidarity arising out of shared lifeworlds, it becomes focused on opposition to an Other: the 'We' is defined not by reference to a framework of shared experiences, common goals and a collective horizon, but by the negation of the Other. Identification takes place through the imposition of otherness in the formation of a binary typology of 'Us' and 'Them'. The purity and stability of the 'We' is guaranteed first in the naming, then in the demonisation and, finally, in the cleansing of otherness. This is frequently what the pursuit of community really is about: the imposition of otherness in the assertion 'we are different from them'. The defining characteristic of the group is not what its members have in common but in what separates them from other groups. By this I do not mean to suggest that difference is somehow bad. Identities are always relational and what matters is not the representation of the Other as such but the actual nature of the difference that is constructed. The issue then is one of diversity or division: self-identity by the recognition of otherness or by the negation of otherness; solidarity or exclusion. When the Other is recognised as such, difference is positive, but when the Other is represented as a threatening stranger, difference is negative. This dichotomy between Self and Other has been pivotal in the making of European identity (Keen, 1986; Hall, 1992; Harle, 1990; Larrain, 1994; Neumann and Welsh, 1991; Neumann, 1992; Said, 1979; Young, 1990).

The concept of identity must be further differentiated into the levels at which identity is possible. It is important to distinguish between personal and collective identities. While a collective European identity existed (at least as part of elite culture) in some form since the sixteenth century, European identity as part of personal identities did not exist until the late nineteenth century though it had gradually evolved since the Enlightenment. In this period the idea of Europe became reflected in the personal life histories of individuals as well as movements.

Much of what is being called 'European' is in fact reconstructed, and in many cases thinly disguised, nineteenth century imperialist ideas (Nederveen Pieterse, 1991). One could even go so far as to argue that there is a similarity between present-day experiments with European identity and late nineteenth century attempts at consciousness-raising by means of a social imperialism and jingoistic nationalism. In both cases the result is the same: the postulates of political discourse are withdrawn from critique and scrutiny by being reified into official cultures. Oppositional currents, sub-cultures and regional and social movements are alienated in the appeal to a meta-community: 'For a part of the public the abstract symbols presented by the various administrative agencies may become a stereo-typed substitute for rigorous thought about their own and others' social needs' (Edelman, 1964, p. 62). The idea of Europe was mostly derived from 'above' and not from 'below' in concrete forms of life and political struggles. It has principally been the ideology of intellectuals and the political class. As such it has tended to be a counter-revolutionary ideology of the elites, those groups who claim to be the representatives of society. It is in their language that the idea of Europe has been codified. Intellectuals generally play a leading role in the shaping and codification of collective identities (Giessen, 1993).

Today, more than ever before, the discourse of Europe is taking on a strongly ideological character. In this transformation Europe becomes part of a hegemonical cultural discourse. Elevated to the status of a consensus, the idea of Europe, by virtue of its own resonance, functions as hegemon which operates to produce an induced consensus – which is less a compliance with power than acquiescence and helplessness – with which a system of power can be mobilised. By a 'hegemon' I mean, following Gramsci (1971), the manifold ways in which consciousness is structured in the soliciting of consent. In the battle of ideas, a single system of thought becomes hegemonic. The rule of the hegemon is rule by a form of consent that does not question its own presuppositions. A world is created which is experienced as objective; it is something that is given, taken for granted, unalterable and self-evident. As a hegemon Europe is a self-enclosure, a coherent subject-matter, a system of thought. It is not something that can easily be chosen or rejected, for it itself structures the field of choices and the epistemological framework in which it is articulated. Thinking, reading and writing about Europe are the intellectual modalities of power through which Europe is constituted as a strategic reality and a subject of knowledge. Europe thus exists as a sub-text which sets the terms for the construction of a field of representations. As a philosophy of history, the idea of Europe serves as a meta-norm of legitimation for the pursuit of a strategy of power. It serves as a substitute for the complexity of modern society, which is characterised by differentiation and abstractness (Luhmann, 1982; Zijderveld, 1972). One of the tasks of a critical theory of Europe is to demonstrate that cultural and political diversity and the heterogeneity of social milieus lie beneath the dominant ideology. The task of the sociologist is to inquire into the process by which realities are constructed out of ideas and to demystify the power of symbolic names; to disentangle the complex web of interconnections by which identities become linked to relations of power. It must also be recognised that the dominant ideology, the hegemon, is never entirely a monolith but is fraught with tensions and contradictions, for where there is consensus there is conflict. The dominant ideas are never controlled by any single ruling elite and can be used to subvert power. So the European idea is not just only a hegemonic idea; it should be seen as a totalising idea that collapses at the point of becoming hegemonic.

Europe is more than an idea and identity; it is also a geo-political reality. One of the central characteristics of Europe as a geo-political entity is the process in which the core penetrated into the periphery to produce a powerful system of control and dependency. It was colonialism and conquest that unified Europe and not peace and solidarity. Every model of Europe ever devised always generated an anti-model. Europe has tended to be a divisive phenomenon; it is not inherently connected with peace and unity. It has been a fact of European history that every attempt made to unite the continent occurred after a period of major division. This presupposes a theory of the historical regions of Europe. It will suffice here to remark that Europe is not a natural geo-political framework but is composed of a core and a number of borderlands which are all closely related to the eastern frontier. To a very significant extent, much of the 'unity' of Europe has been formed in relation to the eastern frontier and it has been possible only by violent homogenisation. Unlike the western frontier, which has been a frontier of expansion, the eastern one has been a frontier of defence and has played a central role in the formation of European identity.

There is another aspect to the discourse of Europe which bears on the present context. The idea of Europe shares with the idea of the nation, or national identity, the characteristic of obscurantism. Though the idea of Europe rarely evokes the same degree of irrational reverence and deification that the ideal of the national community can demand, it is also ultimately based on an obscurantist interpretation of community: a fantasy homeland that goes hand in hand with a retrospective invention of history as well as a moralisation of geography. Underlying this are unifying narratives of origin and destiny. The difference is that in the case of the idea of Europe it is the mystique of civilisation that is cultivated and reinforced by myths of high culture. Europe can be viewed as a discursive strategy which is articulated by shifting signifiers in relational contexts. In other words, what must be analysed are the reference points of the European idea rather than its cultural content. This is because there is no real tradition of Europeanism in the sense that we can speak of a tradition of statehood or nationalism. Today such an 'invented tradition' is clearly in the process of invention with the proliferation of a paraphernalia of emblems and slogans of the new official culture. It must not be forgotten that the nation-state is also not the unified and autonomous entity it is often portrayed to be, but is characterised by the same divisions with which Europe is often equated.

Taking Gellner's (1983) argument that nationalism came into being to serve society in the process of industrialisation with a culturally uniform mode of communication, it could be argued that the idea of Europe is today fulfilling this role. The new politics of Europeanism is very much a product of the media and is exhibited in life styles – food, advertising, tourism, satellite TV – and technocratic ideologies and not in the emotionalism of nationalism. The idea of Europe quite simply does not have the same emotional attachment of the nation. To take an example from history. After the Risorgimento, when Italy was united in 1861 (without the knowledge of most Italians) one of its architects, Massimo d'Azeglio, in a famous phrase, said 'we have made Italy, now we have to make Italians' (Hobsbawm, 1991b, p. 44). The situation is not very different today: Europe has been united, but those elusive citizens, the Europeans, have yet to be invented.

The idea of Europe has all too often been erroneously seen as a cosmopolitan ideal of unity and an alternative to the chauvinism of the nation-state. My thesis, in contrast, is that it must be viewed in the global context of world-views and the nation-state, far from being its enemy, is in fact the condition of its possibility. The European idea has in fact reinforced rather than undermined the ideology of nationality. As Karl Mannheim (1979) argued, many cultural ideas which embody utopian impulses do not always transcend the society with which they are ostensibly in conflict but become ideologies.

When we contemplate the vast range of books, monographs and political manifestos that all bear the word Europe in their titles, it is difficult to deny that there is an element of mystification in the idea of Europe. It projects the language of the life-world and political struggles onto the macro-dimension of a community of states by the invention of a mega-community. The result is not genuine internationalism but a socio-technical framework for the exploitation of scarce resources and the pursuit of unrestrained economic growth. We find that the idea of Europe is becoming the driving force of strategies of macro-political and economic engineering, and, above all, the substitution of a new goal, closely linked to the neo-liberal political programme, for the traditional social democratic programme. It is a unifying theme which links the macro-level of economic and global frameworks to the cultural reproduction of the life-world and enhances the steering-capacity of the former. The most important task for Europe today is the articulation of a new idea of Europe which would be capable of providing an orientation for a post-national European identity. Rather than being the leitmotif for 'disorganised capitalism' (Lash and Urry, 1987) the European idea should, if it is to be anything, be the basis of a new politics of cultural pluralism.

At this point I should like to clarify a theoretical presupposition implicit in what I have been arguing. Essential to a sociological theory of the evolution of modern political culture is a vision of the structures underlying shifts in collective identity and their regulative ideas. By structures I mean, essentially, the state, economy, culture and society. When we survey the history of the European idea it can be seen how it was always articulated in terms of the first three. Europeanism generally signified some notion of political unity, be it that of the Holy Leagues and alliances of Christendom, the Concert of Europe or the European Union. This state-centred model was in modern times closely linked to the pursuit of economic interests. It is also connected with militarism in the sense of Europe as a security agenda. Europe has also been seen as a product of culture: be it that of scientific-technological culture, bourgeois high culture, or the present-day attempts to invent a European official culture. Europeanism has rarely been associated with the politics of society in the sense of 'civil society' or the 'public sphere' understood as a domain distinct from that of the state. If Europeanism is to have any sense at all, this is the model that it should be based upon and not one that uses collective identities as props for macro-institution-building. The discourses with which the idea of Europe has been connected – Christendom, civilisation, the West, imperialism, racism, fascism, modernity – are ones that are based on matters that have little to do with the real experiences of life. The official and codified version of European culture has nothing to say to the silent Europe of minorities. Not surprisingly the charisma and enchantment that it lacks is filled by nationalist and racist ideology and the new politics of materialism. So exactly where the space for identity formation is to be created is a crucial question for the future. It is certain, however, that it is not to be found in the sphere of the state and its administrative and ideological apparatus. Of relevance here, and which I think will seriously challenge the possibility of a European identity, is the fact that in recent times post-national identity is increasingly focused more on collectively mediated goals than on totalising visions of unity. Post-national Europeans do not see themselves as bearers of the whole, be it the totality of the nation or Europe, but as citizens whose identity is formed by their interests. If this is so, then a European identity, unless it is to be a contradiction in terms, could only be formed on the basis of intractable disunity and the democratic pluralism that this entails.

An important theoretical problem concerning the idea of Europe is its relationship to the claims of European culture to universal validity. In other words what is the normative status of the idea of Europe? A book on the idea of Europe cannot escape this thorny philosophical issue. It must be said at the outset that while I have heavily drawn on Foucault's (1980a; 1980b) notion of discourse and Said's (1979) concept of cultural construction, I hope to avoid some of the well-known theoretical pitfalls of their works. My approach is also inspired by the sociology of Max Weber who attempted to provide a theory of 'Occidental rationalism' (Schluchter, 1981). Rather than circumventing the issue of universality by means of cultural relativism, I shall attempt to present a working hypothesis of a concept of universality that does not open itself to the Eurocentric fallacy. The idea of Europe, I have argued, is essentially a cultural value as opposed to a concrete form of identity. As a cultural value it is not in itself a normative postulate. Values are not the same as norms. The latter are closer to ethical principles and can claim to be universalisable in the sense that we can expect them to be of binding force (Habermas, 1984, p. 89). Values, in contrast, are particularistic, they do not carry the same claims to universal validity that we attach to norms. The problem that this presents for the idea of Europe is not whether universal ethical principles exist, but whether they are embodied in European culture.

The equation of the idea of Europe with political identity-building projects has resulted in a distorted idea of Europe. This is because the idea of Europe, since it became an institutionalised discourse in early modern Europe, served as a kind of legitimation for the politics of the secular and territorial state. Now, legitimation presupposes a normative standpoint by means of which power becomes legitimate authority. In usurping the place held by Christendom, the idea of Europe came to acquire the aura of a normative standard of civilisation, but this ultimately was a reification of ethical postulates. The concept of a universal Church was thus preserved in its heir, Europe, which espoused a secular ideology of progress and a philosophy of history. As the geo-political name for a civilisation, Europe also signified its cultural value spheres. This, as I shall argue in the following chapters, was possible because of the tension between the two functions of the idea of Europe: as a geo-political name and as a cultural framework. As a result of the enduring conflict between West and East, Christendom and Islam, Europe failed to devise a geo-political framework capable of uniting European civilisation with a common set of values. Ever since the Muslim expansion of the eighth century, much of Europe lay under non-European rule. After the Fall of Constantinople in 1453 as much as one quarter of European territory lay under Muslim rule and after the advance of the Red Army in 1945 one third of Europe lay under the Russians, who have traditionally been perceived as non-European. Europe, as a civilisation, perpetually under threat from outside forces, particularly on its eastern frontier, evolved a cultural ethos which tended to attribute to its own structures of consciousness a universalistic dimension. With the opening of the western frontier after 1492 and its subsequent path to world mastery, the idea of Europe increasingly signified a universal culture and European modernity was supposed to be the agent of universality. With the exception of China, the only cultures that ever challenged this were eventually either defeated or assimilated.

It is a mistake, as Ernst Troeltsch (1977) argued, to conflate universal structures of consciousness with any one particular culture. This is the essence of Eurocentricism as an ethno-cultural project. Whether or not universalistic structures of consciousness have been more institutionalised in western European culture – which clearly transcends Europe as a geo-political region – than in non-European cultures is not the issue. Habermas (1984, p. 180) has cogently argued this point:

> The universalist position does not have to deny the pluralism and the incompatibility of historical versions of 'civilized humanity', but it regards this multiplicity of forms of life as limited to cultural contents, and it asserts that every culture must share certain formal properties of the modern understanding of the world, if it is at all to attain a certain degree of 'consciousness awareness' or 'sublimation'. Thus the universalist assumption refers to a few necessary structural properties of modern life forms as such.

It is important that these minimal conditions be separated from the idea of Europe. To suppose that the idea of Europe is itself a universal normative standard would be to relate it to a kind of 'cultural violence' (Galtung, 1990). By this I mean the violence that is contained in a cultural world-view which claims to be in possession of a single universal truth. Pertinent to this issue is the thesis, developed in Chapter 5, that European culture was never adequately secularised and that consequently the idea of the universal survived as a cultural absolute, an 'essentialism', in the Europe of the territorial and secular nation-states. To invoke Europe often involves the illusion that there is a privileged 'We' who are the subject of history and a corresponding belief in the universality of western norms. Europe becomes a mirror for the interpretation of the world and European modernity is seen as the culmination of history and the apotheosis of civilisation. The most common form in which this exists today is an highly ambivalent 'anti-racism' which, in appealing to some allegedly self-evident set of abstract rights, is selectively deployed as an pretext for western triumphalism and does not recognise that there is a profound 'antinomy between universalism as regards human beings and universalism as regards human beings' "cultures"' (Castoriadis, 1992).

The thesis I should like to propose, then, is that it is important that the idea of Europe be separated from universal ethical validity claims disguised as an essentialist ethno-culturalism. The idea of Europe, ostensibly a geo-political concept, is a cultural model, a cultural construct, and as such cannot claim universal validity. It is an unreflective category of cultural reproduction. While it can be connected to the moral dimension of society, it itself is not a moral concept. Moreover, in so far as battles for legitimation crystallise in the idea of Europe, the effect can only be one of distortion, a reification of the moral space. The idea of Europe then inevitably becomes a basis of division and a strategy for the construction of difference. The politicisation of the idea of Europe in fact amounts to a definition of Europe not as what its peoples have in common but in what separates them from the non-European world, and, indeed, very often amongst themselves. It is this definition of Europe, which inevitably results from its political hijacking, that should be avoided.

At this point the notion of universality must be further clarified. Universality does not mean uniformity and the intolerance that this necessarily implies, but can refer to plurality and difference. As I have already argued, difference is not in itself bad so long as it is not a question of the negation of otherness. Universality can refer to a notion of otherness than includes rather than alienates the Other. It is for this reason important that what I would call the 'project of autonomy' be disengaged from the dominant social representations that have until now prevailed and be more firmly connected to normatively grounded ideas. A model of citizenship based on participation and solidarity is crucial in this respect. I shall be arguing that the notion of European post-national citizenship is a more important ideal than that of 'European unity' and could offer a more normatively based reference point for a European identity.

The idea of Europe is not, then, without ambivalence. It is Janus-faced: on the one hand, an exclusivist notion of Europe has prevailed; yet, on the other the idea of Europe does appear to occupy the normative space for a universalist project of autonomy. By deconstructing the myth of the unity of

European culture, I hope to be able to open up a critical perspective for a theory of citizenship which no longer appeals to atavistic myths and cultural chauvinism. So what needs to be clarified is the moral universalism that is implicitly connected to the idea of Europe. There is enough within European history with which the idea of Europe can be associated, such as a strong tradition of civil society and anti-authoritarianism. It must, however, be recognised that even these enlightened traditions are not specifically European but transcend the specificity of cultural traditions.

The structure and argument of the book reflect this critique of the universalist claims of European culture. It is written in the spirit of a radical intervention into the debate on a European identity and the attempt to fashion an artificial identity out of what should perhaps be best left as a cultural idea. The unifying theme in the book is the deconstruction of the 'Eurocentric fallacy', the implicit association of the idea of Europe with universally valid norms and the myth of unity. The crux of the problem is the relation of Europe as a cultural idea to concrete forms of collective identity-building and its structuring in the geo-political framework which we call Europe. What is also at stake is the relationship of cultural identity to political identity: the historical process whereby Europe was constituted as a cultural idea and transformed into a political identity. Above all the failure of this identity to constitute a collective identity capable of challenging national identities is my theme.

I can now state a central hypothesis. A theory of the invention of Europe seeks to explain how the idea of Europe becomes attached to processes of collective identity formation, which reinforce the dominance of the centre over the periphery. By a 'European identity' I mean essentially, by definition, a collective identity that is focused on the idea of Europe, but which can also be the basis of personal identity. I shall attempt to outline the historical constitution of the discourse of Europe in the following chapters by reference to these three levels of analysis: Europe as an idea, identity and as a reality. The variables in this are language, religion, consciousness of history, nationality, the frontier, material and aesthetic culture, and law/citizenship. The structures to which these are linked are the economy, the state, culture and society. From a normative-critical point of view, I shall be arguing for a restructuring and re-imagining of the European idea, which should be located on the level of society, so that we can speak of a 'Social Europe' as opposed to a state-centred Europe and link it to citizenship as a normative basis of collective identity. Very schematically, I shall link the idea of Europe to five discourses which can be seen as its 'crystallisations': the discourse of Christendom, the Enlightenment discourse of civilisation, the late nineteenth and early twentieth century discourse of culture, the Cold War discourse after 1945 and the contemporary conflict between the discourses of Fortress Europe and that of a Social or Citizens' Europe.

I begin, in Chapter 2, by tracing the genesis and emergence of the idea of Europe in classical antiquity and its gradual transformation in the course of the Middle Ages from a geographical notion – originally linked to the idea of the Hellenic Occident – into a cultural idea, but one which, nevertheless, was subordinated to the idea of Christendom. With the consolidation of the idea of Europe – which I place at the late fifteenth century – I seek in Chapter 3 to relate this new cultural model to the emerging forms of European identity and their burgeoning geo-political realities. My aim is to assess at exactly what stage European identity became focused on the idea of Europe as opposed to Christendom. Chapter 4 deals with the enclosure of the idea of Europe in western Europe. Its central argument is that the division between Europe and the Orient was reflected in an internal division within Europe and that the eastern frontier – closed after the fall of Constantinople in 1453 – was the determining factor in the shaping of the idea of Europe as the 'West'. It was not until the opening of the western frontier following the reconquest of Spain and the colonisation of the Americas after 1492 that the broader and more hegemonic notion of the 'West' provided the basis for European identity. Chapter 5 looks at the consolidation of the western system of nation-states and the formation of a political concept of the idea of Europe as a debased normative standard in the Concert of Europe. A central concern in this chapter, as well as in Chapter 6, is an attempt to explain the manner in which the idea of Europe came to rest on a universalistic notion of *civilisation*, constructed in opposition to the Orient and the conquest of nature, while the idea of the nation became more focused on the particularistic concept of national *culture*. In Chapter 6 I argue that European identity is very closely linked with racial myths of civilisational superiority and the construction of otherness within an adversarial system of world-views. Chapter 7 proceeds with an argument about the collapse of the idea of Europe: the rise of the idea of *Mitteleuropa*, as a competitor, the conditions of total war and the rise of fascism, which also competed for the idea of Europe. Chapter 8 considers the rebuilding of the idea of Europe as part of post-war reconstruction and its institutionalisation as a pseudo-norm in the European Union. In this context the crucial issue is the wider scenario of the Cold War. Chapter 9 is addressed to the implication of the collapse of the Cold War consensus for the idea of Europe. Its basic thesis is that the idea of Europe has become part of a new state-seeking nationalism that has crystallised in 'Fortress Europe' and far from being a successor to the nation-state, Europe, in fact, is a function of it.

Finally, in Chapter 10, by way of a conclusion I argue that it is important that the ethno-cultural idea of Europe be separated from normative considerations such as the issue of citizenship. Political and legal conceptions should not be made out of unreflective cultural identities. When such unreconstructed cultural ideas are translated into institutional practices by political identity projects, the polymorphous nature of reality will ensure their divisive application. The only way out of this would be to replace the largely unreflective idea of Europe based on self-identity through negation and exclusion with one based on autonomy and participation. Only by means of a commitment to a post-national European citizenship can the idea of Europe be divested of its cultural ambivalence. Since a collective European identity cannot be built on language, religion or nationality without major divisions and conflicts emerging, citizenship may be a possible option. Given the obsolescence of the Cold War idea of Europe, there is now a greater need than ever before for a new definition of Europeanism that does not exclude the stranger. A collective identity based on citizenship could be a starting point for such a reappraisal of the European idea. I am suggesting then that the politics of Europeanism should be seen as an incomplete project in which there can be both regression and a potential for social learning.

2 The Origins
of the Idea of Europe

THEORETICAL PERSPECTIVES

In this chapter I want to focus on the genesis and development of a conceptual demarcation running through western society from classical antiquity to the Middle Ages whereby a particular discourse of power is privileged over against others. The nexus of this discourse is the West–East dualism and the corresponding counter-factualism of an 'us'/'them' polarity. I wish to show that one of the most enduring forms of western identity was the postulation of a centre, anchored in a historical myth of origins, and that this served to reinforce the formation of adversarial world-views. The origins of Eurocentrism, then, lay not in the idea of Europe itself as a cultural model, but in the structures of a discourse which served to reinforce the power of the centre. Thus, when the idea of Europe emerged as a cultural idea it became associated with structures of power and their identity projects. The cultural space for the formation of an autonomous discourse of Europe had not yet formed. Prior to the early modern period the idea of Europe was always articulated through other discourses, of which the most significant was Christendom. In other words, then, 'European' identity, as an ethno-cultural and political project, preceded the formation of the idea of Europe as such. But of course we cannot call this a 'European identity' since it was never focused on the idea of Europe itself. The idea of Europe when it did emerge was embedded in Christendom having become virtually coterminous with the notion of the Occident, which preceded the idea of Europe. It was this latter notion of the Occident or West that provided continuity between Hellenism, Christendom and the idea of Europe.

For the civilisations of antiquity the idea of Europe was relatively unimportant and did not come to designate the continent of Europe until the rise of Islam in the seventh century. For a long time Europe as a concept designated the wider Greek world of Asia Minor and included parts of northern Asia, not the western continent, most of which was unknown and only partly inhabited. We often forget that the culture and civilisation of the Occident owes its origin to the Orient. The world of antiquity was oriental not western. As a geographical entity Europe was a product of the break-up of the civilisation of the Mediterranean. Throughout the Middle Ages, the idea of Europe was linked to the idea of the Christian West and served as a hegemon against the ascendancy of Islam. The limits of Europe in the crucible of Christendom were set by the Muslim advance and Christianity became the territorial identity of medieval Europe. The idea of Europe gave to medieval Christendom a sense of territorial unity, though not a specific identity.

From a very early stage in its history Europe failed to develop a geo-political framework capable of integrating Latin and Greek Christianity into a unitary civilisation. This geo-political split was reflected in the emergence of two cultural frameworks in which the idea of Europe tended to become interchangeable with Latin Christendom. This was, I should like to stress, before the idea of Europe itself became an autonomous cultural framework and a basis of identity. Moreover, an enduring tension remained between the idea of Europe as a geographical concept and the notion of Christendom, the territory of Latin Christianity.

Since it is one of my central contentions that the idea of Europe in the modern period never emancipated itself from the adversarial East–West nexus with its roots deep in Christendom, a considerable amount of space will be devoted to an analysis of the early history of the idea. This will, I hope, have the additional value of demystifying the notion of the unity of Europe as a historical region with its roots in classical culture, the idea expressed by T. S. Eliot (1962, p. 130) that: 'We are all, so far as we inherit the the civilization of Europe, still citizens of the Roman Empire.'

EUROPE AND THE ANCIENTS

The idea of Europe had little meaning for the Ancients. Long before it became even a geographical expression the idea of Europe belonged more to the realm of myth than of science and politics (Hay, 1957, p. 5). Like many proto-national figures, Europe was the name of a woman. As such it had the power of mystification. In the Greek myths the Phoenician princess Europa, having been seduced by Zeus disguised as a white bull, abandoned her homeland in present day Lebanon for the western island of Crete where she later married the King of Crete. That Europe was therefore an eastern import did not worry the Greeks as they did not have a strong sense of division between a western territory extending beyond Greece, but to which Greece belonged, and an eastern or southern continent alien to Hellas. Indeed, in many of the myths, Europa was the half sister of Asia and Libya (the name of Africa) while for Homer Europa was the daughter of Phoenix (Buehler, 1968). This suggests that Europe was not a highly differentiated concept. Europe, after all, was not a Greek discovery but Phoenician and may even have had Semitic roots (Sattler, 1971, p. 19). The notion that Europe was of Greek origin was undoubtedly a later invention and, according to the famous thesis of Bernal (1987), can be traced to the attempts of counter-revolutionary intellectuals – particularly in the period 1815 to 1830 when classics was founded as a conservative discipline – to fabricate a European cultural tradition whose roots lay in a purified ancient Greece that bore no recognition of its roots in the Orient.

It appears that Europe and Asia as individual regions were of little significance to the Greeks for whom everything non-Greek was simply 'barbarian'. Greece was often thought of as being a separate entity, distinct from Europe and Asia. This seems to have been the view of Aristotle who made a threefold distinction between Greeks, Europeans and Asians, but held that the latter two were 'barbarians'. In his reflections on the nature of kinship in *The Politics* (1962, pp. 136 and 269) he argued that the barbarians are more slavish than the Greeks, and Asiatics more so than Europeans. As is well known, the democracy afforded by the fabled Greek polis was based on slavery. Given that most slaves were Asiatic, it was not surprising that Aristotle expressed contempt for Asia and regarded barbarians, that is non-Greeks, in the same light as slaves (Puzzo, 1964, p. 580).

The authors of antiquity rarely used the word Europe. According to Hay (1957, p. 2) in his authoritative study on the early history of the idea of Europe, the term Europe may have been originally used to refer to the mainland areas of Greece and only later came to include the Aegean islands. The principal antithesis in Greek thinking was the dualism of Greeks versus barbarians (Gollwitzer, 1964, p. 20). For Plato in *The Republic* (1974, p. 358) there was a clear distinction between Greeks and barbarians, but we have little evidence to suggest that he attached importance to Europe. Aeschylus in the play *The Persians* constructed an opposition of Greeks versus Persians: the Persians were Asiatic while the Greeks were civilised. To the Greeks the concept of Asia was more firmly linked to a specific territory than Europe, which remained a vague area to the north of Hellas. For Herodotus in the fifth century the feud between the Greeks and the Persians amounted to a virtual conflict of civilisations. It is possible that this feud provided the terms of reference for the conflict of Europe and Asia in later centuries. Herodotus himself, however, had no clear distinction between Europe and Asia and simply called the wilderness north of the Black Sea *Scythia*. Europe and Asia were merely geographical terms while Greece and Persia were cultural-political terms. Isocrates, however, in the fourth century BC constructed an identification of Europe with Greece and Asia with Persia (Hay, 1957, p. 3). Ptolemy, in the second century AD, used the term *Sarmatia* and distinguished between *Sarmatia Europea* and *Sarmatia Asiatica* with the River Don separating them (Halecki, 1950, p. 85). This was to prove an enduring distinction and still remains one of the geographical definitions of Europe. At about this time the earlier twofold division of the world between Asia and Europe, or Persia and Greece, gave way to a threefold division: Europe, Asia and Africa. Earlier, it is thought that Africa may have been considered a part of Asia (Fuhrmann, 1981, p. 7). According to Hippocrates, the Sea of Azov was the boundary between Asia and Europe (Toynbee, 1954, pp. 708–29). The principal frontier known to the Greeks was the Nile, which separated Asia from Africa. It appears the distinction between these two continents was more significant than the singularity of Europe against Asia (Hay, 1957, p. 2). Toynbee (1954, p. 711) has argued that it is possible that Asia and Europe originally emerged as nautical terms used by the Aegean mariners to distinguish between the two land masses that set restrictions to navigation. In general we may conclude that the Greeks did not always consider themselves Europeans. Hellas was seen as the land of culture and civilisation and beyond it was barbarism. What is significant, however, is less the opposition of Europe versus Asia, than the fact of political dualism itself and the ethnocentrism that it constructed.

The idea of Europe began to emerge with the decline of classical Greek civilisation. After the Persian wars, the Greek city states were weakened as a result of internal strife and the ensuing Peloponnesian war between Sparta and Athens prepared the way for the ascendancy of Macedonia in 338 BC. Under Alexander the Great the centre of Greek civilisation moved towards Asia Minor after Macedonia annexed Greece and defeated the Persians in 331 BC. The idea of Europe, which began to take on a proto-political form in the Age of Alexander, served to mystify the territories of the Macedonian conquests by bestowing upon them the identity of a distinct geographical entity. This possibly may have been because Greek culture after Alexander the Great was no longer the property of the Greeks. Greek, which denotes language rather than a people, was able to lend itself to universalistic ambitions. Even though Greek culture and language had spread throughout the region, Greek political hegemony had given way to new political powers which were as much 'oriental' as 'western'. The idea of Greek superiority against the 'barbarians' of Europe diminished and a broader concept of Europe emerged and came increasingly to refer to what is essentially Asia Minor and included Greece, but with Asia still being the focal point of Otherness. Asia was in effect pushed eastwards beyond Persia after the conquests of Alexander (Baldry, 1965, pp. 120–1 and 132). It is interesting to observe that the territories united by Alexander eventually fell under Byzantine rule and only in later centuries ceased to be regarded as the essence of 'European' culture.

For Antiquity the idea of Europe was subordinated to the notion of the Occident. The notion of the Occident first referred to the eastern Mediterranean

world and was not identical to the idea of Europe, which had less meaning as
a cultural idea. It was a Hellenic Occident. It is even possible that the Greeks
were more strongly aware of the world being structured on a north–south axis,
from light and heat to darkness and cold, than on a west–east polarity. While
the notion of the Occident referred, broadly speaking, to the wider Greek
world, the idea of Europe was predominantly geographical. The idea of the
Occident, which predates the usage of the notion of Europe, was in fact, like
the early idea of Europe, what we today would call the Orient. Troy, the cradle of the Occident, for instance, was east of the Dardanelles. The ancient limits of the West were the borders of the known world in the western Mediterranean
and Persia in the East. Orient and Occident, then, had quite different meanings from the connotations they were later to acquire when the centre of civilisation shifted westwards. But the notion of the Occident had another and
more important meaning in Antiquity: it was believed to be the site of paradise, which lay somewhere in the unknown western ocean. It was to this
mystique of the West that Europe was subordinated.

After the defeat of Macedonia by Rome in 197 BC, Greek civilisation
moved from the eastern Mediterranean to its western shores. Like the Greeks
before them, the Romans never had a strong sense of a European identity,
possibly because parts of the Roman empire were spread over non-European
territory and did not include much of the northern parts of the continent. The
heart of the empire was located in the eastern Mediterranean basin. The
Roman Empire was as much oriental as it was Hellenic, and it was only in
a trivial sense 'western'. It included a great diversity of peoples: Celts,
Germans, Romans, Iberians, Berbers, Illyrians, Libyans. The Chinese once
believed that Antioch was the capital of the Roman Empire rather than its
third largest city (Dudley, 1975, p. 243). Like the East, the Roman world was
a maritime civilisation based on cities and written cultures. A great network
of roads and seaways connected areas as far apart as the Thames and the
Euphrates. The encounter of Roman civilisation with the Orient did not always
amount to the same clash of cultures that resulted when the Romans annexed
Europe north of the Alps. It is evident, however, that Europe in Roman times
referred to a geographical region comprising, approximately, most of the
present continent of Europe, with the exception of Scandinavia. The British
Isles and the Iberian Peninsula were often excluded from Europe. Bede, in
his *Ecclesiastical History*, suggests that Britain is separate from Europe.
Europe was not yet a highly politicised concept. Europe had not yet been
'westernised'; nor, for that matter, had the East been 'orientalised'.

So, for much of Antiquity, Europe did not encompass what we associate
with it today. It was at most a region and not a continent in the geo-political
sense of the term: for the Roman Empire Europe did not constitute a cultur-

al model. Nor did it signify cultural unity since much of the continent was inhabited by 'barbarians'. There is little historical congruity between the modern notion of Europe as the West and the ancient idea of Europe. When we look back into early history we find that relatively few claims were made on its behalf. We can detect, however, the beginning of a civilisational struggle towards the cultural hegemony of the West in the sense of the cultural superiority of the Romano-Hellenic world over the unconquered world.

For the Romans the idea of Europe was not as strongly pronounced as it was in the Middle Ages. Roman ethnocentrism was focused, not on the idea of Europe, but on the myth of Rome as the centre of the world. Even in the early Christian era to be a Christian was to be a Roman, not a European. The notion of a European identity as opposed to the idea of Europe had not yet emerged. Yet while Virgil's Aeneas symbolised the unity of Orient and Occident, he ultimately represented the superiority of the Occident. Virgil's great epic poem, *The Aeneid*, gave poetic expression to the myth of the origins of the Roman nation. According to their myth of origins, the Romans could trace their history back to the fall of Troy in Asia Minor. The idea that it was the destiny of the West to inherit the burden of Oriental civilisation is central to the myth of the origins of Rome. This was later to become a major legitimation of western attitudes to the Orient. The myth of Aeneas survived into the Middle Ages in the formation of a European myth of origins: the exiled Trojans were supposed to have established a series of cities in the West and many of the western kingdoms claimed to derive their genealogy from the exiles of Troy (Tazbir, 1986, p. 6; Tanner, 1993). Both the Tudor and Habsburg historical myths of legitimation, for instance, proclaimed the Trojans to be their ancestors, and in the east the Ottomans also appealed to Troy for a myth of origins.

We must not, once again, overstate the difference between east and west as far as Antiquity is concerned. For the peoples of Antiquity the divide between north and south was a more significant one than that of east versus west. It must not be forgotten that in a seafaring age the Alps represented a far greater geographical, and hence cultural, divide than the Mediterranean, which had been the centre of world civilisation for long before it became a Roman lake. The sea served to unite people and civilisations rather than to divide them. The entire trading networks of the ancient world criss-crossed the Mediterranean linking Cadiz, Carthage, Alexandria and Constantinople into a unified trading bloc. For the Romans the Danube and Rhine were more strategic frontiers than the Don (Hay, 1957, p. 5). A geographical image that had far greater reality to the ancient and early medieval mind was that of Ethiopia, which was believed to contain the source of the Nile with which paradise was associated (Baudet, 1976, p. 15).

The ancient idea of Europe, then, did not signify the western continent but rather expressed a vaguely defined Occident, the land of darkness, the land of the evening sun. But even this notion of Europe as the Occident had not yet become a unifying idea of consequence. While the word 'Europe' did exist, the term 'Europeans' was rarely used in ancient times. Thus, the natives of Syria and Iran still call modern Europeans 'Franks' because they have no other word for the crusading Franks who arrived from the West in the twelfth century. Similarly in Greece the Europeans were known as Franks, and in parts of North Africa Europeans are still called Romans (Davis, 1988, p. 3). This suggests that the notion of Europe was at most a geographical idea and was not yet a cultural idea of significance, still less a political identity. The idea of a European identity had yet to be forged. Ethno-culturalism was in general focused on other reference points: Hellenism, Rome and the Christian church after the fourth century.

The division of the Roman Empire into two parts in 286 by the Emperor Diocletian was crucial in the shaping of the future antagonism between east and west. The two basins of the Mediterranean, with Sicily in the centre, became the cores of the West and East. But this early division did not reflect the later civilisations of Orient and Europe. While the eastern half included Egypt, the western half included 'Africa', which meant for the Romans the western parts of North Africa. Greece and the Aegean, and most of the southern Balkans went to the eastern half of the empire and the Italian peninsula remained a natural dividing line between the two halves of the empire (Herrin, 1987, pp. 22/3). Following a brief period of reunification Constantine transferred the capital to Constantinople in 330, and in 395 the Roman Empire finally split into two parts, the Eastern and Western Empires. This division did not mean that the split which was eventually to come about was determined from the very beginning. Constantinople, founded on the bridge between West and East, was simply the New Rome, or the Second Rome, and its citizens called themselves Romans. It was founded as a political expedient in order to protect the empire from attacks from Persia. Western Europe itself was quickly lost to the barbarians coming from the east and north. What then happened was that the Occident shifted eastwards once more towards Asia Minor. Initially the links between Rome and Constantinople remained strong because of the Muslim victories in Palestine, Syria and Egypt. But this was not to endure. Rome had long since outlived its military usefulness and the capital of the western part of the empire had in fact shifted to Ravenna in 402. In 410 Rome itself was sacked by the Goths, and in the sixth century Justinian, the eastern emperor, failed in his bid to recover the western parts of the empire.

In the centuries after its foundation, Constantinople acquired an identity of its own when it became more oriental and in language more Greek than

Latin. The notion of Europe subsequently came to designate the western part while the idea of the Empire came to refer to the Byzantine east, the Orient (Fischer, 1957, p. 44). So, Occident and Orient evolved to refer to the two halves of the Roman Empire. The term Occident, along with Europe, tended to be used increasingly for the western half of the former Roman Empire, making it possible to speak of the European Occident. Then, with the Byzantine empire laying claim to the imperial tradition, the identity of the western half came gradually to rest on Latin Christianity. Europe and Occident became synonyms for Christendom (Wallach, 1972).

The fissures of the conflict between Europe and Orient were slowly becoming apparent in these far-reaching developments. One thing was already clear: in the great transformation that accompanied the decline of the Roman Empire in the West, the notion of the Orient not only gained currency but its parameters were slowly creeping westwards. The Orient was no longer merely Persia, but was gradually coming to designate Asia Minor. With its advent the idea of Europe began to take shape as a cultural idea.

CRUCIFIX AND CRESCENT

From the seventh century the idea of Europe came increasingly to be articulated against Islam, which for many centuries held the upper hand. After the death of Muhammad in 632 his followers spread out from Arabia and conquered the Persian empire of the Sasanids and annexed the Fertile Crescent (the lands of Iraq, Syria and Palestine). In the seventh and eighth centuries the Arabs conquered most of North Africa with Alexandria falling in 642 and Carthage in 698. Muslim power spread over Anatolia, Persia and Mesopotomia, and eventually reached India. The Arab empire of the Umayyad dynasty, established in Damascus in 661, began to look westwards and advanced into Europe with the fall of the kingdom of the Visigoths in Spain in 711. After 711, until the Christian reconquest of Spain, the effective frontier of European Christianity in the West was the Pyrenees. The proximity of the borders of Africa and Europe where there was for centuries an overlapping of civilisations led Napoleon to remark that 'Africa begins at the Pyrenees' (Sertina, 1992, p. 2). The Muslim conquest of Spain was almost extended to France until the Arabs, under Abdier Rahman, were defeated by the Franks at the battle of Tours in 732. Significantly, one of the first references to Europeans was the army with which the Frankish leader, Charles Martel, defeated the Muslims (Hay, 1957, p. 25). This battle was of major significance for the future of Europe. Had the Muslims not been defeated it is not inconceivable that Christianity would have been wiped out in Europe.

Whether this is true or not, the symbolic significance of the battle, as opposed
to its possible military implications, is of greater importance in that it under-
lies the emergence of an adversarial identity in the West. Above all it heralded the arrival of Europe as a proto-cultural idea. Under the signs of the
crucifix and the crescent, the clash of Christianity and Islam was crucial in
the formation of the Eurocentric world-view.

Under the Abbasid caliphate, which emerged after the overthrow of the
Umayyads in 750 and lasted until the mid-thirteenth century when it was sacked
by the Mongols, Arab power, as a result of its non-Arabic conquests, became
transformed into an Islamic political system whose centre had moved from
Damascus to Baghdad, which was the new nerve centre of a vast trading network and linked up the entire Middle East. With the rise and consolidation of
this Muslim world-system, the West was put on the defensive. Charlemagne
failed to defeat the Moors in Spain in 778. The threat was no longer from the
barbarian tribes of the north who had been attacking the Roman Empire since
the fifth century, but from Islam. Many of the barbarian tribes, of which the
most significant were the Franks, had been converted to Christianity and became
the backbone of Christendom. The contours of Christendom became increasingly those of Europe so that the two ideas came to express the same cultural
model. The Orient was thus destined to become the new image of hostility for,
what was now effectively, the European Christian West and is best exemplified in the famous xenophobic paean, the *Song of Roland* (circa 1100).

With the expansion of the Islamic empire, the boundaries of Graeco-Roman
civilisation shrank to the Pyrenees and the Bosporus, which was put under
siege in 674–8 and again in 718. The Muslim civilisation that emerged in
the seventh century was more advanced than the cultural remnants of the
Graeco-Roman civilisation that had survived the fall of the Roman Empire
in the West. In fact Muslim civilisation absorbed more of Greek culture than
did the post-Roman West. Links between Europe and the Orient were broken during the period of Muslim ascendancy and it is believed that it was
the Jews who were the principal links between the two hostile worlds (Lewis,
1993b, p. 95). But we must not get the impression that there were two mutually exclusive civilisations confronting each other. Much of the classical culture, which had been extinguished in the West after the break-up of the Roman
world, was preserved, and indeed expanded, by the Arabs. Muslim Spain, in
particular Cordoba and Toledo, was important in transmitting Islamic culture to Europe in the period after the Reconquest. Sicily had for long been a
crossroads of the two civilisations and it was from there that many ideas
entered the two worlds. Arab culture greatly influenced European civilisation until the sixteenth century, after which it had passed its zenith when
Europe began to take over the leadership of the world.

The West was shaped by the Muslim onslaught in the one hundred years from about 650 to 750. This period, and not the beginning of the so-called Dark Ages after the break-up of the Roman Empire in the fifth century, was the real turning point as far as the formation of a European identity is concerned. After the Roman Empire had shaken off the barbarian menace by shifting to Constantinople, and later the Persian threat, it was confronted by Islam. The battle of Tours and the sieges of Constantinople marked the limits of Muslim expansion in the West. The Byzantine Empire had also reached the limit of its expansion and was unable to prevent Islam from encroaching upon its territory. But the Byzantines were only resilient; they succeeded merely in pushing the Muslims back but could not defeat them. After 700 the Byzantine empire had shrunk to Constantinople itself, parts of Asia Minor, Greece and parts of southern Italy. Nothing could alter the fact that Christendom was beleaguered by Muslim power in the east in Asia Minor, in the south from the southern shores of the Mediterranean and in the west in the Iberian peninsula. The annexation of Crete in 825 and Sicily in 827 imposed further restrictions on western Christendom. Islam by virtue of its possession of these strategic islands was in a position of real strength and virtually controlled the Mediterranean in the ninth century. In 826 Rome itself was sacked and the pope forced to pay tribute. By the twelfth century Christianity disappeared from the Maghreb. The spreading of Christianity was not only halted but was put on the defensive; and within Europe itself a wedge had been driven between the Latin west and the Greek east. Moreover, later conflicts between Persia and Byzantium exhausted both empires, preparing the way for Muslim ascendancy in the peripheries of Europe.

In the wake of the rise of Islam a new idea of Europe began to emerge whereby Europe came to refer to the north-western continent. With the loss of much of the Mediterranean to Islam, the Occident began to embrace the barbarian lands of the north-west. The West more or less abandoned the Mediterranean and the Byzantines were left to take the initiative on the eastern front. In 863 they defeated the Arabs in a major battle and, until the rise of the Seljuq dynasty in the mid-eleventh century, they pursued an offensive policy which held the Arabs at bay (Obolensky, 1971, p. 71).

CHRISTENDOM AND EUROPE

In this period, known as the Dark Ages, conventionally placed between 476, the year of the deposition at Ravenna of the last Roman emperor in the West, and the beginning of the Carolingian empire in the ninth century, Rome ceased to be the centre of Europe. The reforms that were carried out by the emperors Diocletian and Constantine enabled only the eastern part of the Roman Empire, the Byzantine empire, to survive. Following the great population migration of the Germanic tribes in the fifth century and the consolidation of the Anglo-Saxon kingdoms in England in the succeeding centuries, the centre of European civilisation shifted north-westwards, and the Baltic superseded the Mediterranean in importance. While the Germanic tribes were undermining the empire from the north, the Persians were attacking from the east. Western Europe was vulnerable to attack from all sides. In the ninth century the Vikings pressed southwards, the Magyars advanced from the east and the Muslims from the south. It was in this context that the idea of Europe gained currency (Leyser, 1992, pp. 40–1). The idea of Europe's historical uniqueness and autonomy begins to emerge in the face of opposition. The Islamic invasions along with the barbarian and Persian invasions gave a sense of a European identity to Christendom which served as a bulwark against the non-Christian world. It was a siege mentality, an identity born in defeat, not in victory. But with the gradual acceptance of Christianity by the northern tribes, from the Franks to the Vikings, the barbarian threat to Christendom was over and something like a European order was consolidated. The development towards a European civilisation centred in the north-west was enhanced by the ascendancy of Charlemagne who styled himself the 'father of Europe' (Fischer, 1957 p. 115). Europe had abandoned the Mediterranean for the Baltic. In this retreat it was to acquire a new identity.

Christianity provided the western monarchies with a powerful myth of legitimation which became increasingly consolidated with the encroachment of Islam. The need for cultural cohesion became all the more necessary because there was no central political authority under the system of feudalism that had emerged in the West after the break-up of the Carolingian empire in the tenth century. Christianity, with its ethic of obedience and hierarchy of power, was more adaptable to the settled agrarian world of feudalism than to the urban and secular world of trade and commerce. The notion of Europe as a geographical term became increasingly applied to the Christian parts of the West. Europe became identical with the notion of a Christian commonwealth, with the emphasis being on the north-west. With the rise of Islam, the ancient links between East and West took on the character of an enduring antagonism, and in this great and far-reaching shift in the formation of the identity of modern Europe, the northern and southern parts of Europe, for long separated by the Alps, merged to form medieval Christendom. A new border emerged, stretching from the Baltic Sea to the Black Sea. From then on the greater division between West and East took on the character of a moral-religious divide with the Occident signifying civilisation and goodness and the Orient barbarity and evil. The identity of Europe was constructed out of a sense of spiritual superiority in the disavowal of its own very origin in the Orient. Without the image of hostility afforded by Islam, the Christian West would have been unable to attain a single and high culture capable of unifying the diverse elements of European society.

This sense of western and Christian superiority is expressed in some of the early ideas of Europe. In early Christian times the idea emerged that the peoples of Europe, Asia and Africa were the descendants of Noah's three sons: Japheth, the originator of the Greeks, Gentiles and Christians; Shem, the originator of the Jews and Arabs; and Ham the progenitor of the Negroes. In the Christian mythology Japheth, the father of the Europeans, was accorded superiority over Shem, which meant Asia and designated primarily the Jews, and over Ham meaning Africa and referred to Africans. This idea survived into modern times as a conceptual tool in the service of Eurocentric philosophies of history for dividing the peoples of the world into races (Mudimbe, 1988, p. 46). With the decline of Rome, the notion of the Christian *oecumene*, the civilised world, emerged and Europe became closely identified with the Christian religion and its global aspirations. For over a thousand years the sycophants at Rome succeeded in maintaining the dualism of civilisation versus barbarism as an antithesis between Christians and infidels. Christianity then came to be associated with cultural superiority and civilisation while the non-Christian world was seen as uncivilised and barbarian.

Christianity was effectively 'Europeanised' from the eighth century onwards. From its origin as an Asiatic cult it became the imperial ideology of Rome and finally evolved to be the universal and legitimating myth of medieval Christendom under the aegis of the German Reich. The word Christendom was used from the ninth century (Phillips, 1988, p. 32). That Christendom as an expression was itself such a relatively late development – it was not in common usage until the eleventh century – we should not be surprised to find that the idea of Europe was an even later invention. From the early third century the notion of a Christian age had been established as the basis of historical chronology, while Islam established its own system of dating after the death of Muhammad in 632 (Herrin, 1987, pp. 1–6). The idea of a universal empire was taken over by the Church, which cultivated a historical memory based on nostalgia for the imperial past: the universal empire became the universal church and the cult of emperor worship was transposed to the papacy. In this transformation the Roman citizen became a Christian subject. The quest for universal imperialism was thus destined to become a crucial component in the identity of Europe. But, as Wallace-Hadrill (1985, p. 151) points out, 'the truth is that most people did not see the situation in this light and thought that European unity was an overrated ideal, like that of its parent, the *Imperium Christianum*.'

The word Europe, however, was rarely used until the fifteenth century. This was not surprising because Christianity, with which Europe was usually associated, was not a territorially unified culture. This inevitably led to ambiguity since Christian unity transcended European unity and was in its early phase a universal religion that was not specifically European. The Greek, or Byzantine, church became increasingly identified with the Orient. The Byzantine Empire never tried to monopolise the notion of Europe, which came to be applied, but never exclusively, to the former western empire after its restoration by the Franks and their Germanic successors, the Ottonians. In time the separation of the two empires would become a division of *ecclesia* versus *imperium*, or Christendom versus Empire. This enduring division, which has shaped the face of Europe until the present day, was also reflected in the schism within the Christian church itself, whose two halves spoke different languages and eventually acquired different cultural and ecclesiastical customs (Chadwick, 1990, p. 228). The attempt to enforce orthodoxy at the Council of Chalcedon in 451 prepared the ground for future secession. This, of course did not become irreversible until much later. Charlemagne's defeat of the Byzantines in 789 hastened the split within Europe. After the burning of the papal bull issued to excommunicate the eastern church at Constantinople in 1054, the division between the eastern Orthodox church and the western Roman church finally became permanent. The culmination of this was the sacking of Constantinople in 1204 by the Fourth Crusade. The idea of Europe as it became articulated in this period served as a means of alienating the Greek church from the Latin West.

It is significant that the identity of the Byzantine empire was constructed by the state which fused the sacred with the secular. In the Latin West, in contrast, the pattern of cultural and political identity formation rested on a separation of state and church. This was the basis of the West's divergent path of development. It meant that in the West, the state could decouple itself from the burden of legitimation with which the Byzantine state was encumbered. This was to be to the long-term advantage of the West, which was able to undergo a more differentiated logic of development. In this it is possible to see how the idea of Europe would become the secular identity of the West while Christendom would be its religious identity.

With the limits of Europe being set by the Muslim advance, Christianity had effectively become the territorial religion of medieval Europe. Christ was Europeanised and the crucifixion, after the tenth century, became the universal symbol of European mastery. To be a Christian was to be no longer merely a Roman or an imitator of Rome but to be a member of the universal Christian polity, the *oecumene*. Europe was the secular identity of Christendom which was for long associated with the Frankish empire. The idea of Europe gave to medieval Christendom a certain territorial unity with which it could confront the Orient. But this was a unity constituted only in confrontation and did not succeed in concealing the real divisions within the western system of medieval kingdoms. The notion of the Orient came to refer to the entire heathen lands of Asia Minor, Asia, India and the Maghreb. The rise of Christianity in the West, in effect, led to the equation of the Occident with Europe.

CONCLUSION

The aim of this chapter has been to show that the early history of the idea of Europe reveals a tension between its function as a geographical construct and as a cultural-political idea. The principal political polarisation with which the idea of Europe was linked, Christendom versus Islam, had in reality very little to do with the idea of Europe, but nevertheless influenced the future history of the notion to a great extent. We can conclude that by the tenth century the idea of Europe had evolved from a mere geographical expression to a cultural idea which had political uses but which had not yet stabilised to be the basis of a specifically European identity. The consolidation of the idea of Europe and the formation of an identity focused on it is the theme of the next chapter.

3 The Westernisation of Europe

THEORETICAL PERSPECTIVES

This chapter is mostly concerned with the consolidation of the idea of Europe as a cultural framework and the formation of a European identity in the Middle Ages. The counter-offensive, in the form of the crusades that the West launched against the Muslim Orient, failed to restore western fortunes, and, as a result, the identity of Europe as the Christian West found its focus of hostility in Islam. But the idea of Europe as a cultural model was mostly overshadowed by the rise of the Holy Roman Empire as the centre of Europe moved from the Mediterranean towards the Baltic. The foundation was thus provided for an enduring tension between the idea of Europe and the Holy Roman Empire, which sought to legitimate itself as the guardian of civilisation. Modern western Europe can be seen as the result of the failure of the empire to impose its rule over its vast territories.

Until the late fifteenth century the idea of Europe was principally a geographical expression and subordinated to Christendom which was the dominant identity system in the West. The idea of Europe as the West began to be consolidated in the foreign conquests of the age of 'discovery'. Europe then begins to shed itself of its association with Christendom and slowly becomes an autonomous discourse. As a result of the fall of Constantinople to the Turks in 1453 and the subsequent colonial expansion of the western European powers after 1492, the idea of Europe became linked to a system of what was coming to be regarded as specifically European values, though these did not become fully articulated as a European identity until the late seventeenth century. It was thus in the encounter with non-European peoples and in resistance to Ottoman expansion that the idea of Europe itself became the focus for the construction of a specifically European identity.

What we are therefore witnessing, in the period under discussion in this chapter, is the transformation of the idea of Europe into a European identity whereby Europe refers not merely to a geographical area but a system of 'civilisational' values. In this movement the idea of Europe supplanted Christendom as the cultural frame of reference for new processes of identity formation and the rise of new centres of power. In doing so, however, a tension emerged between the cultural idea of Europe and the geographical framework to which it referred. As a cultural framework Europe became the normative idea of a civilisation that was in the process of expanding overseas, but as the name of that civilisation's geographical territory it was faced with the problem that a considerable part lay under Ottoman suzerainty. This tension could not easily be reconciled, and so we find that the idea of Europe tended to be overshadowed by the hegemonic notion of the West, which became the driving force of the ascending European powers in their conquest of the Americas. The older ambivalence between Christendom and Europe was thus replaced by a new one with Europe and the West as the shifting signifiers of a rapidly expanding world-system with its epicentre in western Europe.

With expansion in the East for a time closed off, the lands beyond the seas provided room for European expansionary zeal. The age of discovery was a renewal of the crusading idea but with the difference that it was primarily western bound and the product of the new absolutist regimes and Counter-Reformation Roman Catholicism. In this transformation a new being was born: the European. The acquisition of the New World greatly strengthened a sense of European superiority at a time when the West had failed to defeat the Muslim Orient. In its colonising thrust across the Atlantic a myth was created. This was the European myth of the West, which was in subsequent centuries to become an important part of the identity of North America in the myth of the limitless frontier of the West. And, Europe, as the Old World, became the cultural repository of the New World. The myth of European civilisation was thus given substance.

In this period Europe emerged to become a clearly defined region, the centre of what Wallerstein (1974 and 1980) has called a 'world-system', and acquired an enduring identity based on its westward thrust. Up until the sixteenth century there were several world-systems, of which the European was relatively insignificant (Braudel, 1979, pp. 80–5). What may have been of greater significance was the Oriental-western world-system in the thirteenth and fourteenth centuries and the Mediterranean civilisation of the sixteenth century (Abu-Lugnod, 1989). It may therefore have been, as Marshall Hodgson (1962/3, p. 250) once suggested, that European modernity was 'the outcome of a breakdown of the common historical conditions on which rested the premodern Afro-Eurasian historical complex as a whole'. It is important to appreciate that the 'unity of Europe' which was constituted in this transformation was an invented unity. To imagine Europe involves the privileging of a particular discourse over others. In the Middle Ages this was Christianity against Islam; in the early modern period it was the victory of civilisation over nature.

THE EMERGENCE OF A EUROPEAN POLITY

What we today understand as Europe in its strict geographical definition was throughout the Middle Ages merely, to use Paul Valery's apt phrase, a 'peninsula of Asia' and was considerably less populated. It consists of not more than 7 per cent of the land surface of the earth, depending on how far the eastern limit is taken. Until the tenth century 'Europe' was less than one third its present size since the entity it designated did not include the northern regions. In comparison to China it was technologically backward (Needham, 1961). From the seventh to the late thirteenth centuries, China under the T'ang and Sung dynasties attained a higher level of development than the West. In this period western Europe was undermined by a process of fragmentation resulting from population movement and the decline of the Roman Empire. Medieval Europe consisted of some 500 political entities, including duchies, bishoprics, principalities and city states (Tilly, 1990, p. 45). Western Europe was weak in comparison with the Orient. The 'Little Ice Age' of the early fourteenth century and the ensuing Black Death of 1347–50 greatly weakened western Europe, which suffered a loss of as much as one third of its population. In contrast, the Byzantine east suffered less from these setbacks and, in fact, experienced a period of growth in the fourteenth century. Moreover, Europe was militarily ill-equipped to defend itself against Muslim expansion.

Only in the High Middle Ages (c.900–1250) did the West begin to overtake China, which underwent a process of stagnation following the Mongol invasions (Jones, 1987; Chirot, 1985). Western Europe, according to Hodgson (1962/3, p. 248), played a peripheral and until well into the Middle Ages a backward role. Though Chinese decline was offset by a period of recovery following the rise of the Ming dynasty (1368–1644), the development of capitalism and the system of nation-states that emerged in the West finally outpaced China (Mann, 1986).

So the relative underdevelopment of the West was to its eventual longterm advantage. Europe, as a result of the process of disintegration during the Dark Ages, in fact succeeded in discarding the burden of Antiquity, in the form of the ancient empires, and could therefore outpace the eastern empire and the oriental civilisations whose development had been retarded by the yoke of pre-feudal modes of production (Anderson, 1974a). The Black Death, for instance, in removing a large surplus population, may have provided a crucial condition for the emergence of capitalism in the West. The relative advancement of the East was ultimately an expression of the survival of Antiquity. It had surpassed its limits and was living on borrowed time into the second millennium; and the comparative backwardness of the

West was a sign of the transition to the feudal mode of production. Yet, the West did not finally surpass the Orient until the seventeenth century, though the roots of its advance did lie much earlier.

During the Dark Ages, from the fourth to the ninth centuries, 'Europe' – by which of course we mean Christendom – was unable to assert itself against Islam. The first wave of feudalism, from the fifth to the ninth century, had produced a static agrarian world. It was not until the High Middle Ages, from about 900 to 1250, that Christendom, enhanced by a forward thrust in the feudal mode of production – which led to a demographic explosion in which Europe's population doubled and a revival of trade occurred – attempted to launch a counter-offensive against the Orient. This was ultimately a failure, despite a relative expansion of frontiers, and Christendom had to reconcile itself to the fact that it had failed in its ambition for world mastery. But it was a failure that was not without success.

The collapse of the Carolingian empire led to the emergence of a number of independent Christian kingdoms from the ninth century. Strengthened by feudalism, these kingdoms gained a considerable amount of territory during the following centuries. Most notable was the rise of Norman power which, in the aftermath of the conquest of England in 1066, culminated in the capture of Palermo from the Arabs and in 1091 the annexation of Sicily. The thirteenth century reconquest of Spain consolidated these developments and by the early twelfth century the Mediterranean was once again, after some five centuries, recovered for Christian traders. These developments amounted to a general widening of the frontiers of Europe in the form of expansion of the French civilisation. The penetration of Norman power into the British Isles after 1066 and in Sicily after 1072 belong to the same dynamic. Between about 1000 and 1250 a whole new civilisational pattern based upon feudalism expanded as far west as Ireland and as far east as Jerusalem, bringing with it a uniform society (Bartlett, 1993). This new framework is what we call Europe: the watchword for the expansion of Franco-Latin Christendom.

THE RISE OF A CRUSADING IDEOLOGY

What was crucial to the identity of Europe was less its territorial expansion than its increased internal homogeneity. The idea of a Christian community provided not only a legitimating myth for medieval kingship, but also served as a medium of cultural cohesion for groups otherwise separated by language and ethnic traditions. Strengthened with an official liturgy and a centrally organised and militant episcopacy, Europe evolved a new counter-offensive against the Muslim Orient. The ensuing crusading ideology that emerged became an integral component of the identity of the European. The importance of the crusades is that they shaped the formation of an ethno-culturally homogenising identity, which subsequently became a core component of European identity.

The crusades were a collective mobilisation of Christendom and gave a strong sense of territorial identity to medieval Europe. The political energy of the feudal kingdoms in western Europe was transformed into an eastward movement towards colonisation. This was also Christendom's counteroffensive against Islam and the idea of a Holy War against the infidel was born. The crusades were able to take advantage of a period of crisis in the Islamic world in the tenth century when the Abbasid dynasty was overthrown by the Buyids. This period of disintegration and renewal lasted until the twelfth century, when a new centre of power emerged, based on the Seljuks, an ascending Turkish dynasty who adhered to Sunni Islam and who established themselves at Baghdad in 1055 and expanded into Anatolia in Asia Minor. The political unity of Islam split into a number of units, principally those centred around Cordoba, Cairo and Baghdad respectively. The Seljuk victory over the Byzantines at the Battle of Manzikert in 1071 won them most of Anatolia and precipitated four centuries of crusades. The entrenched Byzantines, who now had lost most of Asia Minor, sought the help of Gregory VII, whose successor, Urban II, responded with the First Crusade (1096–99) which he preached at Clermont in 1095. Though there are no records of Urban's famous speech, a English chronicler reports one of the first references to Europe, which is positively identified with Christianity in the context of the Islamic threat (Hay, 1957, p. 32).

This was also a period of Reconquest for the Latin West. The king of Leon and Castile, Alfonso VI, captured Toledo from the Muslims in 1084. This was an event of epochal significance for it signalled the advent of a new and larger Europe and a major victory for Christendom. Spain was the first of the former Christian lands to be reconquered until the recovery of Hungary in 1699 (Lomax, 1978, p. 1). However, further advance in the Iberian peninsula failed until the thirteenth century as a result of a renewal of the Arab power. The Latin West therefore concentrated on its eastern frontier in the confrontation with the Orient. The term 'Cold War' was first applied to the resulting tension between Muslims and Christians in the thirteenth century (Bozeman, 1960, p. 426) and the dichotomy of Self and Other that it postulated remained a determining force in the European identity for centuries.

The crusaders were also unable to overcome the differences that existed between them. The unity of Christendom was only a unity in the face of a common enemy. The crusaders were also disadvantaged by the revival of Muslim military power in the twelfth century. By 1187 Jerusalem had been recaptured by the Muslims. The subsequent crusades that were launched failed to reverse the fortunes of the West. The feudal states that the crusaders set up did not stand the test of time and by the late thirteenth century their lands were recovered by Muslims, with Acre, the last Christian state in the Holy Land, falling in 1291.

The idea of Europe was not central to the crusades; in fact it was probably its negation. Christianity was the principal identity of the crusaders. The symbol of the crusaders was the transnational symbol of the cross, not a national emblem, and they were known as 'the army of God' or 'the host of God' (Bartlett, 1993, p. 261). The crusaders retained the political identity of their respective kingdoms but their collective identity was that of Christian pilgrims taking the cross and sword. However, the term 'Frank' was in more common use than the notion of 'Europeans'. While Europe was in the process of becoming a clearly defined entity, 'Europeans' still hardly existed. Apparently the Byzantines, like the Muslims, labelled any westerners 'Franks' regardless of their origins (Bartlett, 1993, pp. 103–4). To the Chinese in their encounter with Europeans in the fifteenth century, the term Franks, as a pejorative word for Europeans, had found its way into their language (Bitterli, 1993). The dualism of Christians and infidels was more significant than the later opposition of Europeans versus barbarians. But the terms of reference for the construction of an adversarial system of contrasting identities had been created in what was to be an enduring notion of difference, of otherness. The emphasis on Christendom rather than Europe was not surprising since between 1099 and 1187 when Jersusalem was occupied by the crusaders, Christianity extended beyond its European frontiers.

The dominant power in the West was no longer Byzantium. Its age had passed and in 1071 it suffered a double defeat, one by the Turks at Mantzikert and the other by the Normans, the ascending power in the West, who had taken Bari, one of the principal cities of Byzantine Italy. After the Fourth Crusade ended with the pillage of Constantinople the empire never really recovered its former glory. The hostility of the eastern empire to Christendom was enhanced by the crusades. The Byzantines regarded the crusades, not as a Christian counter-force against Islam, but a formidable power which threatened their own existence. It was this divide that outlived the crusades which had effectively divided Europe internally as much as externally.

EUROPEAN IDENTITY AND THE EASTERN FRONTIER

The Ottoman empire established by the Turks became the principal military power in the East. In the early fourteenth century Osman had founded a state in the north-western part of Anatolia which was to become the basis of the future empire. In 1354 the Turks crossed the Dardanelles to Gallipoli and, after 1361, established their capital at Adrianople. Then they began their conquest of the Balkans with the famous battle of Kossovo in 1389 at which the Serbs were defeated and the whole of Christendom was put on the defensive. A further Turkish victory over a crusade that was sent to halt their advance at Nicopolis in 1398 confirmed their power on both sides of the Straits. The Latin West, weakened by the Black Death and destabilised by peasant revolts, was helpless to stop the Islamic revival of the fourteenth century. The fifteenth century saw the consolidation of Ottoman supremacy in the Balkans, Anatolia and the Aegean. In 1453 the Sultan Mehmet II seized Constantinople and, with the death of Constantine XI, the last eastern emperor, brought an end to the Byzantine Empire.

The fall of Constantinople was one of the really decisive events in the formation of European modernity. According to convention, the European Middle Ages came to an end in 1453 when the eastern empire fell to the Turks. Sunni Islam had finally won a major victory over the Christian world. Constantinople, renamed Istanbul, the city of Islam, was now the capital of the Sunni empire of the Ottomans. The capital of the greatest Islamic civilisation in the world was now located in Europe, giving birth to what for centuries was to be known as 'Turkey in Europe'. Within a decade the last Christian enclave in Asia Minor had fallen to the Turks. From then onwards the Latin West was put on the defensive: with the disappearance of the Greek Christian empire of the East, the Latin West was directly exposed to Islam which was within striking distance of the heart of Christendom and had occupied about a quarter of the territory of Europe. Equally important was the fact that both Europe and Islam had to compete for control of the same territory, which became the eastern frontier of the West. Moreover, the danger was not always military, but the fear of mass conversion to Islam (Lewis, 1993a, p. 13). The events of 1453 gained momentum in the following decades with the expansion of Ottoman supremacy over the southern and eastern shores of the Mediterranean, culminating in the conquest of Syria and Egypt in 1517, at the height of the Reformation in Europe, and its expansion across the Maghreb.

Towards the end of the Middle Ages we can speak of an epochal break between the Orient and Occident. A sense of European identity existed by the fifteenth century, but it was an identity that was shaped more by defeat than by victory and was buttressed by the image of the Orient as its common enemy. According to Hay (1957, pp. 86–7) there is a significant increase in the frequency of use of the word Europe in connection with the Turkish advance. Pope Pius II frequently used the word Europe in the context of the Islamic advance, though the traditional notion of Christendom was more frequently employed, and we find such expressions commonplace in the language of diplomacy: 'the common enemy, the Christian republic, the Christian world, the provinces of Christendom' (Hay, 1957, pp. 96 and 114). Burke (1980, p. 23) points out that when Pius II first heard of the fall of Constantinople he remarked: 'Now we have really been struck in Europe, that is, at home.' He was also one of the first to use the adjective 'Europeans', which he did in the context of the Turkish threat (Yapp, 1992, p. 141). His concept of Europe was not only that of Latin Christendom, but in the wake of the Turkish advance, it also included Greece, the Balkans and Byzantium (Barraclough, 1963, p. 24). Even the great humanists of the Renaissance were conscious of the increased importance of the Sublime Porte over the Holy See. This is evidenced by the proliferation of European publications on the Ottoman empire in the sixteenth century (Springborg, 1992, p. 277). Erasmus, who has often been called 'the first European', believed that the Christian princes should stop quarrelling in order to be able to form a united front against Ottoman power (Tazbir, 1986, pp. 11 and 16). He thus exhorted the 'nations of Europe' to a crusade against the Turks (Coles, 1968, p. 148; Curio, 1958, pp. 190–1). Luther, too, had hoped that Latin Christendom would be able to heal its self-inflicted injuries and take up the mission of the cross against the Muslim infidels. In his 'War Sermon' in 1529, Luther gave vent to the 'Great Fear' of peasants in Germany and central Europe that they would be overrun by the Turks in the fulfilment of an ancient prophesy (Bohnstedt, 1968; Coles, 1968, p. 146; Southern, 1962, pp. 104-9).

The origins of European identity can be found in the sixteenth century resistance to the Turks (Beck, 1987; Schwoebel, 1967). It was a consciousness that was sustained by the principle of exclusivity rather than on any kind of immanent collective cohesion. It was this adversarial identity that survived the demise of Ottoman sea supremacy after Lepanto in 1571 and provided the receptacle for a racial notion of European identity in the age of imperialism. At about this time the idea of Europe began to replace Christendom as a cultural frame of reference for the construction of new forms of identification. In this transformation Europe no longer signified a geographical area but a system of values. This is what made it possible for a French poet in 1555 to suggest that Europe might be saved by abandoning European territory and transferring European societies to the New World (Coles, 1968, p. 148). It also made sense to replace Christendom with the word Europe since it was obvious that not all of Europe was Christian. Moreover, the Greek writers who fled to the Latin West after 1453 undoubtedly found the rhetorical use of the Greek word 'Europe' more natural than that of Christendom, a development that was probably also reflected in the more general humanist preference for classical words (Hay, 1957, pp. 87–8). With Bodin in the sixteenth century, a shift is evident that Europe was in the process of replacing Christendom (Fritzemeyer, 1931, p. 90). But the idea of 'Europeans' seems to have been a later development. When Francis Bacon used the phrase 'We Europeans' in 1623, it is probable that it was already clear who they were (Hale, 1993, p. 46). So by the early sixteenth century we can speak of the creation of a discourse of Europe, which did not become a self-conscious identity until the late seventeenth century when the wars of religion petered out.

The formation of a European identity was never a predetermined. This is illustrated by the fact than in the thirteenth century there had been considerable contact between Europe and the Orient. For instance, European kings had their representatives at the Mongol court. In 1245 Pope Innocent IV sent an envoy to the court of the Khan and in 1255 Marco Polo went on his fourteen year journey through Asia. In this period many travellers had set forth to China from where many cultural and aesthetic influences came to Europe (Wittkower, 1977, pp. 10–14). In fact, the possibility of an alliance between Europe and the Mongols had been a very real possibility in the thirteenth century (Phillips, 1988, pp. 22–5). Chinese culture was an important part of the imagination of Europe until the mid-fourteenth century when the Ming Dynasty replaced the Mongol empire and contacts with Europe ceased. It was significant that this occurred at a time when the Latin West was also put on the defensive against the rising tide of Muslim power in Asia Minor.

The idea of a recovery of the Christian lands overseas never died and the ideal of Christian world mastery continued to be a powerful cultural motif in the West, which was never able to accept its diminished status. The idea of the enemy outside enhanced the mystique of Europe as the crucible of Christendom. By its very failure to expand, Christianity gave to Europe its identity. It was fateful that this was to be largely a German identity.

EUROPE AND THE MAKING OF GERMANY

In what follows, I should like to backtrack on the historical narrative in order to sketch the rise of the Holy Roman Empire and its creation of a competing notion of Europe. It is important to appreciate that the identity of Europe was not only formed in opposition to Islam, but was also shaped by tensions within Europe, which was never a homogeneous geo-political entity.

The main contender for the mantle of Christendom was the Germanic empire of the Franks. The shift to the north-west from the south-east was largely associated with the movements of the Germanic tribes. In the early Middle Ages Europe receded northwards following the movement of the Franks from their old capital at Aachen towards the Rhine. The division between the Roman world of the Mediterranean and the barbarian world of northern Europe began to be blurred in the formation of a Frankish-Germanic empire.

An embryonic Europe of nations emerged by the late ninth century with the contours of Germany and France already becoming visible. The borders of Charlemagne's empire coincided to a remarkable extent with those of the original EC and it has frequently been observed that the border between West and East Germany was not very different from the line of Charlemagne's advance into Germany (Seton-Watson, 1989, p. 39). The Frankish empire extended only as far eastward as the Elbe, the mountains of Bohemia and the Alpine districts of Austria; it was a small Europe, which excluded the Slav lands to the east and did not include all of Germanic civilisation (Barraclough, 1976, p. 18). In fact one of the early political uses of the word 'Europe' was at Charlemagne's court at Aachen (Barraclough, 1963, p. 12).

It was the Germans, who by aping the Carolingians, succeeded in evoking the imperial tradition. Ever since the crowning of Charlemagne by Pope Leo III as Emperor of the Romans on Christmas Day in the year 800, this association of imperial authority was bound to the notion of a Christian king. Charlemagne used the church as a bulwark against the aristocracy. Gregory the Great associated the Roman Church with the idea of Europe by making the papacy the centre of European gravity (Ullmann, 1969, p. 135).

The Carolingian Renaissance was also a 'European' movement. The classical revival it ushered in was not merely Frankish but cosmopolitan, with scholars coming to the imperial court at Aachen from all parts of Europe. 'The ideological concept of Europe determined its territorial extent: Europe as conceived in the Carolingian age stopped where Roman Christianity ceased to be effective' (Ullmann, 1969, p. 137). The new idea of Europe was institutionalised in religious institutions and brought about an ideological transformation of Rome into Europe. Following the ascendancy of the papacy, the idea of Rome had been broadened to include Europe with the consequence that a Greek was seen as a non-European and a Roman Christian a European (Ullmann, 1969, p. 139). The ecclesiastical conflict between Rome and Constantinople expressed itself in an enduring tension between the Latin West and the Greek Orient. Christianity effectively took over the ancient notion of the barbarian and applied it to non-Christians. The new dichotomy would therefore be one of Christians versus barbarians, and the hallmark of civilisation came to be membership of the Christian *oecumene*, the 'civilised' world.

The adoption of Christianity in northern Europe – complete with the conversion of the western Slavs in the twelfth century – facilitated the emergence of a new and wider civilisation in the lands of the Carolingian empire (Christiansen, 1980). It was this idea of a Christian empire that outlived the

German empire and became a major part of the culture and identity of Europe. It created the idea of a spiritual unity between Germany and Italy, Emperor and Pope. The wars Charlemagne fought were in the name of Christianity. The most significant of these were the wars against the Muslims in Spain which, like the crusades that were to follow, were conceived of as Holy Wars against the infidel. We can thus see how the contours of Europe became visible with the consolidation of two centres of power: the domains of Frankish emperors and the Byzantine emperor. Europe slowly ceased to be merely a geographical expression and came to denote a cultural unity that referred to the territories under Carolingian rule as opposed to those under Byzantine authority.

From the tenth century onwards in the wake of the break-up of the Carolingian empire the restored Roman empire, under Otto I, shifted to Germany and away from the east Franks. With the collapse of the Carolingian empire – which in fact was more of an international order than a Frankist one – in the late ninth century, the Germans were able to take advantage of the political vacuum that emerged. In 962 Pope John XII crowned Otto, as protector of the papacy, Roman Emperor. Thus the tradition of a Christian emperor that had begun with Charlemagne was reinvoked and the imperial title passed to Germany, providing that country with an abiding aspiration to make its frontiers coterminous with those of Europe.

Throughout the Middle Ages the German rulers contended for a hegemonic concept of European mastery with the invention of the Holy Roman Empire. For the eastern emperors the Holy Roman Emperors were mere usurpers and the gap between East and West widened. With the rise of the German empire, Europe became a more clearly defined territorial entity. This was of enduring significance, for it meant that the idea of Europe would be closely tied to German national identity. This is best exemplified in the tension inherent in that famous piece of political obscurantism: the 'Holy Roman Empire of the German Nation'. With the first part of the equation containing the tacit identification of the empire with Christendom, the second part effectively tied Europe to the 'German Nation'. It was out of this feud that the idea of Europe began to take on the increasing coherence of a cultural frame of reference for the northern princes. This was strengthened by the Habsburgs, who, though ostensibly Germans, were in reality more of a European house.

The German empire – an alliance of princes and counts under oaths of allegiance to the suzerainty of an elected emperor – was sufficiently large to be able to claim to be Europe, though what it in effect engendered was a generic form of *Mitteleuropa*. Dante, for instance, hoped that the German emperors rather than the papacy would unite Europe. According to Denis de Rougement (1980, p. 31) this was one of the first statements of the unity of

Europe. In the Middle Ages the idea of Europe became closely linked with Romano-Germanic culture. Europe had not been a clearly defined geo-political framework until it became fixed as the territory of the German rulers of the Reich. Europe then became 'Mother Europe' and was symbolised by the German Reich (Fischer, 1957, p. 111). The eventual collapse of the empire left its shell, Europe, more or less intact, but nonetheless, not unified. An abiding discord remained between France, heir to the Roman tradition, and Germany, which was only in part Romanised and the focus of its leadership shifted progressively eastwards (Cahnman, 1952, p. 619).

THE MYTH OF UNITY

We should not overstate the political or cultural unity of the Middle Ages. The unity of the Middle Ages is a myth (Balzaretti, 1992; Reuter, 1992; Rubin, 1992). To the extent to which we can speak of a common culture, it was expressed in a great variety of different forms. In western Europe there always had been a more significant difference between the towns and the countryside than in eastern Europe, where towns never reached the same degree of autonomy as in the West. The rise of autonomous cities not subjected to outside influences was a crucial development in the rise of western Europe (Benevolo, 1993, p. 23). According to Weber (1958) the rise of an urban population was the distinctive aspect of the European city. Popular diversity has been the key to the formation of Europeanism. Above all, revolutionary traditions have played a major role in the formation of the identity of Europe (Tilly, 1993; Pillorget, 1988). What was unique to Europe was not so much the nature of power exercised by the state, but the opposition that came from society. The stronger separation of state and society in Europe is often held to be a reason for its divergent path of development (Scüzs, 1988). Europe was never fully integrated from 'above' because of traditions of autonomous rights that had evolved as early as the so-called Dark Ages. In the twelfth and thirteenth centuries various groups succeeded in winning liberties from central authority thereby providing the basis for a lasting and organic process of development (Reynolds, 1984). It was upon the foundations of these traditions that revolutionary ideologies emerged.

Western Europe never reached the same degree of unity as other world empires had. Islam, for instance, like Christianity, is a religion of unity, but unlike Christianity it claims that all laws derive directly from God (Black, 1993). It is possible that the diversity of Europe was precisely as a result of the failure of the Church to unite western Europe into a single bloc. The answer that Europe found to the problem of cultural uniformity was the creation of what could be called a central institution in the form of the Church, which had succeeded in devising master codes for the organisation of knowledge according to a differentiated and rationalised world-view, but a world-view, it must be added, that failed to control political life. So, a civilisation such as India, in contrast, failed to develop unifying master codes to deal with its own diversity (Saberwal, 1986, pp. 23–3). The problem, then, is in using the idea of Europe to describe what are, in fact, structures of polymorphous diversity and manifold opposition to power. The 'unity' of Europe was more the pose of elites than a political reality.

Cultural diversity within Christendom ensured that the unity that Europe was to find was in foreign conquest and a focus of hostility beyond its frontiers. The hegemony Roman Catholicism eventually achieved should not blind one to the fact of the essential disunity of the Middle Ages. As Braudel (1990, p. 190) has remarked, Europe is diversity itself. The One Hundred Years War (1337–1453) between England and France, for instance, prevented the unification of the two countries and the formation of a mega-bloc in western Europe. For much of the fourteenth century there was a major schism in the Church with the popes resident in Avignon. Nor should we forget the long tradition of anti-Roman Catholicism that eventually culminated in the Protestant Reformation. Ironically, as the use of the word Europe increased in the sixteenth and seventeenth centuries, the continent became more divided than ever before. In addition to the international religious orders, other important agents of cultural change were the revival of Roman law, international trade, chartered towns and the universities (Bartlett, 1993, p. 288). The European universities can be seen as constituting a kind of European order and were rarely closely identified with any one particular country. Europeanism, then, did not always mean religious unity but a whole range of other factors as well as a long heretical tradition. The great European architectural styles – Romanesque, Gothic – could also be said to have given Europe a distinct form. So, if we are to speak of the unity of Europe it must be a cultural Europe rather than a political Europe that we are referring to.

THE WESTERNISATION OF EUROPE

As we have seen, the year 1453 was a turning point. After the fall of the Byzantine empire, the Latin West began to look westwards. The great defeat that the Turkish seizure of Constantinople signalled for the West was compensated for within four decades. The year 1492 was symbolically an important one in the formation of a European identity. In that year the Reconquest begun in the twelfth century was completed with the seizure of Granada from the Muslims, their last stronghold in the West. The Jews were expelled from Spain and the Muslims were forcibly converted to Christianity. The Christianised Muslims, the Morescos, were finally expelled from Spain in the early seventeenth century. This event in the history of Europe gave rise to the doctrine of the purity of the blood, which became the core of European racism in subsequent ages and a major legitimation of 'ethnic cleansing' (Poliakov, 1974, p. 137). The destruction of the mosques, the burning of Moorish libraries and the establishment of the Inquisition in the late fifteenth century further enhanced the homogeneity of western civilisation as a Christian polity.

After the late twelfth century the segregation of the Jews established a fear of pollution in Europe. According to R. I. Moore (1987) and Cohen (1993) Europe became a persecuting society in the early twelfth century when the new apparatus of government turned to minorities for a focus of hostility: heretics and Jews, for instance. The repression and persecution of minorities thus became a central component in European modernisation. It is possible that the split in Latin Christianity that occurred with the Reformation was projected onto scapegoats such as the Jews and women. This could explain the mass exodus of Jews from Central Europe and the increased witch-hunting which accompanied the zenith of the Reformation and Counter-Reformation (Israel, 1985, pp. 6–7). With the deliverance of Europe from the external enemy following the final retreat of Islam from the Iberian peninsula, the function of the victim, Europe's Other, was transferred onto the internal enemy, the Jews. This is also a demonstration that European unity was often the result of violent homogenisation.

The ascendant absolute monarchy in Spain required the cultivation of a myth of legitimation based on universal Catholic monarchy in which there could be no room for even the traces of earlier civilisations. From being a frontier land, Spain became a bulwark of a revived and imperialist Roman Catholicism. 'Europe conquered the Peninsula', Braudel (1990, p. 824) has written, 'by way of the Pyrenees and by the Atlantic and Mediterranean shipping routes: along this frontier zone it defeated Islam with the victories of the Reconquest which were victories for Europe.' Europe became subordinated to the notion of the West in the wake of the reconquest of the Iberian peninsula. Until the Reconquest Spain, being under Muslim rule, was not in the 'West' for Christendom. Prior to the Age of Discovery, the West as the Occident was defined by reference to the eastern frontier, that is, in opposition to Islam. After 1492 the ground had been prepared for the invention of a new myth of the West: Columbus replaced Charlemagne as the harbinger of the new age. The notion of the West became transformed into an outward movement.

THE IDENTITY OF EUROPE AND THE WESTERN FRONTIER

It was Portugal that preceded Spain in the 'age of discovery'. With expansion in the Iberian peninsula closed off, Portugal sought its legitimating myth in overseas conquest. What is interesting is the transformation of the reconquest of the Iberian peninsula into a movement towards world domination: reconquest became conquest on a far greater scale than anything that preceded it. The crusading ideal was revived in the making of a new European identity. The Portuguese explorer, Henry the Navigator, for instance, had been a crusader and a member of the Order of Christ (Phillips, 1988, pp. 248–9).

The year 1492 was also the year of the 'discovery' of America, though it was not for about two decades that it was finally recognised that a new continent had been discovered. Of course 'Columbus did not discover a new world; he established contact between two worlds, both already old' (Parry, quoted in Jennings, 1975, p. 39). It was at this time that the concept of the 'continent' entered the consciousness of a burgeoning Europe, which then became a mental image. In 1566 the first book in any modern language bearing the title *History of Europe* was published by a Florentine historian (Dionisotti, 1971, p. 13). Europe became an entity defined in space as well as in time. This was made all the more possible by developments in cartography (Lach, 1965, 1977; Hale, 1993). The advent of the map and the coming of the book made Europe tangible, a visible configuration: the Continent had finally arrived.

The period from the second half of the fifteenth century was one of growth for western Europe, which began to recover from decline in the fourteenth century. The shift from northern Italian city states to the Baltic had been marked by the burgeoning Hansa cities which dominated trade in the fourteenth and fifteenth centuries. Now, even their age was over: the age of exploration saw the rise of larger territorial states, proto-nation-states such as England, the United Provinces of the Netherlands, Spain and France. Preoccupation with the Turks thus shifted to overseas conquest. This was often seen as the only means of 'saving' Europe.

It was significant that this occurred at a time when the Orient seemed to reach the limits of its growth. These developments were consolidated with the gradual dismantling of medieval feudalism and the arrival of the great absolutist states with their mercantilist economies in the latter part of the fifteenth century. The long civil wars of the Middle Ages drew to a close, giving the West a respite from the Ottoman victory of 1453. The year 1453 also saw the ending of the One Hundred Years War (1337–1453) between England and France. The marriage in 1469 of Isabella and Ferdinand heralded the unification of Castile and Aragon in 1479 when the civil wars came to an end. Spain then ceased to be a frontier and became a world power (MacKay, 1977). The union of the crowns in Spain was accompanied by the extension of Spanish domination to North Africa and a new frontier was formed by 1511, the Ibero-African frontier (Hess, 1978). In 1480 the Russians under Ivan the Great finally ended the Tartar Yoke and the foundations of modern Russia were laid. And in 1493 the Pope, Alexander VI, divided the New World between Spain and Portugal. The victory of the Holy League over the Turks at the great sea battle of Lepanto in 1571 secured the conditions for western expansion. At about this time the other Islamic civilisations underwent an irreversible period of decline: the Safavid empire in Persia and the Mughal empire in India had become stagnant by the seventeenth century and were unable to withstand western colonialism (Umar, 1988). According to Toynbee (1953a, p. 21) the West had still not abandoned its desire to crush Islam but decided not to make a fresh frontal attack on the Islamic world, which was far from defeated after 1571. Instead, the West hoped to encircle Islam by conquering the ocean and opening up a new East Asian frontier between Christendom and Islam.

In this period the old polarity of Orient and Europe began to be replaced by a new one, Europe and the 'Overseas' (Gollwitzer, 1964, p. 39). New categories of differentiation emerged. We thus find the emergence of a new discourse of otherness. Cannibalism, for instance, became a major motif in western sterotypes of the non-European world (Hulme, 1986; Arens, 1979). With the decline in Turkish supremacy after Lepanto in 1571 and the completion of the conversion of Europe to Christianity, the idea of Europe tended to lose its strictly religious meaning and acquired a secular resonance. The term 'barbarian', for instance, rather than infidel tended to be increasingly applied to the inhabitants of the non-European parts of the world opened up in the age of exploration (Jones, 1971). Within a few decades the 'discovery' of the Americas impinged itself upon European consciousness to the extent that Europe began to find its identity more in westward expansion than in defensive postures against Islam. America rather than Islam was the great dominating theme in early modern Europe (Chiappelli, 1976; Honour, 1975; Jennings, 1975; Sale, 1991). Christendom was not so much abandoned as transformed into a western crusading movement. The Christian myth was simply transferred from the eastern frontier to the western in the substitution of the Islamic 'infidel' with the new construct the 'savage'. The idea of 'civilisation' became associated with Europe, which gradually began to replace Christendom and became an absolute value. In this migration of symbols the myth of the frontier became an enduring aspect of European identity now based on the nascent notion of the West. This crystallised in what Webb

(1952) has called the 'Great Frontier', which in his view has been one of the primary factors in modern history (Gerhard, 1958). We can now see how a new tension in fact arose between the ideas of Europe and the West. In this the idea of Europe was linked to the formation of a specifically 'western' identity. While the eastern frontier was a frontier of defence, the western frontier was one of expansion. Both frontiers, it should be noted, were created by the same dynamic: the Spanish simply transferred their war-machine from the wars with the Moors to the conquest of the New World. The western frontier was after all originally supposed to be the continuation of the eastern frontier, since it was only by accident that Columbus stumbled on the 'New World'.

It was Europe's mastery of the Atlantic – with the aid of new and improved methods of shipbuilding and navigation – that signalled the arrival of a new age and a specifically European identity. It is noteworthy that these developments coincided with the Galilean revolution in science (Mann, 1988) which enhanced Europe's secular identity. With the discovery of the Atlantic and the new trading routes it opened up, the conquest of the Americas and the Far East began. The Portuguese were the first to set up a vast trading empire and were followed by Spain which established a colonial empire. England and Holland followed in their wake with the foundation of the English and Dutch East India Companies in the early seventeenth century. An important dimension to the Commonwealth, 1649–1660, was the Cromwellian 'Western Design' – the mission to colonise the Caribbean – which provided Puritan consciousness with a means of recovery from the debilitating effects of the Civil War. The Western Design illustrated the manner in which European countries began to focus their identity in the conquest of foreign lands rather than in Europe itself.

European mastery thus passed to the control of the sea with the decline of the old agrarian based economies of the Middle Ages. The Muslims never commanded the sea in the way that the Europeans did. It was this mastery of the sea that helped to shape modern Europe. No point in Western Europe is further than 350 km from the sea, a distance which is doubled in Central Europe and reaches 11,000 km for the Russian plains (Mollat du Jordan, 1993, pp. 4–6). Moreover, the course of European rivers facilitates links between the seas and the agriculturally rich hinterland.

The divergence of European Christendom from the Muslim Orient and its spheres of influence in Europe now took on a new manifestation which was less confrontational. The new collision course between the two civilisations was more for the struggle to gain mastery over the seas than the extension of imperial domains within Europe. At least those countries which were to take over the leadership of the West, Spain, France, Holland and England, looked westwards. It is significant that this was at a time when the Habsburgs were still looking eastwards. The developments of the sixteenth and seventeenth centuries favoured nation-states with maritime and mercantilist economies rather than feudalist-agrarian and polyethnic empires. The development of Europe's maritime trade, however, did not have enough strength, at the end of the sixteenth century, to challenge the near eastern economy and the Ottoman Empire remained a formidable power on land. The result was that the deep discord between western and eastern Europe grew firmer: western Europe evolved to become a polity of mercantilist nation-states with non-European empires, while central and eastern Europe remained agrarian polyethnic conglomerate empires with their focus on the eastern frontier of Europe. The result was the formation of two notions of Europe, the idea of Europe as the West with its destiny beyond the seas – an 'Oceanic' Europe and a 'Continental' Europe (Cahnman, 1952) – and the old idea of Europe as a Christian bastion against the Muslim Orient. These two notions of Europe found their embodiment in the two imperial traditions: the colonial empires and the central European empires. Thus we can see how the construction of European world-views in focusing on a point outside themselves created the conditions for the future internal division of the continent into opposing camps.

CONCLUSION

In this chapter I have tried to show how the idea of Europe in evolving from a geographical concept to a cultural idea came to rest on two different kinds of identity. The first was shaped by the conditions of the eastern frontier in the confrontation with Islam during the crusades and the fall of Constantinople in 1453. The second was formed by the western frontier after 1492 when the European world system was consolidated by the ascending sea powers. These two models were reflected in different forms of empires. From the sixteenth century we can speak of a European identity, in the sense of an identity focused on the idea of Europe as opposed to Christendom. But this was always ambivalent as the cultural shift from Christendom to Europe occurred at a time of the birth of the more hegemonic notion of the West. In this transformation the new dichotomy of Self and Other came to rest on the myth of the savage and on the internal enemy, the Jews.

4 The Limits of Europe: The Shifting Frontier

THEORETICAL PERSPECTIVES

The theme of this chapter is the question of the historical frontiers of Europe, in particular the eastern frontier. One aspect of the argument is that what is often, and misleadingly, called 'Eastern Europe', in fact consists of at least two historical regions which can be contrasted to 'Western Europe', on the one hand, and to Russia and Turkey on the other. These regions are firstly, south-east Europe, comprising principally the Balkans, and, secondly, the 'lands between', that is the lands between Germany and Russia: Poland, the Baltic Republics, the former Czechoslovakia and Hungary. These two regions were the frontier zones of the larger empires of the Tsars, the Sultans, and the Habsburg and Hohenzollern emperors, and were never fully integrated into any of the metropolitan cores. They remained zones of transition between western Europe and Eurasia. The chapter also looks at the complex question of whether Russia is to be considered European or represents an independent phenomenon.

A central theme explored in this chapter is that the internal structure of Europe was shaped by an eastward process of conquest and colonisation. This inevitably led to a conflict with the two principal 'non-European' powers on its eastern frontier. What was crucial in the shaping of Europe was the process by which the core penetrated into the periphery and semi-periphery to forge a powerful system of political and economic control. The diversity of Europe was the product of enforced dependency and much of its unity was the expression of hegemonic forms of identity deriving from the core. The idea of Europe remained the cultural model of the western core states. A major implication of this view is that the eastern frontier of Europe was above all a frontier of exclusion rather than of inclusion; it accelerated and intensified a process by which Europe became the mystique of the West.

The idea of Europe began to take shape as the cultural framework of the western European core in the context of a double conflict. The age-old conflict between Europe and the Islamic East, represented principally by the Ottoman empire, reproduced itself as a conflict within Europe between western and eastern. In its eastward advance Europe in fact prepared the ground for future tensions since eastern Europe was never fully integrated into the new geo-political framework. Eastern Europe was always held in a double bind: on the one hand, it was regarded as being nominally European while being at the same time held in dependency. This was compounded by the fact that the west–east border from the Baltic Sea to the Aegean Sea more or less coincided with the division between Orthodoxy and Latin Christendom. As Russia increasingly began to replace the Ottoman empire as Europe's new arch-enemy, the difference between the eastern European orthodox lands and Russia became a faint one for the West. Opposition to the external enemy reproduced itself in opposition to the internal enemy.

Just as Europe in the Middle Ages had failed to create a geographical framework capable of integrating Greek Christianity and Latin Christendom, secular European modernity likewise failed to integrate the Slav and other eastern European lands into a unitary framework. Moreover, the European idea as a cultural framework was only partially extended to eastern Europe. The idea of Europe in fact drove a wedge through the Slavs, separating the west Slavs (the Poles and Czechs) from the east Slavs (the Russians). Europe as a geo-political framework was never coeval with the cultural model of Europe. Europe as an idea and reality was thus divisive both internally and globally.

THE BALKANS AS A BORDERLAND

The idea of Europe was never constituted by geography alone. It was always politics masquerading as geography that determined the definition of Europe. Of all of Europe's frontiers the eastern one was the most impermanent since there was no natural geographical line of demarcation. The eastern frontier was never fixed: its northern most point was to be found between the White Sea and the Baltic Sea and its southern point variously shifted from the Ural mountains, the River Don, Caspian Sea to the Black Sea and the Aegean Sea. There had always been an 'Eastern Question' as far as Europe was concerned and, indeed, its very existence required it.

Nowhere is the political nature of the definition of Europe more clear than in the case of the Balkan states. The Balkans always occupied an ambivalent position in the European imagination: while geographically they are clearly a part of Europe, politically they were closer to Asia Minor. They were for a long time excluded from Europe and were thought to be an extension of Asia Minor. Indeed, up until recently they were often referred to as the Near East (Hobsbawm, 1991a, p. 17). For Metternich 'Asia begins at the *Landstrasse*' – the road out of Vienna to the East (Taylor, 1942, p. 9). The Balkans were the dividing line of two civilisations, the point of collision between Europe and Asia. In this mountainous terrain – the word Balkan is

Turkish for mountainous terrain – not two but three religions collided, Sunni Islam, Roman Christianity and Christian Orthodoxy. The Ottoman advance into Europe and the European counter-offensive created an ethnic fault-line which in subsequent centuries became a frontier of civilisations. The Balkans lay at the centre of this borderland. They were never fully incorporated into either of the two principal powers, the Habsburg and Ottoman empires, which competed for control of the area.

Until 1919 the Balkans were a Habsburg–Ottoman frontier society, a zone of transition between two civilisations. The Balkans and the Adriatic Sea constituted western Europe's last line of defence against the Muslim East. By the sixteenth century the Black Sea had become a 'Turkish Lake' (Halecki, 1950, p. 79). The western frontier was then effectively the Adriatic, which at its narrowest point, the Straits of Otranto, is a mere 72 km separating Apulia from Albania, and it was across this narrow stretch of water that successive generations of invaders from the West – Normans in the eleventh century and Angevins in the thirteenth – launched their invasions of the Balkan possessions of the Byzantines (Obolensky, 1971, p. 10).

Even in Antiquity the Balkans were a borderland (Cornish, 1936, pp. 81 ff). When the Roman Empire split up into its eastern and western parts in the late fourth century, the new border ran more or less through the Balkans, dividing them into two territories. The line separating Greek from Latin Christianity followed the administrative division of 385 between the two halves of the Roman Empire (Palmer, 1970, p. 17). The Balkans subsequently became the dividing line – the Sava and Danube rivers becoming the northern frontiers of the rising Ottoman empire – between Occident and Orient, and the southern Slavs, who began to settle in these territories in the sixth century, inevitably became the frontier ethnic groups of larger territorial units. When the Slavs occupied these territories, having moved into the vacuum created by the westward migration of the Germans, the indigenous Greek and Latin populations were driven out and the bridge between the two civilisations was broken. Only the Albanians, in their mountainous stronghold, could preserve continuity in their history. The new Slav settlements corresponded closely to the older Greek and Latin divide. This cleavage was also reflected in their conversion to Christianity in the ninth century.

The Balkans represented the outer limits of Europe, the point of collision between the Latin West and the Muslim Orient, and it was here that the struggle for the mastery of Europe expressed itself in the ethnic tensions which have endured to the present day. McNeil (1964) refers to south-east Europe as Europe's 'Steppe frontier', where the only effective choice lay between competing imperial systems. Many of these frontier zones were caught up in a regressive transition from Ottoman–Byzantine rule to Russo-Western affiliations which prevented autonomous development. For the same reason, the Balkans were never entirely assimilated by either side (Braudel, vol. 11, 1987, pp. 776–7). As a consequence of being marcher regions of larger political entities, the Balkan peninsula was never united into a single state so that for most of their history the southern Slavs never had a single political centre.

The lineaments of future conflicts in Europe are recognisable in the original divisions of the Roman Empire: the lands of what were to become Russia, Serbia and Bulgaria went to the Byzantine Empire while Hungary, Croatia, Bohemia and Poland remained in the western half. As I have argued in the previous chapter, it was in the Balkans that the Ottoman Empire made its northernmost drive so that by the middle of the fifteenth century, as the Latin West was beginning to amass great empires in the New World, the Muslim East was rapidly gaining ground on Europe's eastern frontier. The entire Danubian plain and the Levant were under the Turkish Sultan by the end of the sixteenth century. The climax came in 1529, at the height of the Reformation in the Latin West, when Vienna was put under siege by the Ottomans. Though they were eventually resisted, the West, even after the great sea battle of Lepanto in 1571, failed to stage a showdown with Sunni Islam. It was not until 1683, when the Turks, under their leader the Grand Visir Kara Mustapha, again had reached the gates of Vienna that the West mobilised itself in an international campaign, the Holy Alliance, financed by the pope, Innocent XI. But the international counter-offensive that was launched was never able to reach more than a stalemate.

The Ottoman ambition, after storming Vienna and enforcing Islam on it, had been to move against Louis XIV (Vaughan, 1954, pp. 268–78). But after Vienna was delivered from its siege, the prospect of a Muslim victory in Europe was diminished. The Habsburgs remained the only western Catholic power in Eastern Europe and their obsession with Roman Catholicism can be seen in the context of the threat that the Turks represented. This has been called an '*antemurale* myth', the myth of the Christian frontier (Armstrong 1982, p. 91). Until 1918 most of the south-west of Europe remained nominally dominated by the Turkish Sultans (Kortepeter, 1973). Even after the Ottoman advance was halted the West remained weak, particularly as a result of the seventeenth century wars of religion. The Ottoman Empire, however, had reached the limit of its power and economic capacity for sustained growth: it was effectively living on borrowed time. It was crucial that this was at a time when the West was about to break its links with medieval feudalism by establishing proto-capitalism with the commercialisation of agriculture and mercantilism, the basis of its future take-off.

The consequences of the confrontation between the Habsburgs and the Ottomans was the creation of frontier societies in the intermediary lands between the two great powers. Since 1699 Croatia had effectively become a frontier society after the Turks had been repelled from Vienna, following their last great siege of the Habsburg capital. After the Peace of Karlowitz in Croatia in 1699 the northern parts of Croatia had become a permanent line of defence and Hungary, along with Transylvania, was regained by the West. Croatia itself had been a kingdom in the tenth and eleventh centuries, but was absorbed by Hungary, which in turn was assimilated by Austria. Croatia had become a frontier zone in the sixteenth century when the Croatian Military Frontier was established by Ferdinand I of Austria at a time when the Turks, having occupied the Hungarian-Croatian kingdom, were within striking range of Austria (Rothenburg, 1966). Croatia thus became a bulwark of Roman Catholicism while Serbia became a bulwark of Orthodoxy.

The Balkans were caught in a double bind. On the one hand, they were divided between Islam and Christianity and on the other hand there was an abiding division between Roman Catholicism and Christian Orthodoxy. These fissures, in the form of marcher regions, were the price that had to be paid for a European identity. The most enduring mark of the clash of cultures is Bosnia. A Bosnian state had come into existence in the twelfth century and, after a short period under Hungarian rule in the early fourteenth century, had expanded to include the neighbouring province of Hercegovina but became a province of the Ottoman Empire in 1463 after the Turks had conquered Serbia. This Muslim island within the borderlands of the Christian West continued to be loyal to the Turkish sultans. It was in Bosnia that the Christian West had its closest encounter with Sunni Islam and this clash of civilisations was destined to be a complicating factor in European history for centuries (Malcolm, 1994).

The history of south-east Europe was determined not only by the Muslim threat, but also by the division between Christian Orthodoxy and Roman Catholicism. What was to be of great and far-reaching significance for the future history of Europe was the process of Christian conversion in eastern Europe. The Poles, Czechs, Slovaks, Magyars, Croats and Slovenes fell under the influence of Roman Catholicism while the Serbs, Montenegrins, Bulgars, Greeks and Russians looked to the Byzantine Patriarch. This religious divide not only drove a wedge between the Slavs themselves but also shaped the formation of a border between East and West. Since the Schism of 1054, Greek Orthodoxy was regarded by the Latin West as heretical and alien to Christendom. The conflict between Latin and Greek Christianity far exceeded the division between Protestantism and Roman Catholicism. The result of this divide was that the identity of western and eastern Europe came increasingly to be expressed in an enduring cultural animosity. Orthodoxy was seen as semi-oriental and foreign to the identity of the Latin West. After 1204 the difference between Orthodoxy and Latin Christianity was almost as great as the difference between Christianity and Islam.

The conflict between Orthodoxy and Western Christianity was furthermore intensified in the Balkans by the incorporation of the Orthodox Slavs into the Ottoman empire. The Serbs, Bulgars and Montenegrins were assimilated into the Ottoman empire from the fourteenth century. Thus it came about that the consciousness of the Croats and Slovenes was formed by Latin culture and Roman Catholicism, while the identity of the Serbs and Montenegrins was shaped more by the Greek heritage of Byzantine after Roman Catholicism had been abandoned in the early thirteenth century. This division between the two churches was then part of a more general clash of cultures, of West and East. This became all the more pronounced when the northern provinces of the Balkans – Croatia and Slovenia – were assimilated by the Habsburg empire in the seventeenth century after the Turks had been driven out. These provinces had been part of the Napoleonic Illyrian state from 1809 but the Habsburgs regained control of the provinces after the Congress of Vienna in 1815.

The Serbs, in contrast, remained more firmly in the eastern tradition. Serbia had originally been a client state of the Byzantine empire and became a kingdom in the thirteenth century only to fall under Turkish tutelage over a century later. Ever since the fall of the medieval state, Serbian national consciousness was preserved in the Orthodox church (Petrovich, vol. 1,1976, pp. 10–14). Serbia had won autonomy from the Turks by 1830 and in 1878, after the Congress of Berlin, became an independent state, along with Romania (de facto since 1859) and the de facto creation of Bulgaria. Serbia and Montenegro became kingdoms in 1882 and 1905 respectively. Bosnia and Hercegovina, and Croatia and Slovenia remained in the Dual Monarchy, while Albania and Macedonia with their large Muslim populations remained in the Ottoman empire. The Ottomans greatly distrusted the populations of south-east Europe, especially their Orthodox subjects, and it was principally against them that they had fought their greatest battles (Sugar, 1977, p. 254). The Balkans remained an anomaly in the balance of power system. The Congress of Vienna in 1815 integrated Russia into the Concert of Europe, the congress system, and thus provided stability for western–Russian relations. No such measures were undertaken for the Balkans, which remained the Achilles heel of the balance of power.

THE LANDS IN-BETWEEN

It was the fate of the western Slavs, the Poles, Czechs and Slovaks, to find themselves located in a stretch of the continent between eastern central Europe and

Russia. This borderland, once known to German historians as _Zwischeneuropa_, meaning Europe's borderline, is often called the 'lands between' (Palmer, 1970). It comprises the area between Germany and Russia: the Baltic Republics, Poland, Czechoslovakia, Yugoslavia, Bulgaria and Romania. This was a zone of partial and short-lived conquest and for that reason no state ever survived for long. The concept of _Zwischeneuropa_ was popularised by Wirsling (1932) whose ideas reflected the belief that the east central European states were not nation-states and had to be incorporated into Greater Germany. Not surprisingly, for the Germans it signified a war ideology and became a part of political language during the First World War (Conze, 1992, pp. 1–4). The Slavs were thus locked between greater empires and the struggle to attain hegemony in these intermediary regions was never conclusively resolved. All victories were provisional.

The origin of the ethnic tensions in eastern Europe are to be found to a significant extent in the process by which Germanic civilisation shifted from the Rhine to the north-west. With the rise of Prussia in the Middle Ages, the German centre of gravity shifted from the south to the north and the conflict between Germany and Italy came to be overshadowed by the conflict between Prussia and Poland. By pressure of surplus population, the Prussians started to move eastwards in the early twelfth century and occupied the area between the Elbe and the Oder but failed to hold the lands further eastwards in their entirety. East Prussia was colonised by the Teutonic Knights in the thirteenth century while Pomerania and West Prussia were later added to the original kingdom of Brandenburg, linking it with East Prussia.

The tensions in the area were further exacerbated in the thirteenth and fourteenth centuries when the German settlers came into contact with Russians and an enduring conflict emerged between the adherents of two religions, Latin and Greek Christianity. The _Ostsiedlung_, the colonisation of the east, which stretched from the shores of the Baltic to the Carpathians, produced a clash of cultures between those Slavs who were converted by the Russians and those converted by the Germans (Bartlett, 1993, p. 8). The Slavs who accepted Roman Catholicism and those who accepted Greek Orthodoxy formed distinct groups, and were furthermore differentiated from those in the Balkans who accepted Islam. The result of this was that eastern Europe became more culturally heterogeneous than western Europe, despite greater linguistic homogeneity. Western Europe, which is mostly Romano-Germanic, has been shaped by Latin Christianity, while eastern Europe has been shaped by both Greek and Latin Christianity – a cleavage that is arguably greater than that between Roman Catholicism and Protestantism.

As Germany expanded eastwards, the result was that the two great centres of Germanic civilisation, Berlin and Vienna, were isolated on the eastern flank of their empires, precisely at the point of their greatest weakness. In the fourteenth century, when Charles IV became Holy Roman Emperor, Prague became the capital of the empire, and with the foundation of the University of Prague in 1348, the centre of German culture moved outside the traditional lands of the Germans. This led to an unrelenting desire for the recovery of these lands, which lie mid-way between Berlin and Vienna: 'He who is master of Bohemia is master of Europe,' declared Bismarck (Palmer, 1970, p. 6). As a result of the shifting nature of Germany, no single political centre emerged capable of dominating the German-speaking peoples. The result was the formation of several metropolitan centres: Berlin, Vienna, Prague.

The failure of eastern European states to endure was a crucial factor in shaping the course of European history. The medieval monarchies were eventually absorbed by larger dynastic empires and, consequently, much of eastern Europe failed to evolve into nation-states such as were in the process of formation in western Europe. While the fourteenth century was a period of crisis for western Europe, eastern Europe made a rapid recovery from the Mongol invasions of the previous century. Poland, Lithuania, Bohemia and Hungary established themselves as independent monarchies in the fourteenth century and constituted an eastern belt that stretched from the Baltic Sea to the Caspian Sea. One of the most striking features of fifteenth and sixteenth century Europe was the Lithuania-Polish Kingdom which stretched from the Baltic Sea to the Black Sea. In fact, it largely comprised the area which was to become Europe's borderland. The disappearance of this kingdom contributed greatly to the future divisions of eastern and western Europe. These developments lay behind Engels' famous distinction between the historic and the non-historic nations of Europe. The Slavs, in the opinion of Marx and Engels, were a 'non-historic people' because they never formed lasting states in the Middle Ages.

The problem in Poland was that it became a frontier zone between the great powers, not only between Prussia and Austria but also between the larger mega-units of Europe and Eurasia, or Russia. The western powers regarded Poland as little more than a buffer-zone against Russia, which to them was an extension of Asia. Poland itself, from the sixteenth century, struggled against its role as a political football and strove to represent itself as having a historic mission to fulfil as the defender of Christendom (Tazbir, 1977).

One of the principal differences in the consciousness of eastern and western Europe was the manner by which political consciousness was linked to the formation of states. The tendency in western Europe was towards the formation of national states whose territory, in fact, had not significantly changed throughout the early modern period, c. 1450 to 1700. Moreover, these states, England, France, Spain, Portugal, the Netherlands, could be more or less identified with a dominant ethnic group which had gained power. In addition, these proto-nation-states which were in the process of formation in the Middle Ages could be closely related to national dynasties and national consciousness in general was more formed within the structures of the nation-state. However, in eastern Europe there was less congruity between state structures and ethnic-cultural traditions. The great empires of the Habsburgs and Ottomans were polyethnic. The result was that the identity of the Slavs came increasingly to be articulated in ethnic forms. National identities evolved out of ethnic and religious traditions which had existed in the frontiers. The combination of social subordination and political fragmentation had the effect of transforming these traditions into abiding ethnic-national identities.

As Bartlett (1993) has argued, Europe was the product of a process of conquest and colonisation. It was this that shaped the principal forms of identity in eastern Europe. Modern European racism is closely related to patterns of European identity that were consolidated in the process of colonisation in eastern Europe. While the principal forms of identity in eastern Europe were essentially cultural constructions based on language and religion what was to emerge out of these were biological notions of race. Ethnicity became transformed into a category of descent through blood while its medieval and early modern prototypes were entirely cultural (Bartlett, 1993, p. 197).

The weakness of the ever-shifting eastern border provided ample scapegoats for xenophobic myths. The three great bogeys of western Europe which gave it its enduring historical consciousness were the Muslims, the Jews and the Slavs. According to the ancient myth of the threefold division of the world, the Jews were not the true people of Europe but an Asiatic import. They had been expelled from England in 1290, from France in 1394 and from Spain in 1492. From the Middle Ages onwards the identity of Europe was shaped by Latin Christendom. In this narrow world-view there was no room for competing religions. The Jews were to bear the brunt of much of European Christianity's struggle against its eastern frontier with which they were associated. The Jews were most numerous in the Slav lands, especially Poland, and served as scapegoats for the failed ambitions of European expansion eastwards. The external threat that the Turks represented became transformed into an internal threat. After the fall of Napoleon, German reactionaries had need of a new focus of hostility to replace the defeated French and were able to find it in the Jews (Poliakov, 1974, p. 94). Anti-Slavism is deeply rooted in the political psyche of *Mitteleuropa*. Like the Jews and Muslims, the Slavs were regarded as being Asiatic or semi-oriental. They were also one of Europe's principal exports to the Islamic world. Europe, which had little to offer the Islamic lands in return for the huge quantities of oriental products it imported, sold eastern Europeans as slaves, from which term 'Slav' is derived (Lewis, 1993a, pp. 22–3).

It was not only the need for cultural constructions of Otherness that facilitated the creation of a hegemonical concept of Europe. It was also the rivalry between the Great Powers – Austria, Prussia, Russia and the Ottoman empire – that prevented the autonomous development of the Slav peoples and forced their incorporation into larger frameworks. Eastern Europe, as a result of belated development into feudalism, was held in enforced subordination to the West for which it was used as a cheap supplier of grain. While in the West the peasant classes were emancipating themselves from feudalism in the fifteenth and sixteenth centuries, if not before, feudalism was only beginning to be enforced in eastern Europe as landowners saw advantages in the new corn market in the West (Postan, 1970, pp. 166–74). Feudalism, for instance, was introduced to Wallachia in 1595 and as late as 1621 to Moldavia in present-day Romania (McNeil, 1964, p. 103).

At the beginning of the modern age the corn trade ensured that the Elbe represented a permanent line of demarcation between east and west: the Junker-dominated lands east of the Elbe served as a supplier of food for western Europe. Europe thus underwent two distinct phases of feudalism, one in the west and one in the east: from the ninth to the fourteenth century in the west and from the fifteenth to the eighteenth century in the east (Anderson, 1974a, p. 263). It is significant that the introduction of retarded feudalism in the east, where there previously had been none, was partly as a result of the intrusion of the West. The paradox of eastern European history is that the relative progress and prosperity that it had achieved in the pre-modern period, when much of it was still under Byzantine rule, was partially the cause of its decline in the modern age. As the West advanced, the East fell into the very bondage thrown off by the West. Moreover, the kind of feudalism that was belatedly introduced in the east was not based on contractual forms of obligation as had evolved in the west.

The Byzantine heritage and the polyethnic empires of the Habsburgs and Tsars were unable to sustain the advances that had been made in the process of state formation in the Middle Ages and the area regressed after penetration by western capitalism and colonialisation. The problem for eastern Europe is that it developed within the structures of a belated European feudalism while at the same time being exposed to alien states. The result of this uneven development was that much of eastern Europe underwent a regressive transition to Modernity. One illustration of this is that in eastern Europe the cities were more ethnically differentiated (Jews, Germans, Slavs and Magyars were often to be found in the towns) than in the countryside, which was more homogeneous and dominated by peasant life, while in western Europe there were closer links between countryside and town. Anderson (1974a) argues that the roots of the divergent paths of development lay in the fact that there

was great continuity in western Europe, where in early times the communal
mode of production of the Germanic tribes fused with the Roman slave-ori-
ented and urban economy, which, in turn, was absorbed by feudalism, thus
giving way to capitalism (Anderson, 1974a; Scüzs, 1988). In eastern Europe,
however, according again to Anderson, there was greater discontinuity because
the agrarian economy of the early Slavs clashed with the pastoral nomadism
of successive invaders coming from further east, with the result that it failed
to establish feudalism at an early stage and consequently the historical conditions for the emergence of a modernising bourgeoisie were absent.

This general development cannot be disconnected from the fact that western Europe had, by the sixteenth century, become the centre of a world-
system whose economic dictates required an international economy in order
to have access to cheap labour and markets. The penetration of western capitalism into eastern Europe was thus determined by the same forces that brought
about the introduction of slavery in the New World (Braudel, 1979, pp. 92–3).
What then was crucial in the shaping of Europe was the process by which the
core penetrated into the periphery and semi-periphery to forge a powerful system of political and economic control. Indeed, much of the diversity of Europe
was the product of enforced dependency, and, much of its unity was the expression of violent homogenisation deriving from the core.

THE INVENTION OF EURASIA

The Balkans form only one of Europe's frontiers against the East. The other
is Russia. European identity was formed in opposition both to the Muslims
and to the Mongols, with whom Russia became associated. For Europe,
Russia was semi-oriental and a product of Asia, not of Europe (Dukes, 1991;
Groh, 1961; Kristif, 1968; Stökl, 1965; Wittram, 1973).

The conventional geographical limit of Europe is the Ural mountains. This
is the school textbook definition of Europe. However, these relatively low-
lying mountains do not form a real geographical barrier and are as arbitrary
as any other border. They were unknown in the West until the sixteenth century and most seventeenth and eighteenth century maps ignored them (Parker,
1960, p. 284). The Ural mountains were not important enough even to serve
as a boundary between one local province of the Russian empire and another. Moreover, when Russia began to expand eastwards beyond the Urals the
distinction between European and Asiatic Russia did not coincide with what
is conventionally taken to be the limits of Europe (Halecki 1950, pp. 86–7).
There was rarely consensus on the geographical criterion to demarcate Asia
from European Russia. Many disputed the Ural mountains as a natural divide

and argued for the lowland plain beyond the Urals, while Alexander von Humboldt considered the western regions of Siberia to belong to Europe (Louis, 1955, pp.74–5). Russia has generally been regarded as a mixture of Europe and Asia, hence the term 'Eurasia' to describe Russia west of the Urals (Szporluk, 1990). Though Russia did not expand beyond the Urals until the sixteenth century, it had frequently been associated in the western mind with Asia. European Russia, to western eyes, did not always embrace Transcaucasia, the isthmus between the Black Sea and the Caspian Sea, though the Tsars regarded this region as part of European Russia. In fact Transcaucasia was often thought to be an extension of the Steppes until the area came under Russia supremacy in the late eighteenth century. Only then did it come to be associated with Russia and Europe. But the idea remained that Russia itself was an extension of the Steppes, which connected the area of the Black Sea and the lower Danube with the Far East, and was the route by which Asiatic influences from Mongolia entered the West (Hartley, 1992).

It has been argued by Lemberg (1985) that the idea of Russia as Asiatic was a nineteenth century German invention which succeeded in replacing the far older antithesis of north and south with a west–east polarity, so that Russia ceased to be associated with the north and came to be seen as an eastern country. This argument reinforces the argument that the traditional east–west polarity was one shaped by the conflict between Christianity and Islam and its principal protagonists were Latin Christendom and the Ottoman empire. Russia was not then integral to this antithesis until much later. It is also possible that it was the Russians themselves who invented the myth of Europe extending to the Urals. It has been argued that this idea became established in the eighteenth century and expressed the desire of Peter the Great to have the Russian empire identified with Europe, where its capital, St Petersburg, was located, while its colonial peripheries could be identified with Asia (Bassin, 1991). After the victory over Sweden in 1721 the idea of Russia as a tsardom was abolished and replaced by the western notion of an empire with the Ural mountains as the newly invented boundary between the European homeland and the Asiatic empire (Bassin, 1991, pp. 5–7). So according to this view, it was the Romanovs themselves who invented the idea of Europe ending at the Urals. It is also interesting to note that while the Romanovs were opposed to the liberal constitutional ideas of the West, there was a prevalent tendency to define Russia in opposition to China rather than to the West: Russians were Europeans in China, but in Europe they were Russians. They also saw themselves as Europeans when they had to deal with their Asian provinces (Riasanovsky, 1972; Sarkisyanz, 1954).

The problem that Russia presented for the West was a double one. On the one hand, there was a long association of Russia with the Mongols who had ruled the entire country in the thirteenth century. On the other hand, there was the fact that Russia itself, after emancipating itself from the 'Tartar Yoke', turned eastwards and colonised north-eastern Asia. Russia came to be a frontier separating Europe from Asia. Moreover powerful forces within Russian society rejected Europeanisation, a synonym for reform, and advocated the uniqueness of Slavic civilisation. The nineteenth century debate between Slavophils and Westerners on whether Russia owes its origins to an indigenous process of development or to the impact of the West reinforced the attempt of the West to distance itself from Russia. It was in this context that the myth of Eurasia emerged in Russia in the early twentieth century. Eurasia signified the birth of an anti-western Russia and belief that Russia constitutes an independent historical reality between Europe and Asia. Dostoevsky, for instance, regarded Russia's legitimate aspiration to be opposition to British imperialism and to take up the Christian struggle against Islam (Hauner, 1990, p. 49). The idea of Eurasia itself did not always convey anti-Russian prejudices. While the word was coined by a Viennese geologist in the 1880s to describe the unity of the combined landmass of Europe and Asia, it had its origins in the attempt of Enlightenment philologists, such as Alexander von Humboldt, to demonstrate the linguistic unity of the Indo-European family of languages (Bassin, 1991, p. 10).

The problem of Russia, then, was not significantly different from the situation of the Balkans. The entire Slavic belt was seen by the West as a threat since these lands had become a spring-board from which despotic Asiatic powers sought to invade the West. The Mongol tribes, with a population of more than one million, became one of the most powerful forces in the world in the thirteenth century after they had conquered China. When they turned westwards, Europe, including Russia, was helpless to stop their advance and in the early thirteenth century Russia fell under the Tartar Yoke, as it was called, until 1480 when the Muscovite state under Ivan the Great was established. The Mongol conquest severed relations between Europe and the old centre of Russian civilisation based around Kiev. It is possible that Russian resistance to the Mongols provided a buffer-zone for Europe, which was consequently able to expand at the expense of the Muslims against whom crusades were launched (Jones, 1987, p. 52). Europe in fact was the ultimate beneficiary of the Mongol onslaught against Russia, which as a result of being much weakened was unable to stop its western neighbours annexing territory in White Russia and the Ukraine; and, according to Toynbee, it was not until 1945 that Russia was able to recover huge pieces of territory taken by western powers in the thirteenth and fourteenth centuries (Toynbee, 1953b, p. 4). Of major significance for the identity of Europe has been the fact that throughout the Middle Ages, Spain and Russia were under Islamic rule. While

Russia occupied a frontier position against non-European and non-Christian invaders, this role also tended to divide it from the rest of Europe. Spain in contrast succeeded in attaining the mantle of the leadership of Europe in the late fifteenth century.

The westward thrust of Russian power led to the foundation of St Petersburg, as a 'window into Europe', by Peter the Great as the new capital in 1703 (Szamuely, 1988, p. 135). Russia, however, failed in its cherished dream to expand into central Europe and to gain access to the Mediterranean by means of the Balkans and Adriatic. The relatively powerful state of Poland and the Grand Duchy of Lithuania prevented its westward expansion into Central Europe and the Ottoman and Habsburg control of the Balkans prevented access to the Mediterranean. The rise of Sweden after the Thirty Years War prevented Russia from controlling the Baltic. Russia, after acquiring Finland in 1809, was effectively landlocked in the West (Thaden, 1984). It was this failure to expand westwards that sent Russia on an eastward bound process of colonisation beyond the Urals. It was therefore decisive that, at a point when the western powers were increasingly looking westwards in the creation of non-European empires, Russia began to look eastwards in its colonisation of Siberia in the seventeenth century (Diment and Slezkine, 1993). Russia was feared in the West because of the enormous empire it had consolidated by the nineteenth century. Its empire had grown to such an extent that Russia was seen as an extension of Asia.

The conflict between West and East is, in a more general sense, a creation of borderlands. Ever since the Romans developed the *limes* system along the Rhine in the days of Tiberius, the formation of military zones became an essential part of western civilisation (Dudley, 1975, pp. 208–9). In medieval Europe the frontier zones, or peripheries, were built up as bulwarks against invaders and became a major factor in the strength of the empire itself (Rothenburg, 1966, pp. 2–3). Russia also allowed its marcher regions to enjoy special rights and territories in order to guarantee the security of the empire itself (Wieczynski, 1976). According to Szamuely (1988, p. 13) 'Russia had no frontiers: for many centuries she herself was the frontier, the great open, defenceless dividing line between the settled communities of Europe and the nomadic barbarian invaders of the Asian steppes.' In his view Russia had been itself a frontier country until the end of the eighteenth century when it became an empire.

After the fall of Constantinople the Russian Church broke from the Greek tradition. The belief in a direct communication with Rome via Constantinople was the legitimating myth of Russia for centuries and epitomised its divorce from the Latin West. It was this imperial prospect of Christianity's world mission and the myth of the 'third Rome' that lay open to the Tsars in 1453. In this contest for the mastery of Europe and the contending myths of legitimation that accompanied it, Christianity became a dividing rather than a uniting force. The mission to be the heir to Constantinople provided Russia with a major legitimation for expansion in south-east Europe, particularly in the Balkans. The encounter between Russia and the West was destined to be not just a military struggle but also an enduring clash of cultures. The Russian Orthodox church intensified the split between Europe and Russia because it regarded Europe as the territory of Latin Christianity. The identification of Russia with Orthodoxy inevitably involved the rejection of Europe. The older Byzantine–Latin fault line then shifted to Russia in the creation of a new frontier zone. It must, however, be stressed that until the October Revolution Turkey took precedence as the Asiatic bogey, for Russia's redeeming feature was its Christianity.

The myth of Holy Russia as protector of Orthodoxy was directed not only against the Ottoman empire but also against the West and, in particular, against its neighbours, Catholic Poland and Protestant Sweden. Since the time of Charlemagne, the idea of Europe had been associated with Christendom, or Latin Christianity. For Orthodox Russia, Europe therefore signified the domain of the Antichrist. So it was not surprising that Russia would reject the idea of a European identity along with the religion it regarded as an unholy schism. What then was crucial in the formation of two worldviews was that at precisely the moment when Europe was undergoing a process of secularisation, Russia was embracing Christianity as its unifying idea. This split was famously apparent in Alexander I's invention of the 'Holy Alliance of Christian monarchs' – with which he hoped to impress Napoleon's victors at the Congress of Vienna in 1815 – but was laughed at by Metternich and Castlereagh. It was now more clear than ever before that the age of Christendom had passed and Europe had arrived.

The Napoleonic invasions widened the great gulf that had already been formed between Europe and Russia. Alienated from western culture, Russia was accepted as a member of the Concert of Europe largely because of its foreign policy, which was also based on an attempt to crush Prussia, secure the neutrality of France and drive the Ottomans out of Europe. This led to military coalitions with the French and Habsburg powers in the eighteenth and nineteenth centuries. At the Congress of Vienna in 1815 Russia was accepted as one of the Great Powers and was accordingly awarded with a generous measure of Poland. Russia remained from a military perspective an integral part of the Congress System established by Metternich. But the abiding idea remained that Russia was a product of Asia. Napoleon, for instance, saw Russia as an extension of Asia.

European perceptions of Russia in the nineteenth century were deeply influenced by the rise of the United States. Europe was seen as being hemmed in by the rise of two great power blocs to the east and west. Napoleon foresaw that the world will soon be 'the American Republic or the Russian universal monarchy' and that Europe will be insignificant (de Rougement, 1966, p. 294). Alexis de Tocqueville (1948, p. 434) also reiterated this vision of a bi-polar world. It is not inconceivable that European fears of Russia were also in fact inspired by fear of being surpassed by the United States.

The distinctive nature of Russia was not merely the product of incompatible ideas. In Marxist theory, Russia experienced a different path of historical development to the West. According to Marx and Lenin, feudalism was never fully established in Russia; it was the state and not the magnates that extracted the surplus. Moreover, political domination and economic exploitation occurred primarily through the state, not society. This is the essence of so-called 'Asiatic despotism' associated with the 'Asiatic mode of production' (Wittfogel, 1957). Unlike western revolutions, the revolution of 1917 was a total revolution in the sense that it involved the transformation of the entire state, economy and society on a scale hitherto unprecedented in the West. Most European revolutions preserved some continuity with what had gone before and even elements of the Old Order were preserved until the twentieth century. In contrast, Russia's transition to modernity was accomplished by a complete break with the past. It was inevitable that this would also involve a rejection of Europeanism denounced as bourgeois reaction. Communist rejection of Europe was compounded by the fact that the Bolsheviks, paradoxically like the Orthodox church, regarded Europe as a bastion of Christendom and late bourgeois decadence. Also paradoxically, the communist ideology, which was a western import, severed Russia from the West after 1917. This de-Europeanisation of Russia was also reflected in the choice of Moscow as capital and the renaming of St Petersburg, first as Petrograd and, after Lenin's death in 1924, as Leningrad. If Russia ever had a European element it was the aristocracy and intelligentsia; and it was these very strata that disappeared from Russian society after the Bolshevik Revolution, which addressed itself to the least westernised strata. Since the 1920s the traditional Russian image of Europe has been very much influenced by the Russian émigré culture, which saw Europe as the saviour of Russia (Pesonen, 1991).

CONCLUSION

The argument of this chapter has been that Europe's eastern frontier established conditions which led to the formation of borderlands between the Christian west and Muslim east: external uncertainties were reflected in internal disunity.

Consequently there was always a lack of congruity between Europe as an idea and as a geo-political polity. The fact that Europe was deeply politically divided as a result of divergent transitions to modernity led to an association of the idea of Europe with western Europe whose homogeneity was only apparent by contrast to the eastern borderlands.

5 Europe in the Age of Modernity

THEORETICAL PERSPECTIVES

This chapter focuses on the idea of Europe in relation to the great universalist revolutions of modernity: the Renaissance, the Reformation and the Enlightenment. I also attempt to assess the impact of nationalism and romanticism on the idea of Europe. The idea of Europe is a creation of the fifteenth and sixteenth centuries, for it was in these centuries that it entered into its own as a secularised version of Christendom which began to decline as a unifying narrative. The Reformation and the seventeenth century wars of religion shattered the unity of Christendom. The Renaissance and the Enlightenment provided the basis for a new secular identity. The idea of Europe henceforth became the cultural model of the West and served as a unifying theme of modernity. But this did not mean that Europe signified a radical break from the Christian world-view. What happened was that the idea of Europe simply became less subservient to the old nexus of Christendom and its alter ego Islam. The new polarity was one of civilisation versus nature: Europe versus the non-European world, which now covered the 'New World' and signified the 'barbarity' of uncivilised nature. The idea of Europe became increasingly focused on the idea of progress, which became synonymous with European modernity. This was above all an achievement of the Enlightenment.

The American Revolution in 1776 strengthened a sense of the autonomy of Europe at the expense of the notion of the West which had emerged after 1492. Europe came increasingly to be seen as standing between America and Russia, where the Muscovite state was founded in 1480 by Ivan the Great. The French Revolution was the embodiment of the idea of Europe, which came to signify the civilised polity of nation-states. With the final collapse of Christendom as a political system following the great crisis of the Ancien Régime after 1789, new cultural-political spaces were created in which ideology came to play an increased importance. The idea of Europe became closely linked to the emergence of a western European polity of nation-states and gradually came to take the character of a normative idea. It was rarely seen as an alternative to the nation-state.

These developments should not let us lose sight of the fact that the secularised remnants of the Christian world-view, having survived the transition to modernity, continued to provide substance for new forms of European identity based as much on Christian humanism as on 'occidental rationalism'. It was to these identity projects, which included anti-semitism, that the idea of Europe remained tied. What I wish to criticise then in this chapter is the simple equation of the idea of Europe with the notion of modernity, and in particular with the ideals of the Enlightenment (Heller and Fehler, 1988).

The most significant exercise in identity-building in the nineteenth century was the attempt by national intelligentsias to construct national identities for the integration of the masses into industrial society. It was to the national ideal that the idea of Europe was ultimately subordinated. It was for that reason that Europe rarely signified political unity, except as a foil for pursuing colonial wars. The idea of Europe as an international norm of civilisation was more significant as a means of regulating conflicts between the nation-states than of institutionalising a federation of states. A relation of complementarity took shape in the course of the nineteenth century by which the idea of Europe came to signify the normative claims of *civilisation* and which crystallised in the congress system while the national ideal referred to the particularism or the relativism of *culture*. The principal reason why the idea of Europe never surpassed the national ideal was because in Europe, unlike the United States, the state tradition, and in many cases the national ideal, preceded the rise of international norms and their institutional frameworks. Just as the Renaissance found its expression in the Reformation, so too did the Enlightenment find its expression in a distorted modernity that sought re-enchantment in nationalism and the re-Christianisation of the late nineteenth century.

THE SECULARISATION OF EUROPEAN IDENTITY

The Italian quattrocento and the sixteenth century northern European Renaissance shaped the transition to a new and enduring sense of European identity. From the fifteenth century onwards, as we have seen, the frequency of use of the concept of Europe increased significantly. The cultural and geographical names of the continent no longer coincided. The idea of the Christian Occident, or Christendom, began to lose its former significance and was slowly replaced by the more secular notion of Europe. But this was a very gradual transformation. The first step was taken by the Renaissance with its ideas of humanism. The Renaissance can be seen as offering an integrating world-view which became the basis of a European identity in the modern age. In an age when nationalism had not yet made its impact, the culture of the Renaissance made possible a Europe-wide fusion of ideas and styles. This, however, was never an entirely secular identity since the major pacemaker in its evolution was the Reformation.

It was the Reformation that undermined the idea of a universal Christian order and created the space for the emergence of a secular notion of Europe, but one which nevertheless remained tied to the remnants of the Christian world-view. Christian unity was severely impaired after the Reformation, so it is not difficult to see how it made sense to use the word Europe instead of Christendom. But this, however, did not mean that Christianity was unimportant. What happened was that the old antithesis of Christian versus Muslim was replaced by the new polarity of 'civilised Europeans' versus 'uncivilised barbarians'. The contrasting Other shifted from Asia Minor to the Americas, Africa and the newly won Asia. While the vision of the Turkish menace still remained a powerful motif in western political culture, it gradually ceased to be the dominant one. It was not, in fact, unusual for western powers, especially France, to make alliances with the Turks in order to defeat opponents, which in the case of France was the Habsburg empire. Relations between the Ottomans and the European powers became increasingly more secular by the end of the seventeenth century when Europe replaced Christendom as the accepted frame of cultural reference.

After 1648 Christendom was divided between several competing forms of Christianity: Roman Catholicism, Anglicanism, Lutheranism, and Calvinism and its Puritan sects. Christianity in the period after the Reformation was very different from before. What had effectively come to an end was the unifying vision of Christendom. It is important to appreciate that this did not mean that Christianity became less important than before. What in fact happened was that Christianity ceased to be the territorial identity of the European system of states and became a purely religious value-system surviving in a rationalised form. This growing differentiation of society was one of the most far-reaching developments of the age. The English Civil War in the 1640s, the Glorious Revolution of 1688 and the Thirty Years War of 1618–48 were the great formative events in the long process of European secularisation. Roman Catholicism itself also underwent a major transformation after the Counter-Reformation when it embraced the rationalising spirit of the age. The Roman Catholicism of the age before the Council of Trent, 1545–63, was very different from after. What is to be stressed is that while the Reformation divided Europe between a Protestant north and a Catholic south, Christianity continued to be the principal source of cultural identity. It should not be forgotten that the divisions between the Roman Catholic and Protestant regions in western Europe were never as great as the gulf that separated Latin Christianity from Greek Christianity. Despite the seventeenth century wars of religion, northern and southern Europe remained more closely linked than were eastern and western

Europe as a whole. Moreover, Latin Christianity was still united in fear of the Muslim threat, though this became increasingly less significant after Lepanto in 1571. In fact we find that the great representatives of the Reformation and Counter-Reformation, Luther, Calvin and Loyola, rarely used the word Europe. It was still to Christendom, which they hoped to reform, that they appealed. But Christendom, after the Reformation and the wars of religion, was no longer capable of providing the western polity with a uniform political culture.

That the transition to the discourse of Europe was a slow process is evident from an attempt in 1561 to prevent the continent being named after the pagan myth of Europa (Hale, 1993, pp. 48–9). This is also illustrated in one of the early confederal plans for the unity of Europe drawn up by the Quaker William Penn in the late seventeenth century. Penn, a pacifist, proposed that European unity was necessary in order to preserve the integrity of Christianity and unite Christendom against the Turks (Heather, 1992, p. 65). The connection between Christianity and Europe appears to have been quite clear to him for he argued that before the Turks could be allowed to join a future European association they would first have to renounce Islam and convert to Christianity (Lewis, 1993a, p. 33). Ironically as the idea of Europe entered popular consciousness in the seventeenth century Europe was undergoing a period of upheaval in the wars of religion.

The stage was thus set for the emergence of the idea of Europe as an orientation for secular identity. This was the formative period in the evolution of the concept; it was when the idea of Christendom had declined and the idea of the nation had not yet emerged as an autonomous notion. In the period from the Renaissance to the American and French Revolutions the idea of Europe consolidated as the cultural model of the West and became increasingly important as its political identity. The crucial point of convergence was the notion of the West. When the idea of Europe replaced Christendom as the dominant cultural model, the notion of the Occident was retained as its referent. In this way the idea of Europe became a secular surrogate for Christendom.

I am arguing, therefore, that the idea of Europe represents the secularised equivalent of Christendom and is not a break from it. The unresolved tension between Christianity and humanism shaped European identity for centuries. The Christian humanist myth of man, the vision of a redemptive philosophy of history, and the civilising nature of the new bourgeois value system provided the foundation for a European identity that had reconciled itself to its Christian heritage. The anthropological universal values of modern European civilisation have their origin in revealed religion which, in fact, survived in a strengthened form after the wars of religion. Europe was more likely after 1648 than ever before to believe in the universality of truth, the essential unity of humanity and the redemptive idea of history. The thesis of a radical break with the Christian past is, then, a highly questionable notion. While the culture of the cities in Italy was generally secular, and the papacy proved unable to stem the tide of secularism, this was not true for all of Europe, especially in the north where, for a time, as in Stuart Britain, for instance, the doctrine of the divine right of kings was revived. The highly rationalised world of Puritanism also greatly contributed towards the strengthening of a modernising Christianity. The Arabs, it is interesting to note, never saw Europe as a secular civilisation (Abu-Lughod, 1963, p. 159).

It was not until the end of the English Civil War (1649) and on the continent the Thirty Years War (1648) that a new public came into being with the emergence of new forms of communication. Christianity relinquished its privileged position as the unifying theme in western civilisation; it was in this space that the idea of Europe gained its first foothold as an autonomous idea. Yet, the secularised consequences of Christianity remained. Anti-semitism, for instance, which increased after 1648, can be seen as representing the kernel of the European consciousness as a secularised and anti-obscurantist version of the Christian world-view. It is significant that as the wars of religion were coming to an end in the mid-seventeenth century, western Europe, which was experiencing the first wave of arrivals of Jews since the expulsions in the Middle Ages, found a new focus of hostility. The idea of Europe can be seen in the context of what Rabb (1975) calls the 'struggle for stability' in the seventeenth century. The period between the Reformation and the Enlightenment produced for the first time something approaching a secular consciousness which provided a conceptual apparatus for the organisation of an entirely new society.

The Christian humanist ideal of European bourgeois society triumphed over competing ideologies. No other ideal was more capable of integrating the diverse elements of bourgeois society into a unified world-view. The principal components of European identity were the ideas of progress, civilisation and Christian redemption. Anti-semitism thrived along with these ideas and gave them an orientation. Armed with these ideas and ideals Europe confronted the world in the age of nationalism and imperialism.

EUROPE AND THE ENLIGHTENMENT

To what extent, then, can we speak of a break with the past? The famous Quarrel between the Ancients and the Moderns in the late seventeenth and early eighteenth century over whether or not there was progress in history from antiquity was one of the first secular discussions about the break with the past. But the critique of the past did not really come until the eighteenth century Enlightenment, when the notion of a distinct European identity was consolidated (Lively, 1981). The Enlightenment thinkers were the first to perceive the spirit of the age to be secular and dynamic. Church and state were no longer seen as a symbiotic unity but as separate spheres. The Enlightenment can be seen as the expression of a fully fledged European identity. The rationalism and inquiring spirit of the century was fully expressed in the emergence of a more differentiated society in which state and church fulfilled different roles.

But secularism does not necessarily entail a movement against religion. It is above all the institutionalisation of religion in a national church, which then becomes separate from other spheres of society, that distinguishes secular society. As Chadwick (1993, p. 135) has argued in his classic study on secularism in the nineteenth century, the separation of church and state was a political necessity and was not entirely due to a new outlook. Its ultimate function was not simply to protect the state from clericalism but to protect the Christian Church from the anti-clerical ideologies which were gaining a hold over the state. So, the institution of the national church protected Christianity from the full implications of the Enlightenment critique.

Many European countries, such as Great Britain, entered the modern world in opposition to the revolutionary principles of the Enlightenment and French Revolution. The secularism of the age did not extend to a rejection of the prejudices of Christianity. What it did do, however, was simply to accommodate them in a differentiated world-view by which religion was only one cognitive dimension among many others. In many countries – Scotland, England, Germany and Holland – the Enlightenment found a home within the Christian churches (Gilley, 1981, p. 104). While science, formal law and art underwent their own independent logic of development, the Christian world-view remained as the dominant cultural motif by which European civilisation could identify itself. So, while there may have been an increased differentiation in society between church and state, religion – with its missionary preachers and attacks on pagan popular religion – penetrated the social network to a far greater extent than ever before and became an agent of modernisation. Though the churches lost power over the state, they gained it over the family and school in the formation of a new repressive apparatus of power that took as its object the body. In other words, Christianity in the nineteenth century was not a residue of the medieval age but was itself a product of modernity and a process of re-Christianisation: religion was internalised. In this transformation the Jew replaced the Muslim as the Christian bogey. German nationalists, for instance, demanded that a criterion for membership of the German nation was to be a Christian (Katz, 1980, p. 77). According to Mosse (1978), European racism emerged in the intellectual currents of the eighteenth century in Western and Central Europe; in particular the new sciences of the Enlightenment and the Pietist revival of Christianity evolved a blending of the new and the old and found its expression in the rationalised and regressively modernised world-view of antisemitism.

The idea of Europe as a cultural model began to take shape in the eighteenth century. Rousseau had envisioned an age when 'there is no longer a France, a Germany, a Spain, not even England, there are only Europeans. All have the same tastes, the same passions, the same way of life' (Hampson, 1984, p. 71). In the *The Social Contract* Rousseau established the foundation for utopian programmes of political engineering. The idea of Europe was itself a crystallisation of the social contract expressed as an alliance of nations. Saint-Simon wrote about the necessity for the peoples of Europe to reorganise themselves in a new political framework in order to preserve their independence. Voltaire believed that Europe was replacing the nation-state: 'Today, there are no longer Frenchmen, Germans, Spaniards, even Englishmen: whatever people say, there are only Europeans – All have the same tastes, the same feelings, the same customs, because none has experienced any particular national formation' (Dann and Dinwiddy, 1988, p. 14). Kant provided one of the most famous arguments in favour of a 'federation of free states' in *Perpetual Peace* in 1795. Heinrich Heine regarded Paris, 'Garden of Europe', as the centre of civilisation. In 1796 Edmund Burke wrote: 'No European can be an exile in any part of Europe' (Hay, 1957, p. 123). This lofty idea, however, had little reality and was little more than the expression of upper-class tourism and the cosmopolitanism of aristocratic society for which the bourgeois longed.

It cannot be emphasised enough that the notion of Europe as an alternative to the nation-state had little meaning for contemporaries. The conflicts between the national states were too strong. The universalism of the Enlightenment never expressed itself in a strong sense of Europeanism even though the Renaissance idea of Europe as the centre of culture gained currency and became the basis of a new utopian vision of a European political order. The ideas that the Enlightenment did give rise to were the product of a tiny group of intellectuals to whom most statesmen gave little attention (Anderson, 1988, pp. 185–7). Their legacy has undoubtedly been exaggerated. As far as their concept of Europe is concerned, it was a thoroughly French affair and proclaimed the 'superiority of the European religion, the white race, and the French language' (de Rougement, 1966, p. 157). The concept of unity was much more developed in other civilisations, for instance the Chinese (Bozeman, 1960, p. 135; Dubs, 1944). The Chinese world order never lost its sense of all-embracing cultural unity (Fairbank, 1968, p. 5). The Jewish tradition, with its stronger association between religion and nation, can also claim a stronger tradition of cultural unity than Christianity, which has been more culturally divisive.

Cosmopolitan society was closely identified with the French language and French standards of social behaviour throughout the eighteenth and much of the nineteenth century. It was French that replaced Latin as the language of diplomacy and of polite society. To be 'European' was to speak French. Foreign statesmen understandably were not anxious to politicise French culture, which for all practical purposes was the only truly international one. The idea of Europe was not encouraged since a number of contentious claims could be made on its behalf. Thus Bismarck dismissed the notion of Europe as being incompatible with Prussian interests. 'I have always found the word "Europe" on the lips of those statesmen who want something from a foreign power which they would never venture to ask for in their own name' (Crankshaw, 1982, p. 352). Rulers who depended on nationalism for their legitimation were clearly opposed to pan-European ideas.

The divisive and warlike nature of the European idea can be seen in many of the early ideas on European unity. Among the most famous advocates of the Enlightenment ideal were Leibniz and Hume who proposed the formation of an alliance of European states. The basic idea underlying Leibniz's vision of peace in Europe was the notorious 'Egyptian plan' (1672). In his proposal to Louis XIV, he outlined his belief that the most effective means of securing peace in Europe would be a concerted European invasion of Ottoman-ruled Egypt, led by France (Foerster, 1967, pp. 151–60). Such a war would be particularly attractive to France which could then be 'the avenger of outraged justice, leader of Christendom, the delight of Europe and of mankind' (Yapp, 1992, p. 146). Though the plan was never realised in the manner conceived by Leibniz, it did encapsulate the basic idea lying behind notions of European cooperation, namely the concentration of the western war-machine on the non-European world. This was the reality underlying the utopianism of the European Enlightenment: limited peace within Europe for empire-building.

EUROPE AND THE FRENCH REVOLUTION

The French Revolution had double significance for European society. As a revolution against the Old Order, it was not merely French but a Europe-wide movement. Yet nothing could disguise the fact that it was also a French revolution. The universalist ideas and ideals it gave prominence to were ultimately to become subordinated to the narrower nationalism of the bourgeois classes and the imperialist ambitions of the Directory government. From

1793 France was at war with the rest of Europe and the revolutionary doctrine of 'the nation' became transformed into an imperialist programme.

After royal absolutism had been eventually swept away in the tide of revolution, the post-revolutionary state transformed itself into an expansionary movement. The nation became *la grande nation* and soon became an empire. Underlying Napoleon's plans for the reconstruction of Europe was the belief in the possibility of creating a Europe in the image of France (Woolf, 1991, p. 32). At first there was considerable support for the French in the revolutionary wars which brought about the abolition of the last vestiges of feudalism and republics were set up throughout Europe. Europe was on its way to becoming a Republic.

The universalist ideas of the French Revolution both gave to Europe a sense of a common European identity and at the same time took it away. At least three factors were responsible for the failure of the Revolution to lay the basis for an enduring European identity. First, as already mentioned, from about 1793 the Revolution had transformed itself into a French imperialist programme. Napoleon assumed the title of Emperor of the French in 1804 and loyalty to the ideals of 1789 became associated with loyalty to the French. The Roman Empire was thus resurrected in the form of the French Empire. Second, the revolutionary wars begun in 1793 led to a major conflict between western and eastern Europe. Napoleon's Europe was a Roman Europe with the Rhine as its eastern frontier (Cahman, 1952, p. 608). Nowhere was this more clear than in the case of the Holy Roman Empire, which was abolished in 1806 by Napoleon. The Confederation of the Rhine, which replaced it, was a buffer-zone between West and East and had as its eastern frontier the old Germanic-Slavic frontier. The eastern regions of Europe did not experience the same degree of revolutionary upheaval that western Europe did. There the Enlightenment remained more aristocratic than in the West. Moreover, the absolute monarchies in eastern Europe and Russia were more successful at combating the revolutionary challenge than in the West. Though Poland was the first country to give itself a constitution, this did not survive the test of time and disappeared with Poland itself after its second partition in 1793. Third, the spirit of the Revolution had unleashed new ideas of territorial nationalism. These ideas, however, did not develop into the direction of secessionist nationalism until much later, but the foundation of a European order based on nation-states had already been laid.

Napoleon had attempted to fashion Europe in the name of France and had failed. It was precisely to the idea of Europe that his opponents appealed after 1814 when they attempted to restore the Old Order. This use of Europe, needless to say, was an anti-French construct. More importantly, it was also an anti-western construct, for the Holy Alliance united Russia, Prussia and

Austria into an eastern based power-bloc with the Rhine as its western frontier (Cahnman, 1952, p. 609). What is interesting to observe is that the idea of Europe began to enter the discourse of international politics precisely as a result of the collapse of the unity of Europe as a geo-political framework and a Europe of restored monarchies replaced the revolutionary project of republicanism. The failure of republicanism became an essential condition of the subsequent history of the European idea, which became in the post-revolutionary period more associated with the revived Old Order.

EUROPE AND THE NATIONAL IDEA

Though the restored order of Metternich, from 1815 to 1848, did suppress the revolutionary challenge, it nevertheless had to reconcile itself to some of the demands that had been made earlier and moderate constitutions were granted by most states. Post-revolutionary nationalism was the greatest threat to Metternich's restored order. Between 1789 and 1848 nationalism in the form of republicanism was generally associated with liberalism and its hostility to the Old Order. But nothing could alter the fact that the age of nationalism had arrived, and so, on one level, the idea of Europe fragmented into the particularism of the national ideal. But this did not at all mean that the new system of nation-states was without norms. As Europe consolidated into fewer but larger states, the idea of Europe took on a normative role as a regulative idea (Mann, 1993, pp. 35–6, 65, 254–5). To do this it first had to reconcile itself with nationalism.

From 1848 onwards, when liberal, or republican, nationalism failed to stage a successful revolution against the restored Old Order, nationalism became progressively less concerned with the original republican ideal. From 1848 nationalism discarded its earlier revolutionary form and became an instrument of capitalist modernisation. Minimal constitutions had been granted and most states reconciled themselves with liberalism which, in turn, reconciled itself with reactionary conservatism, thus giving birth to modern conservatism. After the unification of Italy in 1861 and Germany in 1871, nationalism, in the form of national patriotism, became increasingly an ideology of the established nation-state and was no longer an emancipatory ideal. On the other hand, it also became a movement towards secession, though this was generally a later development. This led in the pre-1848 period to the early independence of Greece from the Ottoman empire in 1830 and the separation of Belgium from the Netherlands in 1831, and later, after the Treaty of Berlin, the de facto creation of Romania, Bulgaria, Serbia and Montenegro in 1878, of Norway in 1905 and Albania in 1913.

So how are we to speak of Europe as an idea in the age of nationalism? As far as the nineteenth century is concerned there are two senses in which it is meaningful to talk about a European ideal as opposed to the narrower nationalist ideal. First, there is the notion of Europe that evolved in the movement from the Renaissance to the Enlightenment. This is the Christian humanist ideal and the belief in a universal value system based on Reason, Progress and Science. These ideals lie at the core of European identity and are embodied in the idea of modernity. Second, there is the ideal of European political unity which developed in the course of the nineteenth century. This was essentially an adaptation of the national ideal and its most famous proponent was Mazzini. These two dimensions of the European idea – the cultural and the political – are quite separate, but nevertheless they have together shaped the modern idea of the unity of Europe. By this I mean that Europe, as the embodiment of the Christian humanist ideal of the West, is anchored in the nation-state, which is the agent of European modernity. So, while the culture of the West crystallised in the idea of Europe as a cultural model, it is the nation-state that is the carrier of European modernity. Underlying this is a potent notion of 'the people'.

The idea of 'the people' evolved from the original notion of the French Revolution, which was essentially political, but turned into a cultural construct. National communities were discovered by intelligentsias and subsequently politicised by patriots and nationalist movements (Hobsbawm, 1991b). The national ideal was supposed to be the expression of historical communities whose definition depended on language, and by the early twentieth century religion and ethnicity were added to the list of national attributes. With regard to the problem of European identity this had the implication that an identity of a more universal nature would have to reconcile itself to the particularist assumptions of culture. Anti-semitism is the most potent instance of this hostility of national cultures to trans-cultural influences. Nineteenth century cultural nationalists believed that civilisation was based on national-historical cultures: the foundation of Europe was the nation-state. The Jews were excluded from the national community because they were supposed to have been a people without a nation. While Jews regarded the idea of Europe in the late eighteenth century in an optimistic light, in the course of the nineteenth century Jewish historical consciousness became increasingly disenchanted with Europe and the West and, particularly after 1870, the East was regarded by many to be of greater potential (Shavit, 1992). It is possible that Jewish ambivalence about Europe was related to the growing link between nationality and anti-semitism after 1870.

In the nineteenth century framework of the post-Napoleonic order as laid down at the Congress of Vienna in 1815, the system of the balance of powers made a substantive notion of European political unity impossible. The dominant idea of Europe after the Congress of Vienna was the balance of power, the essence of the Concert of Europe, which was seen to be the basis of a *pax Europaea*. This idea goes back, not to the Enlightenment, but to the age of absolutism when it became a political necessity.

Generally the idea of Europe was associated with the particularistic interests of one country. For the British, Europe was associated with France while for the French Europe signified something Teutonic. Between the Napoleonic Wars and the First World War Britain preferred to turn to its colonies and was largely uninterested in Europe. For the Germans, on the other hand, Europe was too closely associated with French aspirations. This was strongly voiced by Bismarck, who opposed the idea of a European order and held the idea of Europe to be one of the heresies of the age (Schieder, 1962). For Metternich, Europe was an Austrian necessity (Taylor, 1942, p. 34). Europe was a counterweight to France and Russia, but beyond that it had no further use. This was also the view of Peter the Great: 'We shall need Europe for a few decades, and then we can turn our backside to her' (Szamuely, 1988, p. 136). The British were the most opposed to the notion of Europe, which was referred to as 'the Continent'. In its 'splendid isolation', Britain preferred to remain externally associated with Europe, which had for long signified Catholic despotism. English national identity since the Reformation had been formed in opposition to the continental powers and gallophobia remained one of the most pervasive forms that English national identity took.

In the sixteenth century the idea of a Christian republic had emerged as a counter-ideology to Charles V's bid for universal monarchy (Foerster, 1967, p. 107). One of the most famous of these early ambitions of a European political order was the 'Grand Design of Henry IV' worked out by the Duke of Sully in the late sixteenth and early seventeenth centuries. Sully envisioned a new Europe but one that was essentially an extension of France (Souleyman, 1941). An important aspect of this idea was the concept of a united western alliance against the Turks. While the idea of Europe was very much associated with the world vision of Spain in the sixteenth century, the seventeenth century idea of a universal European order of peace was strongly associated with French aspirations and the ambitions of Richelieu. Louis XIV aspired to be 'the arbiter of Europe' (Kennedy, 1989, p. 132). An idiosyncratic play titled *Europe*, performed in 1642, was written as a political allegory with the purpose of defining Richelieu's foreign policy (Najam, 1956). Given the context of the strong association of the Habsburgs for the mastery of Europe, the Bourbons, especially after 1648, represented another bid for Europe and the idea of Europe became very much bound up with hostility to France (Burke, 1980). Yet, the idea of Europe as a universal republic suggests that

Europe could not be unified through the hegemony of any one power, though in practice this was usually a disguised bid for French supremacy (Barraclough, 1963, p. 28). There was also a strong association of the idea of Europe with the aspiration of the Orange cause. Indeed, in the late seventeenth century the idea of the 'liberty of Europe' was closely linked with the Protestant cause, particularly as fostered by the English Whigs, and it was in the name of Europe that William landed in England in 1688 (Schmidt, 1966). The idea of Europe was later invoked on behalf of Protestant interests in the context of the Spanish War of Succession in 1700 (in opposition to the French succession to the Spanish Netherlands) and the Hanoverian succession after 1701 (in opposition to the Catholic Stuart cause).

There were few international institutions. The Red Cross, founded in Geneva in 1859, and the Universal Postal Union, founded in Berne in 1874, were two of the few enduring products of European cooperation (Joll, 1980, p. 14; Lyons, 1963). But it was war, and the permanent preparation for war, that was the reality in European society. Politically Europe was destructive. Yet that did not mean that the idea of Europe remained totally divorced from politics. As I have argued, international politics was not entirely free of norms.

Europe as a normative idea became institutionalised in the congress system of the Concert of Europe. This was above all a response to the growth of 'international society' in the nineteenth century when it became increasingly important for the European powers to regulate the world stage. The scramble for the colonies and the desire to keep Russia out of Ottoman territories were two factors that made this all the more necessary. Its origins are to be found in the Peace of Westphalia in 1648, which brought the Thirty Years War to an end, and in the Peace of Utrecht in 1713, which ended the War of the Spanish Succession. These events underlie my contention that the idea of Europe did not reflect peace and unity but was a normative necessity in order to prevent the continent from being dominated by either the Habsburgs or the Bourbons.

The Concert of Europe, or the congress system of the restored Old Order, was composed of a negative unity. More of one power meant less of another. It was a balance between states and not a unity of states; its unity consisted of the paradoxical ability of each of the Great Powers to find in the single entity the means of bringing about, if not the downfall, at least the containment of the other. If the notion of Europe existed at all, it was composed of its very differences, as a delicate unity of differences. Moreover, if the Concert of Europe had any common focus, it was concentrated on empire-building and maintaining the eastern border of *Mitteleuropa* and, nearer home, on opposition to democratic liberalism and worker radicalism.

The Congress of Vienna did bring peace to Europe, but only so that war could be transferred to Africa and Asia. Peace in Europe was the precondition for colonisation. While there was always the danger that the Great Powers would clash on the colonial question, it was precisely through imperialism that many alliances were formed: the Triple Entente was not only an alliance against Germany but was also an alliance against its colonial peoples (Kiernan, 1980, p. 45). Another pertinent example of this was the independence of the United States after 1776. That year could be said to have signalled the establishment of a new civilisation. A notion of Europe developed which attempted to forge a new identity for Europe as a civilisation standing between America and Russia. It was also in this context that new ideas of a European federation emerged in the nineteenth century (Foerster, 1967, pp. 266–71). The global context in which the idea of Europe emerged cannot be ignored.

In 1856, after the Crimean War, the Ottoman empire was finally admitted to the Concert of Europe and the 'law between Christian nations' was renamed the 'law between civilized nations' – this was granted in order to gain Turkey's assistance against Russia (Alting, 1975, p. 53). Europe became closely identified with the new norms of international politics which it provided with a cultural frame of reference. Civilisation effectively signified the norms of liberal European civilisation, which replaced Christendom as a cultural framework while retaining many of its presuppositions (Gong, 1984, p. 15). The idea of Europe, along with its close identification with the standard of civilisation, therefore became very much linked with international law. This was principally focused on matters dealing with diplomacy, commerce and the conduct of war (Best, 1986, p. 215). It was not 'international' law at all, but European law and hankered after a moral universalism which had been submerged by the rise of the nation-state (Best, 1986, p. 219). But this was a perverted moral universalism, a distortion of the moral law which was reduced to western rationalism and the rule of war.

Even though the idea of Europe was in common usage by the mid-nineteenth century, it was generally subordinated to the principle of nationality. By the early nineteenth century the Enlightenment idea of a citizen of the world (*Weltbürger*) became obsolete and was replaced by the national citizen (Schlereth, 1977 and Meinecke, 1970). What stirred the Great Powers far more than the spectre of a united continent was the death of Byron at Missolonghi in 1826, an event that symbolically marked the birth of modern nationalism when the Great Powers intervened against the Ottoman empire and opened the way for the independence of Greece, which was claimed as the epitome of Europe. The nationalism unleashed by the Greek War of Independence – which concided with a period of counter-revolutionary conservatism in western Europe – was a particularly potent cultural instrument in uniting Europe against the traditional Islamic enemies in Asia and Africa (Bernal, 1987, p. 441). The notion of a European order was limited by nascent nationalism and the system of the balance of power. Nationalism was not, however, a negation of Europeanism, but was the condition of its very possibility. And it was to nationalism that the Great Powers eventually sacrificed Europe both in theory and on the battlefield by 1914.

Even nationalists themselves had to struggle to make the idea of the nation-state popular. The idea of a historical nation-state did not always win widespread popular support. But there was even less enthusiasm for Europeanism, which never became a major public issue. Victor Hugo's ideal of a 'United States of Europe' or Voltaire's vision of a 'European Republic' were anomalies in the age of nationalism. One of the more far-reaching developments in this direction was the foundation of Young Europe in Berne in 1834 by Giuseppe Mazzini (Salvatorelli, 1964, pp. 339–47). The idea of this movement was not to form a united European state as such, but was rather intended to be a support for the struggle of European nationalist movements and to be a basis for a future federal Europe of free states. Ideas for the political unity of Europe along the lines of a united federal state were generally unpopular. Mazzini's Young Europe, for instance, lasted two years and never enjoyed the success of Young Italy and the nationalist movements that it was to inspire, such as Young Germany, Young France and Young Ireland. It is noteworthy that the two countries with the strongest traditions of Europeanism, Italy and Germany, were not yet unified. Both the Risorgimento and the drive for German unity exalted the idea of Europe. However, once these countries became unified, the earlier enthusiasm for Europe degenerated into national chauvinism and irredentism. The universalistic principles associated with Europe were overshadowed by the particularism of national cultures.

THE ROMANTIC REDISCOVERY OF EUROPE

The nineteenth century was not only the age of nationalism, it was also the age of romanticism. While both nationalism and romanticism were closely linked, they were quite separate in their concepts. Nationalism was above all a political idea that frequently looked to the future while romanticism was essentially a non-political movement that looked to the past. Romanticism laid great stress on the rediscovery of the past and, in its revolutionary form, it extolled notions of heroic self-assertion. However, it became increasingly associated in the course of the nineteenth century with the former idea than with the latter revolutionary form. But what it did draw off the revolutionary impulse was the notion of a dynamic and creative force underlying the European spirit.

One of the most famous expressions of romanticism was Novalis's *Christendom or Europe* (1968) written in 1799. For Novalis medieval

Christianity was a utopian alternative to European modernity and its secular ideologies, which he associates with the Reformation, philosophy and the Enlightenment. Moreover, he suggests that Christendom is not coeval with Europe and could be a regenerating force in the world. For Novalis Europe suggests something divisive while Christendom symbolises the unity of tradition. The rediscovery of the Middle Ages through reactionary Catholic romanticism served as a cultural compensation for the divisions of the Reformation and the disenchantment of the Enlightenment. This notion of Europe as the decadent heir of Christendom and the apotheosis of history crystallised in the formation of one of the first magazines to bear the title *Europa*, which was edited by the German romantic philosopher Friederich von Schlegel (de Rougement, 1966, p. 239).

For Fichte, Germany was the cradle of Europe and heir of Latin civilisation. The Germans, by which he meant the Prussians, were 'to serve Europe' by bringing it under their control (Taylor, 1988, p. 38). Hegel saw Europe as a spiritual synthesis of Christianity and Germanic culture whose highest embodiment was in the state. In his philosophy of history Europe represented the world-spirit becoming consciousness of itself at the 'end of history' (Hegel, 1956, p. 103). Leopold von Ranke believed that there was a natural bond between the Latin and Germanic nations and that this constituted the essence of Europe (Schulen, 1985). Language and race became closely linked in the construction of the Aryan myth, which postulated an original race, the Germanic race, to all the peoples of Europe. The Slavs were thus excluded from the European race. According to Poliakov (1974, pp. 99–101), in his classic study on the Aryan myth, the anthropological unity of the German race was accepted as self-evident and in time came to be considered the quintessence of the European or white race. The Germans thus began to impose a regressive notion of culture on Europe, which was linked with the myth of the Aryan race.

In the romantic ideas of Europe that prevailed in the nineteenth century nostalgia played a major role. Nostalgia, in particular for the older European empires, was also a construction of the past. Every age and every nation identifies itself with what has gone before it. But in this identification with the past what is being perpetuated is not the past but an invented past. Few ideologies have influenced our thinking of the past more than romanticism. Continuities are seen where there are only ruptures and great ages are worshipped which were perceived differently by contemporaries. One of the fictions to have emerged out of this is the mystique of the European past. So given the politically divisive nature of the European polity, the idea of Europe as a culturally homogenising notion made sense only on the level of culture. In this sense, then, the European cultural tradition has been invented retrospectively. Europe became identified with its cultural artefacts: the great cathedrals, opera houses, cafés and royal houses. Romanticism provided the discourse of Europe with a memory, without which it would be an empty aphorism.

This sense of Europe as an embodiment of the past was also expressed in the new culture of tourism. Bourgeois society in northern Europe, especially in England and Germany, rediscovered the wonders of ancient Rome and Greece and Renaissance Italy. The Grand Tour became an essential part of the education of the bourgeois gentleman and gave full expression to romantic Protestant disenchantment with modern civilisation. The past that was being rediscovered was a product of Restoration Europe. It was ironic that it was the Protestant north that was rediscovering the Catholic south. The Europe that Burke admired was not that of modern liberalism but that of the Old Regime. A famous passage in his *Reflections on the French Revolution* (1967, p. 76), written in 1790, sums up his view of Europe: '...our manners, our civilization, and all the good things which are connected with manners and civilization, in this European world of ours, depended for ages on two principles, and were, indeed, the result of both combined: I mean the spirit of a gentleman, and the spirit of religion.' Cosmopolitan European culture was largely an aesthetic construction and became a part of the cultural apparatus of the bourgeoisie. The notion of humanism survived and became a major component of European literary culture. It was embodied in Goethe's concept of *Weltliteratur*, or cosmopolitan literature, and the idea of a specifically European literature. This was a tendency reflected in the increased use of the word Europe in titles of books, and the notion of a history of European civilisation gained currency. There is also a sense in which it could be said that Europeanism as a cultural spirit was embodied in music. It was this cultural unity which writers such as T. S. Eliot, Karl Jaspers and Paul Valery later defended against modernity as the unity of European tradition. Yet, throughout the nineteenth century the only really concrete manifestation of Europeanism was in aristocratic cosmopolitanism – which was best exemplified in the royal households, for it was only the aristocracy and royalty who transcended national borders. But European culture since the Enlightenment had undeniably for long abandoned the Renaissance spirit and became, with the catalyst of romanticism, codified as national cultures.

For conservatives Europe was also a political construction. The fiction of a European political order helped to strengthen conservative opposition to liberalism and republican nationalism. For reactionary conservatives, Europe, if it signified anything at all, stood for the vanished Europe of the Old Order. De Maistre equated Europe with the jurisdiction of the Pope and hoped for a revival of Christendom to combat liberalism. For Metternich himself the French Revolution marked the end of the Old Order. He liked to think of Europe as an alternative to nationalism. Europe was already a nation and Italy was merely a 'geographical expression'. The idea of Europe became closely tied to this sense of nostalgia for Roman Catholic autocracy. After Napoleon German romanticists regarded Europe as the past. The rise of liberalism and nationalism gave weight to the idea that Europe had once existed but since disappeared. The idea of Europe then became a conservative counter-revolutionary interpretation of the past and was not a theory of the present nor a guide to action for the future. As such it was a striking contrast to the Enlightenment idea of Europe as a utopia for the future. Europe thus re-embraced the past disavowed by the Enlightenment critique.

So in general it appears that the idea of Europe was counter-revolutionary. People could be united against Jacobinism, against the 'Yellow Peril', against democracy (Barraclough, 1963, p. 41). Bismarck, as we have seen no friend of the European idea, promised help to Russia in 1863 to suppress rebellion, claiming it was 'in the interests of Europe' (Wittram, 1973, p. 105). Apart from such figures as Mazzini and Hugo, it is difficult to find examples of progressive forces that appealed to the idea of Europe. The overwhelming impression one gets is that the idea of Europe was in fact imposed by the Old Order on liberal and democratic movements for reform as a chimera of a unity once contained in Christendom.

Modernity was ultimately seen as residing in the New World. In Baudrillard's words (1988, pp. 73 and 76), Europe is a 'nineteenth-century bourgeois dream' while America is the 'original version of modernity'. The American Revolution, in contrast to the European revolutions, was successful and the self-image of the new society was modern in spirit, while the European idea was claimed by many in Europe to represent the past. This parting of the Old and New Worlds is best exemplified in the representation of Europe and America in Japan of the Meiji Restoration, 1868, which sought to 'modernise' itself by appealing to an image of modernity modelled on the United States with Europe as the spiritual culture of the West and the home of tradition (Kishida, 1992, p. 46).

CONCLUSION

It was from these diverse traditions that the identity of modern Europe was born as a self-negating modernity. Europe as a secularising anti-obscurantist normative idea became an aesthetic impulse. The Renaissance and Enlightenment and the ideals and ideas they gave birth to – Christian humanism and the nation-state – provided Europe with its identity. The unifying ideas of these great universalistic movements ultimately served to reinforce ethno-culturalism and diversity became tolerated only within the context of the particularism of national cultures. The two universal symbols of modern Europe thus became the crucifix and the patriotic victory column. Throne and altar found their common expression in European modernity and its enduring watchword – progress. It was upon this foundation of a distorted modernity that the idea of Europe as a civilisation of national cultures crystallised.

6 Europe in the Mirror of the Orient

THEORETICAL PERSPECTIVES

The theme of this chapter is the idea of Europe as an expression of western civilisation. One of the central contentions of this book is that the idea of Europe found its most enduring expression in the confrontation with the Orient in the age of imperialism. It was in the encounter with other civilisations that the identity of Europe was shaped. Europe did not derive its identity from itself but from the formation of a set of global contrasts. In the discourse that sustained this dichotomy of Self and Other, Europe and the Orient were opposite poles in a system of civilisational values which were defined by Europe.

It should now be clear to the reader that the cultural and political reference points on which the idea of Europe was focused failed to provide the basis for an enduring and culturally homogeneous European identity. To briefly overview these: Language in the form of Latin ceased to be a unifying *lingua franca* by the late sixteenth century when it was replaced by French and later national vernaculars. Religion was a source of division since the schism of the Latin and Greek churches and the Reformation which split Christendom. The geographical idea of Europe, as we have seen, is as arbitrary as any other and was closely associated with its eastern frontier and the confrontation with Islam. Consciousness of a shared history was an impossible criterion: the divisions and discontinuities in European history were too great to produce a unified European identity. The divisions between eastern and western Europe and the internal struggles between the nation-states made the articulation of an immanently constructed European identity extremely questionable. As an aesthetic category, Europe had some reality in so far as it referred to material and aesthetic culture, but this could never be the basis of a European identity except for intellectuals. So it was in adversity that European identity was born. The idea of Europe was subordinated to national chauvinism within the European context, but viewed in the global context, European consciousness emerged in the context of a clash of world civilisations and was closely linked to racism and the imperialist mission of the West.

The value in looking at western views of the Orient – and more generally the non-European world – is that they can tell us a lot about the nature of European identity, for the Orient was to a significant extent the mirror, albeit a very distorted one, of the West. What I principally wish to point to, however, is the way in which the idea of Europe became tied to processes of bipolar identity formation. In the encounter with the non-European world, the idea of Europe served as a cultural model of reference for the formation of what I have been calling European identity projects. These postulated the universality of European values and the identification of civilisation with European modernity. Underlying this was a strategy by which Europe succeeded in foisting an identity on the non-European world which was identified with its perceived negative aspects. The core component of secular European identity was race, with which the idea of Europe became linked. In order to sustain the hegemonic strategies underlying this, the monolithic construction of the Orient served as a distorted mirror image of the West, its surrogate otherness. The universal validity claims of European modernity tended to cohere around the idea of a European civilisation and its racial myth, which functioned to provide a normative model of evaluation against which other societies could be judged. By creating a one-dimensional vision of the Orient, the identity of Europe as a universalising and unifying worldview was secured.

At this point in the book I hope to be able to demonstrate how the idea of Europe, by becoming embedded in regressive forms of identity, ceased to be merely a cultural model and became the regulative idea of universal ethical culture. This had the inescapable implication that the idea of Europe itself became a self-postulated norm. The ethno-culturalism that this resulted in had a distorting effect since cultural spheres of reference are not in themselves universalisable; they cannot claim absolute validity; they are merely cultural resources of meaning. The idea of Europe is not then a normative model and its continued association with universal ethical claims is an invasion and reification of the moral space, which is not the privilege of any single culture.

Europe solved the age-old problem of the universal versus the particular by consigning the sphere of the particular to the relativism of national cultures while the idea of Europe was designated to be the realm of the universal. Culture was seen to be relative and embodied in national histories, while civilisation was universal and transfixed in the crucible of Europe. Europeans thus evolved the capacity to hold two kinds of identity: one national and the other European. Europe is thus subjectively experienced as national identity. This dual identity was a specifically European phenomenon.

The idea of Europe can be seen, in fact, as an expression of the universalist project of nationalism and the unfulfilled claims of the nation-state to universality. This was a universality that had to be sacrificed for the particularism of national culture. The legal framework of the nation-state had to acknowledge the universality of its constitution in order to secure the loyalty of its citizens. Nationalism needed a reference point beyond itself to be recognised as legitimate, hence the myth of universal humanity. At the same time it had to assert the primacy of national culture, for national identity was generally defined against other nations: the identity of 'We' being defined by the counter-factualism of 'Them'. The result of this double bind was the projection onto Europe of the nation-state's incomplete claims to universality which then served as a meta-narrative of legitimation. The cultural framework is thus invaded by the political and transformed into an ideology for the mobilisation of identity projects. There is another dimension to this. The basis of the modern nation-state, particularly those formed in the twentieth century, is ethnic-linguistic nationalism. Given that this was always an impossible project, the idea of Europe provided a means by which a common collective identity could be focused on an imaginary realm outside the nation-state. The idea of Europe is then more of a surrogate nation than an abandonment of the principle of nationality and functions as a safety-valve for the preservation of fragile national identities.

While the principle of universality can be surrendered in favour of the particularism of nationality, the fiction of a European civilisation is the device by which universality can be surreptitiously preserved in the invention of a meta-norm, a 'grand narrative of meta-legitimation' (Lyotard, 1984). Europe thus becomes the representation of a unity destroyed by nationalism. The battle for legitimation takes place at the level of an imaginary reality, which in the final instance is a philosophical myth of modernity. It is at this 'meta-level' that universal ethical norms are postulated in the evocation of an imaginary Other.

THE INVENTION OF THE ORIENT

In order to define itself, Europe needed an Other against whom it could construct an identity of its own. If the Other did not exist it would be invented: between 1800 and 1900 some 60,000 books were written on the Near East (Said, 1979, p. 204). The age of imperialism was also the age of travel literature and orientalism as a cultural and scientific vogue (Cole, 1972). The West strove for intellectual mastery and economic control over the East which it defined in its own terms and the East was forced to perceive itself in the mirror of the West. The identity of the East as the Orient was imposed upon it by the colonial powers in order to conquer and exploit it, and, indeed, also for purposes which were ultimately tied to regressive identity-building in the West: the tensions and divisions within Europe induced it to find its identity as a civilisation in the mastery and subjection of a contrasting Other.

Since the Koran was translated into Latin in 1143, western society was familiar with Islam, but it was a distorted version that haunted the Christian mind (Southern, 1962). Islam was seen as a preparation for the final appearance of the Antichrist as forecast in the Book of Daniel, and Muhammad was seen as a parody of Christ. Pope Innocent III characterised Muhammad as the Beast of the Apocalypse. This was the spectre that conferred legitimacy on western counter-offensives against Islam throughout the Middle Ages. The idea of the barbarous Muslim world inhabited by evil tribes was a dominant theme in medieval literature. Medieval England fed assiduously on the myth of the Orient (Metlitzki, 1977). The medieval taste for the fantastic also expressed itself in tales of unusual races, the 'monstrous races' (Friedmann, 1981).

The Renaissance responded to the Orient with the invention of the notion of oriental despotism (Chabod, 1961). For Dante, Muhammad was the evil opposite of Christ and was relegated to the depths of hell. The Orient was not only represented as despotic and evil but also as cruel. This is particularly apparent in the case of Machiavelli, who contrasted the despotism of the Orient to the free spirit of the West. The Orient was characterised by single despotic kings while in the West there were numerous republics and many kings (Curio, 1958, pp. 208–13). It has been argued that the tradition of western republicanism relied heavily on the idea of the despotic oriental prince for its legitimation (Springborg, 1992). Absolute monarchy was depicted by the proponents of republican government as an Asiatic yoke and therefore a contrast to the supposedly authentic western tradition which had its origins in the Athenian polis and Roman Republic. In this way European identity became constructed around an antithesis of East–West. This of course was a distortion of reality. The Turks were in fact often more religiously tolerant than their counterparts in Christendom and were rarely systematically tyrannical; indeed, as they swept across south eastern Europe they were frequently welcomed as liberators (Coles, 1968, pp. 116 and 145).

European attitudes originally were mostly defensive and also reflected an intense curiosity about the East. Only later did they become imperialistic. Christian Europe did not have a single image of the Orient, but several. The Islamic world was seen as a hostile politico-ideological structure, a different civilisation and an alien economic region (Rodison, 1974; Djait, 1985; Hourani, 1991). Once the Orient ceased to be a major threat to the West, images were created which emphasised less the despotic and cruel nature of the Orient than its romantic Otherness. The contrast between Christianity and Islam was replaced by the more secular one of civilisation versus barbarism (Jones, 1971). The idea of the Turkish infidel was replaced by the idea of the Turkish barbarian. Edmund Burke told the House of Commons that the Turks were 'worse than savages' and that 'any Christian power was to be preferred to these destructive savages' (Marshall and Williams, 1982, p. 165). The new nexus of civilisation and barbarism of course extended beyond the Europe/Orient dichotomy to encompass the greater global encounter of Europe with the non-European worlds beyond the seas (Dudley and Novak, 1972; Hodgen, 1964; Smith, 1985). As the representation of the non-European world shifted from an emphasis on Islam to nature and its conquest, we also find a corresponding change in the representation of Europe. The old myth of Europa becomes a triumphalist Queen Europe, who is portrayed in the famous sixteenth century atlas as sitting on a throne holding the sceptre of world domination (Hale, 1993, p. 49).

The hegemony of the West consisted in its ability to control the means of communication, to impose definitions of otherness on non-Europeans and to ensure that they perceived themselves in the language of the dominant. The idea of the barbarian reflected this preoccupation with associating identity with language, and in particular with written language. Thus a barbarian for the Greeks was anyone who did not speak Greek, for the Romans someone who did not speak Latin. Europe, of course, was not alone in having images of otherness and it is in fact possible that Europeans took over ethnographic legends from the Arabs (Al-Azmeh, 1992; Thapar, 1971). Europe's mastery over the non-European rested very much on intellectual mastery by which the Orient in particular was constituted as an object of knowledge. While Europe constituted the Orient as an object of knowledge, the Orient was largely ignorant of the civilisation of the West (Abu-Lughod, 1963). For instance, under the Tokugawa Shogunate, from the early seventeenth to mid-nineteenth century, Japan was completely isolated from the rest of the world and did not become westernised until under the Meiji in the second half of the nineteenth century (Keene, 1969; Massarella, 1990). In the Ottoman empire no Muslim of rank learnt a European language until the eighteenth century (Lewis, 1993a, p. 34). With its control of the means of communication, Europe was able to create the structures of a discourse in which other civilisations were forced to forge their identity.

The Orient was constructed in such a way that it existed to be conquered by the West. Kabbani (1988, p. 21) has argued that Europe's interest in dominating the Orient was expressed in the predominance of female stereotypes which served to portray the Orient as a domain awaiting the intervention of Europe: the West could be characterised as social stability while the East is pleasure. The idea of the Orient as the love-object of the West, and at the same time despotic and exotic, served to define the identity of the West as a civilised conqueror. Patriarchal culture was fundamental to European identity. The Orient, constructed as an alluring woman, was an invitation to male conquest. It existed for the eye, not for the intellect, and was therefore portrayed as static while the West was dynamic and forward-looking. The Orient was constructed in such a way that it was both a source of fascination and horror; it was at one and the same time beautiful and cruel. Europe was portrayed as virile and the non-European world as effeminate (Kiernan, 1980, p. 41). The otherness of the Orient justified the intervention of European civilisation. The infusion of fantasy and desire into Europe's relationship to the Orient bound the latter to the role of serving the expectations of the West. Islam was especially seen as something enchanting, exotic and romantic, but at the same time it repelled. It was an attitude that oscillated between fear and fascination (Rodison, 1987). But the final effect was to stress the difference between Islam and Europe, the unbridgeable gulf between the Christian God and Allah (Daniel, 1966, p. 60). The genre of travel writing that grew up around the Orient from Marco Polo to Lawrence of Arabia ga\ ⌣ full expression to western expectations of the Orient as the domain of fantasy and gratification (Patnaik, 1990). Most of these, along with the genre of oriental romances such as the *Arabian Nights*, had no real connection to reality. Fantasy stories about the perils and exotica of the Orient provided the European public with a focus for articulating a discourse of sublimated sensuality (Alloula, 1986). As an object of desire the Orient could only be conceived of as a servile object, an object to be possessed and at the same time to be despised. Its desirability consisted in its otherness, in its difference. The opposition of the female oriental slave and the male western traveller was the perfect foil for the invention of a specifically western identity based on patriarchal notions of superiority and intellectual mastery. Thus in the representation of Orient and Occident, the myth of oriental powerlessness was confronted by western mastery and rationalism. Europe represented progress and rationality while the Orient represented stagnation and decay. In contrast to western rationalism, the Orient was the domain of transgression, of irrationality. The invention of the Orient offered Europe a means of finding its own identity in the uncertain world of modernity: the West was what the Orient was not. In this way the identity of the West came to rest on a negation, the denial of the Orient.

This was above all apparent in the Enlightenment. The Enlightenment had created a great interest in other cultures, and the Orient was especially an object of western curiosity. This was the expression of the Enlightenment's preoccupation with the universality of human nature. European ideas were judged to be universally valid for all peoples while non-European ideas were seen as deviations from the norms established by western rationalism. Occasionally they could be used as a mild reproach against Europe, as in the genre of letters from the Orient (Harbsmeir, 1985). The Enlightenment critique of Europe in no way altered European attitudes and identity and may even have deepened western commitment to 'humanising' the non-European world. The favourable treatment many Enlightenment thinkers gave to the non-European world was frequently in fact a political strategy in order to criticise the civilisation of the court society (Bernal, 1987, p. 172). The 'noble savage' was a contrast to the court society and did not represent a fundamental critique of European society (Woolf, 1992, p. 80).

The Enlightenment laid the basis for a new framework of world civilisation. By freeing the human imagination and science from the traditional constraints of the Christian world-view, the Enlightenment sought to inaugurate the ascendancy of a new secular philosophy of history erected upon the foundations of industrial capitalism. The new ideas of western rationalism were not post-metaphysical. Absolute values were not rejected; they were simply secularised and made material. Under Saint-Simon and Auguste Comte, the prophets of industrial society, these ideas amounted to a mystification of capitalist modernity. The most enduring of these new ideas was the notion of progress and civilisation. This was a particularly European notion and was utterly alien to, for instance, the Chinese, whose world-view was more deeply rooted in the past (Marcus, 1961, p. 134). The idea of progress, according to Bury, was 'the animating and controlling idea of western civilization' (Carr, 1964, p. 112). It found one of its most programmatic expressions in the great edifices of late nineteenth century capitalist society, the Great Exhibitions and cathedrals and opera houses (Greenhalgh, 1988).

One of the prejudices of the Enlightenment was the belief that the Orient was a domain of innocent nature. While Europe was progress and civilisation, the sentimentality and innocence of humanity was to be found in the Orient. The Orient thus represented what the West had overcome. The Orient was immature and childlike and inherently incapable of progress; it was stagnant, lacking in innovation and rationality. Exoticism was the reverse of progress (Rousseau and Porter, 1990). But of course Europe did not want the Orient to make progress. Such ideas served only as a distorted mirror image of Europe's own identity, a foil for the articulation of a discourse of civilisation.

By the eighteenth century Europe had ceased to fear Islam. With the abeyance of this fear a loss of respect ensued. The only country that earned the, albeit qualified, respect of the West was China (Davies, 1983) and possibly to a lesser extent Egypt, whose culture was central to the Freemasons. Opposition to Egypt was inextricably bound up with resistance to Freemasonry (Bernal, 1987, p. 161). Reverence for high culture cultivated a natural contempt for both low culture and non-European cultures. Aristocratic contempt for the bourgeois ethos and bourgeois cultural assertion over proletarian popular culture found its natural outlet in racist notions of Europeanism. The new attitudes were those of a patronising benevolence and condescending interference. If the element of fear lived on it was more likely to be fear of the enemy in Europe where the forces of militarism were mounting. European powers often confronted each other in Asia and Africa in the race for colonies. Thus, for instance, the British feared the Near East not because of the threat it offered in itself but because of the spectre of it becoming an ally of France (Daniel, 1966, p.175). The 'Yellow Peril', too, was in reality the fear that Russia would outbid the West in the conquest of China (Kiernan 1969, pp. 170–1; Gillard, 1990).

Underlying many of these attitudes to the Orient was the fact that by the eighteenth century the Muslim Orient, in particular the Ottoman empire, had ceased to be a military threat to the European powers, who were in fact competing for its territory. Romanticism enhanced the European idea and the Orient became the expression of the longing of the romantic sensibility for far-off places. Schlegel, for instance, believed that oriental culture was superior to European culture in its lack of materialist greed. The cult of the romantic Orient was also an expression of the reaction against classicism. Romantics rejected the rationalism of their age for a more sentimental sensibility which they saw in the image of the Orient. In the nineteenth century the Orient became a firmly established theme in western romanticism which sought to find itself in an Other (Sieverich and Budde, 1989). The longing for far-away places is a very deeply rooted motif in romanticism. India, in particular, was a major theme in the British romantic imagination (Parry, 1974). The old myth of the Turk as a despotic and infidel gave way to a more romantic image. A later development was the myth, cultivated by T. E. Lawrence, of the freedom-loving Arab who was contrasted to the image of the despotic Turks. This, of course, was a ploy the British used in order to win Arab support against the Ottoman empire (Nasir, 1976). The myth of the freedom-loving primitive man gave full expression to Victorian paternalism with its conviction that the conquered peoples were incapable of self-government.

But it was not always the longing for innocence that inspired the romantic flights of fantasy; it was also reaction to the revolutionary tendencies within Europe. Revolutionary ideologies – radical democracy and liberalism, anarchism, socialism – were transforming the Europe of the Old Regime. The image of the Orient provided a much needed focal point for strategies of counter-revolution. Moreover, much of European fascination with the Orient was an expression of power relations: authority versus powerlessness was the basic structure that underlined the interaction of the two world-views. In representing the Orient as weak, the West was expressing an attitude of dominance. Great nations sentimentalise weak nations, not their competitors. This can be seen in western representations of the Orient and the myth of the 'noble savage'. 'Primitive man' was an embodiment of simple values which could renew western civilisation so long as they were carefully harnessed. Expressed as an abstract ideal of freedom, the cult of primitiveness became a core component of bourgeois consciousness and served, not as an alternative to civilisation, but as a convenient tool against socialism and radical ideas. It could also be deployed as an instrument of anti-semitism (Kiernan, 1969, p. 173).

The medieval representations of the Orient emphasised its despotic and cruel nature, while Enlightenment and romantic constructions tended to stress the servitude and innocence of the Orient. This was not surprising, for in the Middle Ages the Muslim Orient was a world power, while in the eighteenth and nineteenth centuries it had been opened up to the European empires for conquest. The Orient was noble only in its submission to the West. Once the Orient had ceased to be a major threat to European civilisation it was romanticised. Napoleon's invasion of Egypt opened the Orient to the romantic imagination and it was in France that the cult of the exotic became firmly established with the growing popularity of divans, turbans, perfumes, carpets, tobacco and opium. The increasing penetration of Europe into the East brought with it the discovery of exotic forms of spirituality, such as Buddhism and the cult of individual spirituality, which provided a respite from the bleak Victorian world. This was related to the religious preoccupation of the age when the Victorians sought to rediscover the geographical roots of Christianity in the Holy Lands. Egyptology, antiquarianism and philanthropist archaeology rehabilitated the study of ancient civilisations. But this was purely a paternalistic scientific curiosity, for, as Bernal (1987) has argued, it was at this time that Europeans were intent on fabricating the myth that the origins of Greek culture were European and owed nothing to Egyptian influences. The upper-class custom of wintering in warm climates and the Victorian penchant for travel and collecting exotica established the Orient as a discourse in which the unity and cohesion of western civilisation was placed on a new level. The growing interest of Europe in the Orient did not mean the acceptance of non-European ways of life. The real encounter between Europe and the Orient was limited to superficial and romanticised pursuits. The adoption of eastern clothes, food and furniture as well as the aesthetic appeal and scientific curiosity the Orient had for the European mind suggested less acceptance than a process of selective assimilation (Panikkar, 1953; Todorov, 1993).

Underlying these developments was the relatively new idea of civilisation.

CIVILISATION AND CULTURE

The concept of *civilisation* was first used in the late eighteenth century, though the verbal forms of *civilise* and *civilised* already existed (Braudel, 1980;

Williams, 1976, pp. 48–50). It first entered the French language in the 1760s through the *'philosophes'*, for whom it designated the progress of reason (Woolf, 1989, p. 96). The idea of being civilised, in contrast, referred more to social behaviour – bourgeois norms of politeness – than to the nature of society. The invention of the notion of civilisation designated something more pervasive than the behaviour of the individual. Civilisation was social, moral and intellectual progress. The French Revolution embodied this notion of a civilising society based on rational laws (Bauman, 1985). Then, towards the middle of the nineteenth century, the idea emerged that there are *civilisations,* so it became possible to speak of the 'civilisation of the Renaissance' or 'Roman civilisation'. Civilisation could exist in time and space. This idea of civilisation also replaced the older Renaissance notion of *civilita,* meaning the civic duty of the citizen, an idea that had its origins in Cicero's *societas civilis.* This notion was transformed into the idea of 'civil society', that is bourgeois society, and was also expressed in the idea of civil government and early ideas of citizenship.

While for the Germans the idea of *Kultur,* which was essentially the life of the mind, had priority over civilisation, which designated material life, for the British and French the idea of civilisation did not necessarily signify something secondary to culture. The romantic movement nevertheless did succeed in elevating culture above civilisation which was associated with the material ethos of modernity. According to Elias (1978; Mennel, 1989, pp. 35–6) the German *Zivilisation* is derived from the idea of civility, meaning merely outward behaviour, and is inferior to *Kultur,* the life of the mind. Civilisation was the expression of the court and the banality of public ceremony. *Kultur* was more associated with the new bourgeois intelligentsia who sought to demarcate themselves from the French-speaking courtiers. After the French Revolution the idea of civilisation began to be associated with France and the West and *Kultur* came to designate something specifically German.

Though largely interchangeable, the word 'civilisation' is more likely to be used when the totality of the European society is being referred to, while 'culture' usually designates intellectual achievements. Civilisation is generally seen to rest on culture, in the sense of bourgeois high culture. Undoubtedly this is one major reason why Europeans regarded non-European culture as inferior and comparable to plebeian popular culture. For the Enlightenment civilisation was a contrast to nature.

The nineteenth century use of the term 'civilisation' referred to European civilisation, while 'cultures' designated non-European cultures. Asia and Africa were 'cultures' while Europe was a 'civilisation'. In the English sense, then, the notion of civilisation was superior to culture as used in the plural and conveyed a strong sense of Eurocentrism. Civilisation represents order and moral-

ity while Africa represents chaos, darkness and unfathomable mysteries. So
we can say that the concept of civilisation, with its origin in the idea of civilised
behaviour, was rationalised into a wider category and was transferred from the
behaviour of individuals onto the state and came to be wedded to the bourgeois notion of progress (Kuzmics, 1988, p. 152). Civilisation became the
monopoly of Eurocentricism and could also be deployed as an instrument of
anti-semitism. It is noteworthy that the notion of civilisation, like that of Europe,
often designated French aspirations: the progress of civilisation was closely
linked to the struggle for hegemony by the French against their other European
competitors (Woolf, 1989, p. 119). In general, however, the notion of civilisation became a scale by which all countries could be categorised into 'civilised',
'barbarous' and 'savage' spheres (Gong, 1984, p. 55).

The non-European world had no concept of civilisation in the European
sense of the term. Even the geographical idea of Europe had little meaning
for classical Arabic geographers, who used the Iranian concept of a world
of seven circles rather than the Ptolemaic system of three or four continents
(Yapp, 1992, p. 139). Since the globe is round, notions of East and West are
entirely relative (Lewis, 1985). What for Europe is the Near East is west for
what we call the Far East. This relativity is illustrated in the meaning of the
word Maghreb: for the West it is simply a part of the Orient, even though
geographically it covers Arabic North Africa and is therefore geographically south of Europe; for the Near East, the term actually means the Arabic
west. The politicisation of geography is particularly apparent in the inclusion of Morocco as part of the East, while it is in fact more western than
Spain. For the Chinese the concept of the west signalled India and Muslim
Asia. The hegemony of the West consisted of its ability to construct a world
in its own image. One of the most abiding manifestations of this Eurocentricism
is in cartography (Rabasa, 1985). Our perception of the globe has been shaped
by the sixteenth century Dutch map-maker, Mercator, whose representation
of the world reflected Eurocentricism in the undue emphasis given to the
northern hemisphere. Even today, despite alternative forms of cartography
the old Renaissance model still holds sway, a testimony to the enduring power
of European ethno-culturalism.

EUROPE AND THE WHITE MAN'S BURDEN

In the nineteenth century a new myth was born which gave expression to the
Eurocentric notion that the Orient needed the West to rejuvenate it. This consisted of the conviction that the original spirit of the Orient had passed over
to the Occident whose burden was now to reintroduce it to the Orient. The

Orient was conceived of as a dying culture which needed the intervention of the West to restore its lost sense of civilisation. This was the idea of what Kipling, the poet laureate of high imperialism, celebrated in his famous poem 'The White Man's Burden'. Its basic message was that Europe was the ideal of world civilisation and its historical mission was to civilise the world. In Kipling's rendering of the myth the Anglo-Saxon race, which included the Americans, were the most fit to bear the burden of civilisation. The poem, written in 1899, was in fact addressed to the Americans to take up the imperialist challenge. The idea of progress allowed Europe to assert its superiority over the Orient in the philosophy of history it afforded: the notion of a hierarchy of civilisations determined according to a linear progression. The non-European world was seen as what Europe once had been; hence it could be both romanticised and rejected. Indians, Africans and Orientals were seen as the past of Europe whose imperial mission was to bear the burden of civilisation. In order to explain obvious deviations from this, for instance Moorish civilisation, European historians assumed the existence of a Caucasoid origin or the infusion of European blood to explain non-European achievements (Sertina, 1992, p. 21). The kernel of European consciousness was a philosophical myth of history which ranked other societies by reference to western values posing as universal norms.

These ideas of the moral superiority of European civilisation were used as an ideological justification of colonialism. The belief was propagated that the character of Africans could only be improved through their contact with their European masters. Slavery was even held to be a means of the salvation of Africa since it would introduce Africa to Christianity and civilisation (Hammond and Jablow, 1977, p. 23). Even arguments for the suppression of the slave trade – which had led to the transportation of some 15 million Africans across the Atlantic since the discovery of the New World – only reinforced the conviction that Africa needed the protection of European civilisation without which it would be like a child lost in a storm. In India the transition from Tory to Liberal policy, which sought the transformation of Indian society, enhanced the civilising ideal of European imperialism.

The idea of Europe as being the repository of civilisation and progress provided a major legitimation of imperialism and of the extermination of other cultures: the superior white races believed they had the divinely bestowed right to take on the responsibility for the weak and inferior. The Orient was interpreted as a fallen civilisation, the heir of which was European Christian humanism. It was portrayed as degenerate, backward and inferior to the West. The Orient was also represented as a danger to the West and was thought to be pervaded by dark and mysterious forces of terror. Africa, for instance, was portrayed as the 'Dark Continent', but it was a 'darkness' that required the civilising light of a British administration and British values (Hammond and Jablow, 1977, p. 23). The invention of the notion of the 'Asiatic character' also expressed chauvinist attitudes of civilised superiority. Orientals were seen as being fundamentally prone to internal strife, rejecting freedom and independence, which were portrayed as being hostile to the Asiatic character. At the root of European chauvinism was a racist doctrine which held that even if Africans and Asians were converted to Christianity they would still be imperfect, for the superior races were white.

In the age of imperialism the identity of Europe as a Christian civilisation became more pronounced than in the age of the Enlightenment. The nineteenth century rediscovered the Christian identity which the eighteenth century had struggled with. It was in the confrontation with non-Christian civilisations that Europe sought to construct a hegemonic Christian identity. By portraying the Orient as morally backward, the Christian West was able to justify its imperialist drive with moral and religious arguments. Ostensibly opposed to Islam, the imperial nations were in fact keenly interested in deploying it as an instrument of stability, and exploiting its uses as a religion of a fallen people.

The renewal of the crusading ideal by missionary evangelism and Roman Catholicism in the later half of the nineteenth century contributed to the new imperial identity of Europe. The nineteenth century was the greatest century for the spread of Christianity since the first century and its diffusion ensured the spreading of a 'Christian, legalistic Europe' (Roberts, 1978, pp. 51–2). Between 1876 and 1902 there were 119 translations of the Bible, compared to 74 in the previous thirty years and 40 in the years 1816–45. The number of new Protestant missions in Africa during the period 1886–95 was 23 or about three times as many as in the previous decade (Hobsbawm, 1991a, p. 71). This illustrates a fundamental aspect of what I have been calling the process of re-Christianisation, which accompanied modernisation.

Christianity is a redemptive religion. By means of the myth of the 'fall of man' and the promise of salvation through Christ's crucifixion, it claims that fallen humanity can be redeemed. This is the basic tenet of the Christian religion and it is this belief that it is in possession of an ultimate truth that led to its participation in imperialist programmes. When the European powers amassed huge colonial empires overseas, the Christian humanist identity of the West evolved an even more pronounced racial character than ever before. The evolutionary ideas of Darwin coupled with the Enlightenment's watchword of progress provided the foundation for the new ideas of the racial supremacy of the Europeans.

Social Darwinism, or social evolutionism, essentially the application of Darwin's ideas to society, provided substance for the deeply ingrained ideas in the Victorian psyche of progress and moral improvement. Social and racial inequality was seen by Victorian imperialists as a product of natural selection (Jones, 1980). The theory of the 'survival of the fittest' was modified to be a justification for imperialism, class rule and aristocratic privilege. The ideological justification of imperialism was expressed in the language of power and authority. The expression the 'subject races' entered the language and the idea of racial differences based on colour became fixed. 'Colonial' and 'primitive' peoples were associated with the category of biological inferiority.

The language of race, clothed in an atavistic myth, became the core component of European identity from the late nineteenth century onwards (Miles, 1989; Huttenback, 1976; Curtain 1964; Nederveen Pieterse, 1992; Walvin, 1973). It was race, not language and religion, that unified Europe in the nineteenth century (Poliakov, 1974). The Christian churches modified their initial hostility to evolutionism, which became a justification for missionary crusades (Cairns, 1965, p. 154). The word race had entered the English language in 1508 in an intellectual context in which the Bible was the accepted authority on human affairs (Banton, 1987, p. 1). The redemption of primitive peoples from heresy and paganism was postulated as the legitimation of what, in fact, was the hegemony of European culture. It was from the institutions of church and family that the language of race borrowed its terms. While the theories of social Darwinism, modified by eugenics, supplied the intellectual justification for racism, it was the Christian humanist ideology that provided a framework that predisposed people to think in terms of racial supremacy. Church and family, the two basic social institutions of bourgeois repression, made available a discourse of power and authority based on patriarchal conceptions of hierarchy, dependency and control. The British obsession with benevolent reform and intellectual control lent itself to notions of racial supremacy. The British Empire, which in 1900 covered one quarter of the earth's surface and numbered some 400 million people, was justified as a necessary means of fostering civilisation. Anthropology, the science of 'primitive' peoples (as opposed to sociology, the science of the advanced societies, and orientalism, the science of the exotic East) was one of the means by which the West attempted to exercise intellectual hegemony over non-European civilisations.

The mystique of Europe and its myth of civilisation was particularly attractive to colonial elites. In India a tiny elite of over 6000 officials governed almost 300 million Indians with the help of some 70,000 soldiers, the greatest proportion of whom were drawn from Ireland (Hobsbawm, 1991a, p. 81). The imperial ideal and the myth of European civilisation was an important link in connecting the colonial garrison to the mother country. The only link between them was common descent, common origin and common language (Arendt, 1968, p. 181). Going to India and the sense of membership of a white master race was for much of the middle class the only means of aspiring to distinction. This was also true of the white colonists in Africa and is especially exemplified in the concepts of European civilisation constructed by the Boers in South Africa. The myth of civilisation versus barbarity was a major component to the siege mentality of white South Africa. Few countries have a stronger 'European' identity than South Africa.

It is important to remember that the division, whether in India or China, was generally between Europeans and natives, and not between specific nationalities and natives. The colonial garrison was above all a European one and transcended the national rivalries in Europe (Hammond and Jablow, 1977, p. 82). Colonial missions were often international ventures and it was also this that helped to shape a European consciousness (Kiernan, 1980, p. 43). And, in Africa what was at stake was not merely British supremacy alone but the whole issue of white supremacy. Europeans who went to the colonies were able to wield power on a scale impossible at home and, even if they perceived themselves as English, French or Germans, in the eyes of the colonial people there was little difference between the European nationalities (Hargreaves, 1982). Language also played its role in shaping a European consciousness in the colonies. European languages took with them European concepts (Roberts, 1978, p. 52). The exclusive clubs in India were not only for the English, but for Europeans (Panikkar, 1953, p. 494). These examples illustrate that much of the religious and moral fervour which led to the formation of the modern idea of European civilisation was formed in the colonies. There the mystique of Europeanism was addressed to all classes and nationalities and served to link colonial civil servants, soldiers, officers into a moral community united by race.

But why was European identity so embroiled in racist myths of superiority? I think this can be explained by the core characteristic of racism. I should like to define racism simply as the refusal to recognise oneself in the Other, who is then reduced to the condition of nature. The history of European civilisation demonstrates that it is possible to speak of the unity of a distinct European civilisation only by ignoring the 'non-European' elements, in particular the Oriental and Jewish contributions. But these are non-European only by virtue of the ability of the dominant culture to construct an ideology of Europeanism as a myth of civilisation with its roots in nature.

CONCLUSION

Racism was not something incidental to Europeanism but lay at the very core of European identity. The identity of Europe emerged out of violence and colonialism. It was by means of its imperial face that Europe was able to display a unified identity to the rest of the world. This illustrates quite forcibly the role played by the Outsider, or the perpetual Other whose existence always had to be maintained in order for it to be denied. In the relationship between Europe and the Orient a dualism was constructed in which the hegemomic identity of Europe could be sustained as one representing Freedom, Progress, Civilisation and Christian Humanism. The contrast to this, and the condition of its existence, was the notion of primitive man, the despotic and mysterious Orient, backward and degenerate cultures, the noble savage.

7 The Crisis of European Identity

THEORETICAL PERSPECTIVES

This chapter is principally addressed to the question of *Mitteleuropa*. This slippery concept has generally been considered to apply not only to a region but also to a cultural-political idea. The term suggests something much more ideological than the idea of Europe. Today there is a strong tendency to revive the idea of Central Europe, which is seen as the true historical heritage of the area which, since the Second World War, has become known as 'Eastern Europe'. According to this view, *Mitteleuropa* is an emancipatory ideal and suggests an alternative to communism and its redundant construct, Eastern Europe.

The chapter looks at the origin and genesis of *Mitteleuropa* as a political programme and argues that the idea cannot, in fact, be easily separated from anti-semitism, the reactionary politics of pan-Germanism and the spectre of German expansionism with which it had been closely associated in its formative phase; and also that it was the constellation of political forces comprising *Mitteleuropa* that finally engendered European fascism. I am suggesting that *Mitteleuropa* is an obscurantist notion and one which sentimentalises a category of historical experience of doubtful merit.

The chapter then looks at the origin of the twentieth century idea of Europe in the circumstances created by the First World War and the programme of nation-state building which followed. In 1919 the central European powers were dismantled and a whole series of new nation-states were created in the ensuing political vacuum. The decisive event behind the programme of post-war reconstruction was the October Revolution. The spectre of communism stalking the stage of war-torn Europe was the new bogey and gave the western liberal democracies a potent ideological focus of unity, which transcended the traditional rivalries of the nation-states. With the collapse of the Sublime Porte, the abolition of the Sunni empire and the flight of the last Sultan, Turkey had virtually ceased to be the oriental despotism that it had been for centuries in the European imagination and became, after 1923, a secular European republic. Russia, which was not defeated by the great powers, took the place of the fallen Ottoman republic. Instead of Islam, communism fulfilled the adversarial role.

A central point in this chapter is that the idea of Europe that lay behind post-First World War reconstruction was very much linked to the attempt to forcibly create nation-states in the territories of the former central European empires. The sheer impossibility of creating a peaceful European order based on ethnically defined nation-states ultimately led to the failure of the European idea. It has been a fact of European history that every attempt to unify the continent occurred after a period of major division and the solutions found rarely stood the test of time. What in fact ultimately sustained the European idea was the communist bogey.

Finally, the relationship between the idea of Europe and fascism is discussed. While the idea of Europe after the Second World War became very much associated with post-fascist reconstruction through economic and political cooperation, it had also been an essential part of the fascist political agenda which had envisaged a new European order.

My aim is to demonstrate that the idea of Europe failed to provide a cultural frame of reference capable of integrating antagonistic nation-states into a broader polity. As a result of this lack of congruence between the principle of nationality and the idea of Europe the latter became ensnared in identity projects, which were ambivalently linked with war ideologies. The notion of *Mitteleuropa* was one of these identity projects which was deployed by German expansionists as an ideological instrument to secure the unity of Europe in the image of an aggressive Germany. We can thus see how the idea of Europe, from being a normative component of the Congress System in the nineteenth century balance of power system, became, in the wake of the Great War and the October Revolution, a bastion of capitalist opposition to communism and the regulative idea of the Versailles Order, which gave birth to the system of nation-states.

THE INVENTION OF *MITTELEUROPA*

The notion of *Mitteleuropa* cannot be adequately translated. The English term, Central Europe, does not convey the same connotations of the German word *Mitteleuropa* which suggests a certain historical mystique. The German word also conveys the sense of an idea or a cultural ethos that is missed in the English term. As a cultural concept it is closely bound up with *fin-de-siècle* Vienna and Berlin of the *Günderjahre* (the foundation years) and it received its most famous form as a political idea in the programmatic designs for a united Central European order under the leadership of Germany and Austria in the early twentieth century and was also closely connected to the ambitions of the pan-German movement. Though never exclusively a war ideology, it was closer to war than peace. A fundamentally contested concept, it has been called 'a great territory of unanswered questions and unresolved contradictions' (Epstein, 1973, p. 67).

Mitteleuropa is not just a geographical expression referring to the ever-changing region which could be described as lying east of western Europe and west of eastern Europe; it is also a political ideology connected with identity-building projects. As a political construction *Mitteleuropa* may be said to have emerged in opposition to Napoleon's Europe and represented a kind of anti-Europe. Indeed, the enlarged Prussia that emerged out of the Vienna Congress was designed to be a counter-revolutionary bloc between France and Russia. Napoleonic Europe was based on the revolutionary ideas of republican nationalism while the political culture of *Mitteleuropa* remained one of the great bastions of the restored Old Order.

The centre of gravity in Europe shifted to Germany following the Prussian wars against Denmark in 1864 and Austria in 1866, and the unification of Germany in 1871 after the Prussian war with France. Europe became closely identified with *Mitteleuropa* and everything associated with German expansion: *Ostpolitik* (the eastern policy) the *Drang nach Osten* (expansion eastwards) and *Lebensraum* (living space). By the time of the foundation of the Second German Empire under the leadership of Prussia in 1871, a major division had evolved in the identity of Europe. We can speak of two historical Europes: Europe as a product of the French Revolution on the one hand, and Europe as a product of counter-revolution on the other. This dualism was reflected in the dismantling of Napoleon's Confederation of the Rhine and the formation of the Confederation of Germany after the Vienna Congress in 1815. In Germany and Austria the obscurantist tradition of counter-revolution predominated after 1815, while the heritage of the French Revolution remained stronger in the rest of Europe. Even after Napoleon's final defeat, the Napoleonic Civil Code remained a major factor in the political cultures of Europe west of the Rhine.

From Bismarck's fall from the leadership of Prussia in 1890 to the defeat of Nazi Germany in 1945 the idea of Europe became closely bound up with the notion of *Mitteleuropa*. This was the period during which *Mitteleuropa* was at the height of its relatively short life as a political idea and programme. It was a highly contentious notion and there was no unanimity on exactly what constituted *Mitteleuropa* or on how it was to be mobilised as a political programme. The two main contenders for the mantle of *Mitteleuropa* were Germany and the Habsburg empire. *Mitteleuropapolitik* developed in the reign of Wilhelm II, whose main ambition was for Germany to have a colonial empire overseas comparable to that of the British. The World Policy and the *Mitteleuropapolitik* were to an extent contradictory policies, though it was the former, the imperial policy, that was by far the more important and which preceded the latter. The policy of expansion in Central Europe, *Mitteleuropapolitik*, remained unrealised but continued as a confused national aspiration and provided an ideological instrument of legitimation for German expansion in Europe.

Mitteleuropapolitik, which was never exclusively a war aim, was originally a question of economic unity around 1850, and was widely supported by the population as a whole, though the term was not in common usage until the First World War. Even though German nationalists tried to trace the idea back to the Carolingian empire, the concept was unknown before modern times (Okey, 1992 p. 106). One of the first statements of the idea was Joseph Partsche's book *Mitteleuropa*, written in 1904, which envisaged a Greater Germany stretching from Ostend to Geneva to the Black Sea (Meyer, 1955, p. 110; Droz, 1960; Sinnhuber, 1954). The idea of *Mitteleuropa* was popularised in 1914 by Friedrich List for whom it also included the Low Countries. List investigated the prospects of German emigration in south-east Europe and the Near East and estimated that it would cost German colonists one-fifth of the cost of travelling to the United States (Meyer, 1955, p. 13). The idea was later promoted by Friedrich Naumann's (1915) famous book *Mitteleuropa*. Naumann stated the case for the unification of Germany and Austria as the basis for a pan-European order based on a federated super-state, completely integrated economically and surrounded by a tariff wall (Neumann, 1942, p. 119).

A. J. P. Taylor (1988, p. 192) argues that the idea of *Mitteleuropa* was the product of a coalition of interests of Roman Catholic romantics and pan-Germans and included an attempt to free Poland from Russia. *Mitteleuropa* was a counter-revolutionary bulwark between the nascent pan-Slavism in the east and the liberal democracies in the West. Indeed, the tradition of *Mitteleuropa* makes the very notion of 'Western Europe' questionable.

Though the idea of *Mitteleuropa* has been largely associated with reactionary obscurantism, the notion has also been used by Austrian Marxists to a different end. Karl Renner, for example, saw *Mitteleuropa* as a mega-economic unit including the Balkans, Turkey and even Persia. For him, the greater the area the better the chances of success for international socialism. For the left, *Mitteleuropa* held out a promise of a post-imperial unification of the former provinces of the old empires which fell in 1918. The new order was conceived as a multinational Central European state system (Meyer, 1955, pp. 156 and 181). Moreover, the idea of *Mitteleuropa* suggested an alternative to the tide of nationalism that was sweeping Central Europe. In general, however, socialists did not appeal to the European idea but to the principle of internationalism which formed the basis of the Second International Working Men's Association founded in 1889 and later the Third International founded by Lenin in Moscow in 1917. In contrast to notions of European unity, whether those of pan-Europeanism or *Mitteleuropa*, internationalism was a revolutionary idea based on proletarian and socialist sol-idarity. The idea of internationalism, which was reflected in the emerging concept of international law, is also an interesting example of a transnation-al ideal that can be contrasted to the more obscurantist ideas of *Mitteleuropa* and pan-Europeanism. Nevertheless the European idea remained for many communists, such as Rosa Luxemburg, an alternative to the war psychosis of nationalism. Trotsky (1971, p. 26) said, in a speech in 1926, that in a 'uni-fied Europe' the 'toilers of Europe and Asia will be indissolubly linked'.

The idea of Europe, suitably redefined, had more appeal to the Germans whose country was perceived to exist only as a *Kulturstaat* and not as a nation-state. Even after the foundation of the Second Empire in 1871, the German state that emerged was merely an extension of Prussia. The idea of a German nation-state coextensive with the German-speaking peoples was buried after 1866 in the wake of Prussia's victory over Austria. German national identi-ty could not then be focused on the existing state since that state did not include the entire German nation. It was only a 'Little Germany' that was united in 1871 when the old liberal principle of nationalism was laid to rest. The iden-tity of the Second Empire was based less on national identity than on the obscurantist ideas of the *Reich* and the *Volk* (Dann, 1993). The year 1866 saw the dissolution of the defunct German Confederation and a year later Austria opted for the *Ausgleich*, the Compromise, with Hungary in the establishment of the Dual Monarchy in which the Magyars became the most powerful non-German population in the empire. For Germany to exist as a nation-state it would first have to become an empire. Hence the attraction of the idea of Europe as *Mitteleuropa*. The other Great Powers, France and Britain, had already existed for long as centralised states whose national identity did not require territorial expansion in Europe. But the German historical community did not coincide with the Hohenzollern and Habsburg states which by the late nineteenth century had gone their separate courses. The Western European powers possessed empires which were non-European while the German and Habsburg empires were essentially European territorial empires. The former was mainly an empire of German-speaking peoples, while the Habsburg empire was polyethnic. By means of the idea of *Mitteleuropa*, Germany's path to national unification took on a supra-national dimension. Thus one major dimen-sion to the problem of Europe was the German question and as long as this remained unanswered Europe would be a contentious issue.

The national awakening of Germany in late nineteenth century involved a sense of historical mission which invoked the spirit of Charlemagne's Europe. Many German nationalists saw Europe as an expression of *Deutschtum*, or Germanness, so the spectre of a unified Europe after 1890 carried with it the vision of German expansion. Even the sociologist Max

Weber, for instance, saw the special mission of German culture to be 'between Anglo-Saxon materialism and Russian barbarism' (Treverton, 1992, p. 175). This was partly the expression of a general tendency of the turn of the century, when the European powers, for reasons of internal politics, cultivated the political strategy and ideology of social imperialism by which the nation state became closely identified with the empire: hence the invention of Greater Britain, *France Outre Mer*, *La Grande Italia* and *Grossdeutschland*.

Up until now I have discussed the German aspirations behind *Mitteleuropa* without looking at the significance of Austria. The idea of *Mitteleuropa* was popular in Austria, where there was an attempt to deploy it as a historical myth of legitimation for the Habsburgs in the period prior to the unification of Germany The idea served perfectly to express the common homeland of the Dual Monarchy, linking Austria and Hungary into a unitary mega-bloc. *Mitteleuropa* also signified nostalgia for pre-revolutionary Europe and was the expression of an imperial order in decline. In addition to its reactionary and nostalgic associations, the obscurantist idea of *Mitteleuropa* also had a very strong anti-communist bias. Underlying such programmatic ideas as *Mitteleuropa* and pan-Germanism was clearly the ambition to take over the provinces of the crumbling Ottoman Empire, which was being kept alive as a political expedient in the balance of power system.

The Habsburgs, however, failed to sustain their bid for *Mitteleuropa* and, with the disappearance of their empire in 1918, Germany became the main contender for *Mitteleuropa*. By the 1930s and 1940s the pan-German idea had gained prominence. The *Mitteleuropa* of the Habsburgs was a more limited one than that of Greater Germany or the pan-German idea. It was confined to the Danubian basin of the Habsburg empire and their domains in northern Italy, parts of Czechoslovakia and the Balkans. This was the dark and sinister world of the decaying Old Regime explored by Freud, Kafka, Svevo and Musil and which is today once again in vogue (Schlorske, 1980). The mystique of *fin-de siècle* Vienna, its aesthetic and decadent milieu and the aristocratic culture of the Habsburg monarchy gave rise to an enduring dream of recovering former greatness.

Mitteleuropa differs greatly from the more homogeneous Western Europe in the large number of ethnic frontier groups it contains, including the German-speaking groups who found themselves isolated in 1918 and again in 1945. These pockets of Germans located in Poland, Russia, Hungary, Czechoslovakia and northern Italy remained vociferous supporters of the idea of *Mitteleuropa* which has always had special appeal to German irredentas for whom it presumably has a certain nationalistic resonance.

The abundance of books today on the idea of *Mitteleuropa* testifies to the abiding appeal of the idea, which has been reinvented as a kind of nostalgia and a potential collective identity for the future (Schöpflin and Wood, 1989). But the idea that it in fact reflected was the belief that nationalism, and in particular German expansion, would provide stability and identity for Central Europe. While *Mitteleuropa* is supposed to be an emancipatory ideal of historical romanticism today, it was closer to a nightmare for contemporaries. As Hobsbawm (1991c) has pointed out, *Mitteleuropa* is a dangerous concept and we should not forget that in the nineteenth century there was less enthusiasm for monarchy than there is today. For those who lived under its oppressive rule it was known as the *Volkerkerker*, the 'prison of nations', and few mourned its passing in 1918. No country in Central or Eastern Europe thought of itself as belonging to *Mitteleuropa* – all looked for their model somewhere else: London or Paris for instance (Hobsbawm, 1993). It must also be borne in mind that Adolf Hitler, who absorbed his anti-semitism in Vienna, was one of the pathological expressions of *Mitteleuropa*, which also gave rise to fascist aspirations as, for instance, the ideal of *Donauraum* (a Danube area) or a *Donau-Europa* (a 'Danube-Europe'). My argument then is that the idea of *Mitteleuropa* cannot be separated from fascism and anti-semitism. The rebirth of the term today is, I think, more indicative of a strategy of forgetting history, which is only selectively appropriated, than of really coming to terms with the past. So, while nationalism can be debunked for its misdemeanours, *Mitteleuropa* is supposed to be innocent and untainted by the violence of the nation-state and forty years of communism. As an alternative to nationalism and as a means of forgetting the past, the idea clearly has its advantages. Today, as well as in the past, the idea also serves as an anti-communist ideal. But this, too, obscures a lot. The spirit of *Mitteleuropa* was not killed by Soviet communism, as is so often claimed today, but by national socialism. Fascism and anti-semitism were products of *Mitteleuropa* and created the self-destructive conditions which led to the occupation by the Red Army in the closing stages of the war. It was there, too, that the fanatical hatred of the *Ostjuden* (the Eastern Jews) took an unprecedented and grotesque form. Austria, the core of Central Europe, played a role in the Holocaust out of all proportion to its numbers: the Austrians provided one third of the personnel of the SS extermination units, commanded four out of the six death camps and killed almost half of the six million Jews (Johnson, 1993, p. 499). Any attempt to revive the spirit of Central Europe will have to face this brutal fact.

THE BREAK-UP OF EUROPE

No account of the idea of Europe can ignore the impact of the First World War on the identity and unity of Europe. The Great War effectively laid to rest the concept of a European order. After 1918 the idea of Europe could never be the same as before. Unlike all previous wars, the First World War was a 'total war' and marked the beginning of the permanent war economy of industrial society. From 1914 onwards the western states would be in a permanent state of preparation for war (Giddens, 1985). The eight million deaths that the war had cost, the collapse of empires, the 1919 settlements leading to the formation of new nation-states and the process of decolonisation signalled, in effect, the political collapse of Europe as a system of alliances based upon the balance of power.

After the First World War Europe ceased to be at the centre of world politics and the centre of gravity shifted across the Atlantic. After the Great War and the changes in international finance capital that followed in its wake, Europe was superseded by the United States which replaced Britain as the foremost creditor nation in the world (Gilpin, 1987, p. 309). The Bolshevik Revolution turned the war, in its final stages, into a battle of the western capitalist powers against communism. The Russian surrender at Brest-Litovsk in March 1918, after the imperial army had ceased to exist, placed Germany in command of eastern Europe. But by this stage the war aims of Britain, France and the US also included a strategy to contain communism: the spectre of communism engulfing Germany was not an unrealistic one in 1918. Trotsky led the Russian delegation at Brest-Litovsk, where he abandoned the traditional principles of diplomacy by attempting to promote the cause of international revolution (Carr, 1979, p. 10). The circumstances surrounding the collapse of the Central European powers led to a power vacuum which allowed communist movements the space to emerge and gain control of the crumbling states.

The new Europe that emerged after the war with the Versailles peace treaties was constructed in opposition to Soviet communism, which had declared world revolution to be one of its goals (Mayer, 1968). Two worlds confronted each other after 1918: the liberal democracies of the capitalist West and Soviet communism. The ancient adversaries were now defined by opposed political ideologies. Visions of the coming revolution, perceived as an event of apocalyptic proportions, helped to shape the identity of Europe as a counter-revolutionary bastion against international communism. The reality, however, was that the Red Army, after the Russian civil war, was exhausted and if the West was in any danger at all of being overrun by communism, it would not have been from the Red Army.

The emergence of pan-European organisations after the war reflected the changing identity of Europe (Pegg, 1983). The most famous of these was the 'Pan-Europe' movement founded by Counenhove-Kalergi in the 1920s. The US with its federal system became for a time the model for the new Europe.

However, the dominant tendency was the programme of state-building which accompanied the process of dismantling the Central European empires after the war. The nation-state, as opposed to the more programmatic ideas of pan-Europeanism, was generally seen as the best substitute for the defeated Central European empires and the basis of the new Europe. Post-war organisations such as the League of Nations and the Pan-Europe Union reflected the creation of new states in the aftermath of the collapse of the European empires. The new spirit of internationalism was, however, more a reflection of the prevailing belief in the principle of nationality than a radical desire to replace the nation-state with a transnational federation of states.

Europe both as a region and as an idea after 1918 was remarkably different from that before the war. The Europe of the twentieth century was a product of war, not of peace. War was the basis of the Versailles Order, which in fact remained more or less unaltered after the Second World War. Europe after 1945 did not look fundamentally different from its appearance in 1919. At no time in European history were more states created than in 1919 after the partition of the Ottoman empire. Though this was to be surpassed between 1991 and 1994 with the de facto formation of even more states, many of these had been ones originally established in 1919. In 1871 there were 14 states in Europe, in 1914 there were 20 and in 1924 there were 26 (Carr, 1945, p. 24). In 1992 there were 54.

Many of the new states that were created were more 'ethnic' states than nation-states, with language as the defining characteristic of ethnicity. The principle of 'self-determination' amounted to the politicisation of ethnicity since mutually antagonistic groups were placed in the same state. The older principle of polyethnicity was rejected in favour of mono-ethnic states (McNeil, 1986). The project of creating new states along ethnic lines brought about an ethnic-nationalist fault-line stretching from the Baltic to the Balkans and from the Caucasus to the Middle East. This was particularly potent in the case of Yugoslavia where the ethnic conflict, which had been contained in the old polyethnic Ottoman and Habsburg empires, was provided with a receptacle to ferment into a new wave of ethnic nationalism. While the old nationalism had been more directed against the cores of the empires, the new nationalism that evolved after the foundation of Yugoslavia was more an expression of ethnic tensions within the new state. Indeed, many of the new states created in 1919 were the product of nationalism imposed from above and there had generally been little popular agitation for their creation. In Eastern Europe most national identities evolved within the provinces of the Central European empires. In contrast, national identities in western Europe were generally shaped within the structures of the existing nation-states (Mayer, 1966). When the imperial provinces of the Central European powers were converted into independent states in 1919, what had been relatively unimportant ethnic identities became transformed into potent political identities.

The act of creating new states, often with arbitrarily drawn borders, produced enduring ethnic tensions which evolved to become new forces of nationalism in the peripheries of Europe (Hobsbawm, 1992a). The problem was that the ethnic borders did not always coincide with the states' borders. This fundamental lack of congruence between the political and the ethnic was of major importance in the modern history of eastern Europe. What in fact happened was that regressively modernised national identities evolved out of the ethnic and religious traditions which had ossified in the frontiers of the empires. The problem was not so much the artificial nature of the new states, for all states are in a sense arbitrary, as the process by which ancient empires were belatedly dismantled and their provinces transformed to construct new states based on ethnic criteria. This led to the inevitable consequence of massive population upheaval and genocide. It was not demographically possible to create new states without large-scale population upheaval. Since 1915 – with the massacre of 1.5 million Armenians by the Turks – the price that has been paid for the creation of ethnic nation-states in eastern Europe has been the expulsion and genocide of populations.

Moreover the new order established in 1919 contained within itself the seeds of its own destruction. The formation of states out of what, in fact, had been ethnic frontier regions in the old empires proved catastrophic. In the longer perspective of the twentieth century we can now see that many of the states created in 1919 did not survive the collapse of the USSR in the early 1990s. Autonomy has been restored to the Baltic states while Poland and Hungary have survived, but the states of Czechoslovakia and Yugoslavia have collapsed. It is hardly necessary to point out how the Weimar Republic epitomised the failure of the Versailles Order to create a lasting European peace and identity and the Spanish Civil War revealed that Europe was divided between fascism and democracy.

EUROPEAN PESSIMISM

The idea of civilisation did not survive into the twentieth century. One of the great themes in *fin-de-siècle* thinking was the critique of civilisation: the idea that civilisation engendered barbarism. All of the great promises of the Enlightenment were seen as failures and the European mind abandoned civilisation for culture. Oswald Spengler's book *The Decline of the West* (1971), written in 1918, with its motif of the doom of western civilisation, was one of the most widely read books of the Weimar Republic. The theme of the Great War as a portent for western civilization also dominated the writing of Arnold Toynbee, whose great unifying theme was the decline of western civilisation as part of a universal cyclical pattern by which all world civilisations undergo a process of decline on reaching their peak. For Toynbee the West had reached the zenith of its glory by the twentieth century. The idea of the consummation of civilisation – which Spengler dated as early as the beginning of the nineteenth century – led to an abandonment of the idea of civilisation for culture. A profound anti-modernism underlay this movement, by which the idea of Europe came increasingly to be equated with the cultural and intellectual apparatus of the bourgeoisie who found refuge in the comfort of high culture. Thus we find a return to a supposedly authentic European culture as a substitute for the intellectual void of modernity and technological civilisation. Some famous examples of this 'cultural pessimism' are Nietzsche's critique of the 'malaise of modern European civilisation', Max Weber's sociology of 'Occidental rationalism' as a disenchanted and rationalised world-view, Carl Schmitt's (1990) attempt to find an authentic European jurisprudence with its roots deep in the Judeo-Christian traditions and Roman Law, Husserl's (1965) attempt to abandon positivism for a new philosophy which in its most exalted form would fuse with the European spirit and Heidegger's quest for the original European ontology of 'being' as revealed in early Greek philosophy. Freud, in *Civilization and its Discontents*, portrayed civilisation to be the sublimation of deeply rooted neuroses. The rejection of the idea of civilisation for the anti-modern penchant of an 'authentic' European culture embodied the pessimism that grew out of the nineteenth century cult of progress and had special appeal for conservative Catholic intellectuals (Belloc, 1973; Jaspers, 1947; Ortega y Gasset, 1932) for whom the Great War had undermined the unity of European culture and tradition. The result, in Ortega y Gasset's (1932, p. 195) idiosyncratic vision: 'The world to-day is suffering a grave demoralisation which, amongst other symptoms, manifests itself by an extraordinary rebellion of the masses, and has its origin in the demoralisation of Europe.' The appeal to the 'spirit of Europe' was also a means of expressing intellectual disdain for 'mass society'. The idea of European decline and degeneration is also to be found in the writing of Emile Durkheim, Jacques Maritain, Paul Valery and T. S. Eliot, whose work *The Wasteland*, written in 1922, gave ultimate testimony to the idea of European demise under the conditions of modernity. A curious tension thus entered the distinction between culture and civilisation and crystallised in the attempt to rescue the idea of Europe from the nihilism of modernity.

European identity was born in the inter-wars years out of the experience of cultural pessimism and decadence. In a sense it was the cross-cultural avant-garde and the modernist movement in art and literature that really gave Europe an identity. It was an identity that was more associated with European cities – London, Paris, Amsterdam, Berlin, Zurich – than with nations which had engendered a war psychosis. These cities were in a very particular sense cultural metropoles in the inter-war years and embody what was for many the dynamism of the European spirit. The close association between modernism and the city as a motif in the first half of the twentieth century amounts to what could be called an aesthetic Europe of the imagination. Some examples of this are the two novels by Robert Briffault, *Europa: A Novel in the Age of Ignorance* (1936) and *Europa in Limbo* (1937). In these works the idea of Europe becomes intertwined in the personal life histories of individuals whose destinies reflect the decadent spirit of the *fin-de-siècle* period and its sense of impending disaster. The idea of Europe had earlier appeared in Henry James's novel *The Europeans*, written in 1878, and was also reflected in Pierre Drieu La Rochelle's essay *Le Jeune Européen* (1927). The *Todessehnsucht* (the longing for death) of the age received its greatest expression in what is perhaps the quintessential novel on European civilisation, Thomas Mann's *Magic Mountain,* written in 1924. In no other work has the idea of a European identity reached the same degree of eloquent expression and self-consciousness. Its themes are those of the late-bourgeois world obsessed with a foreboding sense of an ending: Europe, death, war. As with Hegel's Owl of Minerva, who symbolises the European mind achieving self-consciousness at the point of its culmination, Europe, in Mann's vision, reaches the fullness of self-consciousness in the anticipation of death. From another perspective the connection between the European idea and love was examined by Denis de Rougement in his famous book, *Love in the Western World* (1983), written in 1939. What we can establish is that in the first half of the twentieth century a European identity had certainly consolidated as a personal identity of intellectuals and was closely linked to the contemporary *Zeitgeist* of decadence and pessimism.

THE FASCIST MYTH OF EUROPE

The idea of Europe took on a new dimension during the twenty-five years in which fascism spread throughout western Europe. It has been conveniently forgotten today that fascism and anti-semitism were two of the major expressions of the idea of Europe. The notion of the essential unity of Europe was central to fascist ideology. Fascism in its classic Italian and Nazi forms was a supra-national ideology. While it was a variant of nationalism, it sought, at the same time, to transcend nationalism in the creation of a new European civilisation. Most people today would probably prefer to associate the idea of Europe with the polis than with the concentration camp, democracy than with totalitarianism, but the truth is that the European idea cannot be separated from fascist ideas and practice. The Jews, for instance, 'saw anti-semitism both as a major pathological symptom of the European essence and as a result of *fin-de-siècle* decadence' (Shavit, 1992). Mosse (1978) has persuasively argued that racism cannot be regarded as a marginal aberration in European history but was an integral part of the European experience.

It was the dream of all fascists from Mosley via Mussolini to Hitler to create a truly European supra-national civilisation. This was to be a post-historical aesthetic order that would both include and transcend the national traditions of the chosen nations. To this end the idea of the 'New Europe' was an aesthetic fiction for a future fascist Europe. Fascism was compatible with the European ideal. The vision of a homogeneous and unitary bond of nations based on a superior culture with a world historical mission was not anyway, as I have argued, antithetical to the idea of Europeanism. In 1932 Mussolini presided over a Europe congress, one of whose themes was the 'crisis and rebirth of Europe' (Gollwitzer, 1964, pp. 6–7; Neulen, 1987). – The idea of Europe – with the important exception of the resistance (Wyrwa, 1987) – was never associated with democracy or the rights of the individual. In fact, fascist ideology can even be seen as the apotheosis of the idea of Europe since, along with doctrines of racism and imperialism, fascism explicitly promoted the notion of a European civilisation. Hitler's speeches, it has often been observed, were full of appeals to the spirit of Europe (Trevor-Roper, 1953). The One-Thousand-Year Reich was to be a European Order, not just a German Reich, and the annihilation of the Jews was seen as part of a cleansing of Europe of an 'Asiatic race'.

The myth of the Nazis appealed to an older idea of Europe in which the spirit of the Middle Ages was reinvoked. The twelfth century German Emperor Frederick I of the Hohenstaufens, known by the name of Barbarossa, was chosen as an archaic symbol for *Lebensraum* because of his crusading mission against the Muslim East and for his ambition to unite all the German lands as well as Italy. The obscurantist legend of Barbarossa served as a historical legitimation to complete an unfulfilled historical mission to restore the medieval Holy Roman Empire of the German Nation.

Arno Mayer has argued that Operation Barbarossa – the code name for the offensive against Russia – was ideologically conceived as a Holy War, a crusade against the East. 'The general idea of the crusade', according to Mayer (1988, p. 217), 'was anchored in a distant past in which Christians had marched to defend Europe against the Muslim infidels or to liberate Jerusalem for the true faith. In the collective memory the crusades of the eleventh to the thirteenth centuries were exalted as the apotheosis of righteous aggressiveness and violence. Usurping this memory, or legend, the Nazis mounted a "holy war" to protect Europe from godless Bolshevism and to capture Moscow, the centre of this heresy.' The campaign against the USSR, with its origins deep in medieval Christendom, could appeal to the spirit of Barbarossa. The old campaigns against the East were recovered in the Nazi cult of Barbarossa. Hitler was successful in appropriating the historical symbols of Europe's collective memory in order to legitimate violence and territorial expansion eastwards, a mission that was fully endorsed by the Christian churches (Mayer, 1988, pp. 216–19). The Nazi conception of *Lebensraum* was the basis of its expansionary thrust. This was essentially an attempt to initiate a process of colonisation in south-eastern Europe and stretching as far as the Ural mountains: Russia, not western Europe, was the original target for *Lebensraum.*

Though the Nazis deployed secular myths of history and rarely made pleas to religion, the Christian idea of the redemption of Europe lay at the core of their thinking. The Jews were accused of kidnapping German culture, of corrupting the purity of the Aryan race, and the Weimar Republic itself, the *Judenrepublik,* was associated with the Jews who were responsible for a cultural theft, which was called 'culturalbolschevism' (Johnson, 1993, p. 477). The assault on Bolschevism became closely linked to anti-semitism in the onslaught on what Hitler called 'Judeobolschevism' (Mayer, 1988, p. 346). The entire campaign was ideologically conceived as a tirade against 'Asiatic bolshevism'. The Nazi myth thus fully expressed the essence of Germanic expansionism eastwards. The annexation of Poland and the drive towards the Urals was not only the principal territorial ambition of Nazi ideology, but a *Judenfrei* European Russia was deemed to be the site for German *Lebensraum.* The onslaught against Russia was portrayed as a struggle for the very existence not only of Germany but of Europe. The Nazis believed in the inherent superiority of the western European nationalities, such as the British and French, over the Slavs.

The extermination of European Jewry in effect led to the destruction of European culture and the possibility of a genuinely cosmopolitan European identity. For centuries the Jews had been integral to European consciousness, and especially in central Europe, but also in all the great European metropoles. The exodus of those Jews who survived the Holocaust symbolised for many the end of European modernity. The European past became a burden rather than a utopia. According to Jean-Paul Sartre (1978, p. 209), writing in 1948: 'The word Europe formerly referred to the geographical, economic and political unity of the old continent. Today it preserves a musty smell of Germanism and servitude.'

CONCLUSION

The idea of Europe cannot be separated from European fascism and its myth of the unity of Europe. Nor can the idea of Europe be separated from the Nazi Holocaust, which was perpetrated in the name of the cultural homogeneity of Europe (Bauman, 1989). The reshaping of the political map of Europe after 1945 was largely shaped by Germany's so-called *Sonderweg* (its divergent path) in its bid for the mastery of Europe. The inescapable conclusion is that it was Germany, advantaged by being located in the centre of Europe, that came the nearest to unifying Europe. Neither the western powers with their experiments in international regulation nor the Red Army succeeded in unifying Europe after 1918. This task became a German mission and the spectre of a united Europe always carried with it the vision of a German dominated Europe.

8 Europe as a Cold War Construction

THEORETICAL PERSPECTIVES

There is another sense apart from the political in which it is possible to speak of Europe as a construction. Europe is also a cultural construction. In this the United States played a leading role. To Americans Europe was a unitary and homogeneous entity and served as a racial myth of national origins. The chapter begins by looking at the representation of Europe in the American historical imagination. It focuses, more specifically, on the theme of the western frontier as a myth of civilisational origins. The central theme of the chapter is the role the Cold War played in constructing the identity of Europe as part of the bi-polar system of West versus East. Finally, the issue of post-fascist European identity in relation to the German question and the foundation of the European Community is considered.

The idea of Europe during the greater part of the twentieth century was subordinated to the notion of the West. The American construction of the West created the conditions for the emergence of an adversarial system in which Europe, as a result of two world wars, was forced to be the battlefield. The West was no longer merely Europe, which was an instrument of the 'Atlantic' West in the global confrontation of a mega-West versus a mega-East. It was within the confines of the Cold War politics that the idea of Europe entered the political framework as a normative model for post-war reconstruction. With the foundation of the EEC in the 1950s, for the first time in history the idea of Europe was institutionalised in a political framework with which, in time, it inevitably became wedded: the idea of Europe finally ceased to be merely a cultural model and became a reality, but one whose identity was less European than 'western'. For even in the space that the EEC created for itself, the idea of Europe still remained a Cold War construct and a bastion of a mega-West.

As a Cold War construct the idea of Europe became a legitimation of war, or rather of a political system based on the permanent preparation for war. The culturally and politically homogenising nature of the European idea thus contained within its discourse a form of 'cultural violence' (Galtung, 1990). This is the violence that is contained in a world-view whose postulates legitimate war.

At this point we can identify a new dimension to the discourse of Europe. In the second half of the twentieth century the idea of Europe articulated a particular way of life which can be said to be distinctively European. Until now I have stressed the political, military and economic significance of Europe. As a cultural construct Europe signified more than the ideals of high culture: the culture of everyday life is also an important dimension to Europeanism.

AMERICA'S MYTH OF EUROPE

With the political neutralisation of Europe after the Second World War, Americans were able to construct new myths of Europe. These are not just American myths of Europe but have become part of the identity of Europe. After the war Europe became once again the Old World, a cultural compensation for a historically impoverished America and the dislocations of urbanism. Tourism played its role in converting the battlefields of Europe into a Great Museum. The recovery of the past was seen as essential to the renewal of the present. But it was an invented past that was restored in post-war Europe and it was not without its political content. As David Horne (1984, p. 21) has pointed out in his study of European museums, one of the aims of western museums is to demonstrate the superiority of the West over the East.

What was rediscovered was a pastiche version of Old Europe with its centre in the West, which then came to be represented as the true Europe. Just as Europeans had earlier constructed their myths of the Orient, so too did Americans construct their myths of Europe. Europe for Americans was a compensation for their own perceived lack of history and cultural inferiority. It was a fascination that had its roots in the American quest for historical identity. After the war Americans rediscovered Europe which was reduced to the monuments of the past. Europe was no longer the sinister *Mitteleuropa* of *fin-de-siècle* Vienna or the Europe of fascism, but an aesthetic category, romantic and nostalgic, designed for the gaze of the tourist. Europe could be viewed as an undifferentiated spectacle: the Tate, St Mark's Square, the Berlin Wall, the Vatican, Dachau and the Eiffel Tower could all be viewed with the same undiscerning eye expressing the same fascination with the past.

The idea of Europe as an aesthetic construction had been for long a part of the American literary imagination. One of the most famous versions of this is Henry James's nostalgia for the aristocratic order of Old Europe. The Anglo-Saxon construction of Europe had a long history and originated in the days of the English aristocracy's Grand Tour of Italy, which was held to be the repository of the true Europe of sensuality, nature and Renaissance splendour. In the same way, Americans romanticised a Europe which had been rendered politically harmless. Twice in the twentieth century America had rescued Europe from the clutches of Germany. The American romanticisation of Europe was also a hankering after the past and expressed the myth of a greater western civilisation. By romanticising Europe, Americans were defining themselves as members of an ancient civilisation over which they themselves had triumphed (Lowenthal, 1990, pp 114–17).

The American myth of Europe can also be traced back to the emigration of Puritan English settlers in the seventeenth century. Escaping from the religious persecution by the Anglican regime of the Stuarts, Europe served as a contrast to Restoration England. In England throughout the eighteenth century dissenters continued to be discriminated against and in the early nineteenth century emigrants fleeing from poverty in early industrial England looked to the new revolutionary ideas emanating from the sentimentalised continent. Europe was perceived as a motherland which was a contrast to the harsh and repressive conditions from which the settlers had fled. But as settlers started arriving from the continent, the image of Europe changed. It was America, and not Europe, that personified a freedom that had been destroyed. But this was to change by the mid-nineteenth century when 'many Americans were less concerned with the liberation of other peoples by the spreading of Republicanism than with the limitless expansion of a superior Anglo-Saxon race' (Horsman, 1981, p. 6). Nevertheless the myth endured and a sharp antithesis emerged between Europe and America in the nineteenth century. The self-perception of Americans was no longer that of Europeans. Europe became associated with oppression and inequality while America was the land of freedom, a freedom personified in the mystique of the limitless frontier of the Old West. The Old World was the land of ruins and tyranny for Mark Twain. The United States of America had, after all, been born in an act of rebellion against a European country. Europe was a mirror for American identity in its formative period in the nineteenth century, a contrasting picture which it could both appeal to and at the same time define itself against. In the confrontation with the native population of America, their identity as Europeans, and equally important Christian dissenters, provided the settlers with a historical myth of legitimation and an ethic of racial superiority. So while Europe was overtly rejected, the racial category of Europeanism was retained.

From the late 1920s America began to re-embrace Europe: the Great Depression of 1929 brought with it self-doubt and Roosevelt's New Deal helped to steer American thinking in a European direction (Boorstin, 1976, p. 37). American intellectuals began to find America decadent and Europe more alive and modern, a tendency epitomised in Hemingway's 'discovery' of Europe in the 1920s and 1930s. For Henry Miller, too, Europe became for this brief moment a stimulus for art (Strout, 1963, pp. 194–5). But the dominant tendency in this period was undoubtedly one towards an inward-looking America that sought its past within itself (Jones, 1971). The antithesis of Europe and America remained unresolved.

The essence of the American view of Europe was that Europe represented the past: Europe, even for Hemingway, secure in his American identity, was decadence, death and oppression. T. S. Eliot's *The Wasteland* was the ultimate expression of this idea of Europe as a malignant city. The creation of republican and federal institutions in the United States provided substance for the myth of the New World as the triumph of liberty and progress over the decadent Old World. Europe, in Jefferson's vision, was loaded 'with misery, by kings, nobles and priests' while America was the land of 'the dreams of the future' (Strout, 1963, pp. 27 and 33). Connected with this was the myth of Europe as the decadent metropolis, which was both fascinating and repelling. American cities are places of industry and commerce; the European city was the vehicle of history. Europe ultimately represented the twin evils of class and nation, over which Americans had supposedly triumphed.

One of the most enduring ideas of Europe civilization was the idea of the West. The old European idea of the West became a major part of American identity in the nineteenth and twentieth centuries. It was no longer a European West but an Americanised West that was consolidated in the creation of the myth of the limitless western frontier. Long before world leadership fell into the hands of the Americans, the idea of the West in the form of the 'Old West' had already entered the American national consciousness as far back as the seventeenth century. Originally signifying the thirteen colonies, it shifted westwards of the Mississippi to finally embrace California, the 'Far West' (Athearn, 1986; Billington, 1949).

It was Thomas Jefferson who invented the notion of the Far West following the purchase of Louisiana from France in 1803. This vision of the West was solidified in the Monroe Doctrine in 1823 which claimed that the colonisation of the Americas was the prerogative of the US government. The European powers were thus forced to concentrate their colonisation in Africa and Asia. The result of this was that America signified not just a continent but a hemisphere. In his famous study of the idea of the western frontier in American history, F. J. Turner (1921, p. 41) argued that the western frontier rather than the north–south conflict shaped the national character of modern America and gave it its enduring tenacity of spirit, democratic and individualistic in form: 'In American thought and speech "frontier" has come to mean the edge of settlement, rather than, as in Europe, the political boundary.' The western frontier was always understood, according to Carlton Hays (1946), as the frontier of European civilisation.

The myth of the West took on a new form with the idea of Manifest Destiny (Berge, 1983; Horsman, 1981). The idea originally was linked to a fated course of empire-building leading Americans to the Pacific and bringing them into contact with Asia (Smith, 1950, p. 45). The sanctity of the myth of 'the West as America' – fully endorsed by Turner – has recently been demolished by Truettner (1991), who has argued that the fiction of the limitless frontier of the West was a hegemonic notion. This was the belief in America's role in the world and that the white Anglo-Saxon settlers had a divinely bestowed mission to fulfil in the conquest of the western frontier, which became the basis of a racial myth (Horsman, 1981, p. 189). Few ideas have given more explicit testimony to the stature of the West as a hegemon. After the American Revolution land-hungry settlers moved westwards into Ohio, Kentucky and Tennessee and occupied the Mississippi valley, displacing the native population. When Texas was annexed in 1846 the idea of Manifest Destiny took on a mythical character and became a major expression of American national consciousness. This can be seen as a revival of the European idea of the Occident as the guarantee of progress and Christian redemption. The idea of the West was a hegemonic notion which disguised conquest and mass extermination as a providential mission.

The theme of a free-moving people pushing westwards conquering virgin territory – the mastery of the Wild Prairie and the Great Plains and the Taming of the West – gave profound expression to the European myth of the Occident. The settlers brought with them the old European ideas of Christianity, progress and republican democracy. The myth of the limitless frontier of the West signalled the transference of civilisation from East to West. Since Columbus, progress and colonisation had always been linked together as a providential mission in which conquest was divinely sanctioned. The transference of the western limits of European civilisation to the Far West was accomplished at the cost of the destruction of a native civilisation. The native Americans were originally driven westwards in the wake of the early colonisation, but when settlers began to move further westwards in the second half of the nineteenth century the native population was gradually decimated from constant upheaval and warfare.

The myth of the frontier is a very powerful motif in the history of Europe whose identity was shaped in its territorial conquests. It found one of its most perverse expressions in the Nazi *Drang nach Osten,* the eastward thrust. Even Hitler had often seen himself as a German Roosevelt and the ambitious futuristic goal of a Nazi Europe was modelled on the American conquest of the West. The Nazi attempt to conquer eastern Europe and push forward to the Urals was compared to the American myth of the boundless western frontier (James, 1989, p. 267; Weinberg, 1964).

The American construction of the West and the romanticisation of Europe shaped the framework for the formation of an adversarial system. The concrete manifestation of this global confrontation between West and East was the Cold War. It is to this that I should now like to turn.

EUROPE AND THE ORIGIN OF THE COLD WAR

The Cold War was undoubtedly the single most important event in the history of the twentieth century that shaped the identity of Europe. It is difficult to think of another event of comparable significance in the formation of European identity in the second half of the twentieth century. But exactly what was the Cold War and how did it shape the identity of Europe?

The Cold War had its origins in the October Revolution, though it was not until the closing stages of the Second World War that we can speak of a major confrontation between West and East (Fleming, 1961). The events which led to the Cold War were effectively decided in February 1943 when the German Sixth Army under General von Paulus was defeated at Stalingrad and the Red Army began its westward advance. A final attempt by the Germans was defeated at Kursk in July 1943. By January 1945 Poland was occupied, Hungary the following month, in April Vienna was occupied and in May the war came to an end when the Red Army and the Allies faced each other in Berlin. By this time the Red Army was in possession of Eastern and Central Europe. With the defeat of Germany the fate of Europe was once again in the balance, for instead of a Nazi Europe the beleaguered West was now faced with the spectre of a communist Europe. So for the second time in the twentieth century Germany was the scene of a global confrontation between capitalism and communism. Since the Middle Ages Germany had been the site of confrontations between West and East. From its historical lands west of the Rhine, Germany over the centuries, from Charlemagne to the Teutonic Knights to Bismarck, expanded east of the Elbe and colonised the eastern areas of the Baltic Sea. It was in keeping with the logic of German history that West and East would finally confront each other on German soil for the dismemberment of Europe. The self-destructive forces within German history had sealed the fate of Germany which was ultimately unable to resist its traditional enemy, Russia. Unable to beat the Red Army in the race for Berlin in the closing stages of the war, the Allies tacitly opted for the division of Germany into western and eastern zones.

What was to outlive the war was the problem of the eastern frontier. Even after the Jews had ceased to inhabit the cities of Central and Eastern Europe where they had lived for centuries and were an essential part of their culture, the East–West frontier remained more unbridgeable than ever before. For the first time a Russian presence formed a direct frontier to western Europe after 1945. The old western Slavic frontier, presented principally by Poland and the Balkans, became part of an overarching East bloc, which symbolically cut itself off from the West on the night of 13 August 1961 when the Berlin Wall was erected. The Berlin Wall epitomised the internal division of Europe and the centuries-long struggle between West and East. While this has always been a shifting frontier, with its limits having been variously determined somewhere between Germany and Russia, what has remained constant is the frontier itself. The abiding nature of this great divide was even reflected in the attitude of westernised Jews to the eastern Jews, whom they resented and often discriminated against. The enduring nature of the Eastern question with which the German question has been inextricably linked can be seen as both an expression of historical reality, of social and economic structures that evolved over centuries to produce two different kinds of societies with antagonistic political structures, and at the same time as part of the construction of historical reality. Clearly the two cannot be separated. Ideas are not simply products of the mind but have their roots in the real world and are a part not only of the way the world is seen, but also shape the world by influencing historical choices. The East–West conflict, then, is not merely the product of abstract ideas, a struggle of civilisations or incompatible world-views, but is reproduced in social, political and economic conflicts. The mutual hostility between East and West was always focused on specific groups who were forced to bear the burden of history. What is to be emphasised is the way in which the cultural representations of reality crystallise in the formation of regressive identities based on racial categories, xenophobic myths of nationality and obscurantist irrationalism.

The idea of Europe is not free of these prejudices. While guilt for the war became a problem for German national identity, the idea of Europe was purified of its past and transformed into a programme for the future. The idea of Europe became a utopia rather than a romantisation of the past. But Europe, as the crucible of the West, was also America's eastern frontier and a reconstructed power bloc against the new bogey, communism. So, for a time, Europe became a substitute for nationalism which had revealed its true colours in the form of national socialism.

The fundamental dualism of West versus East, upon which the edifice of European civilisation was based, was not, then, fundamentally altered after the war. For western Europe this signalled the American Age and the arrival of a new culture that owed nothing to the heritage of *Mitteleuropa*. Europe had in effect become America's eastern frontier. The Cold War division of Europe into two hostile camps, the liberal democracies of the West and, on the other side, the communist states of eastern Europe, then, has its origin in the conditions of the Second World War. It was ultimately the expansionary

ambitions of national socialism in Germany that led to the Cold War. This
point is important to appreciate because the Cold War was not, as the conservative rhetoricians of the West always maintained, created by the USSR.
It was capitalist over-production and the self-destructive German expansion
in eastern Europe and the onslaught on Russia that brought the Red Army
into Central Europe, not communism. Communism, like western liberal
democracy, had already settled for containment, and while it was clearly anxious to gain as much territory as possible in the westward march of the Red
Army in 1945, the principal motivation was in fact defensive.

The idea of 'Western Europe' took on an enhanced significance in the formation of a new eastern frontier. Poland, which had lost about one fifth of
its population during the Second World War, was moved physically westwards by several hundred kilometres, having acquired what had been previously German territory, and in the process having lost territory to the east.
The new German–Polish frontier became the Oder–Neisse line. The Soviet
Union also moved further westwards with the acquisition of the Baltic republics
and the eastern territory of Poland. This was part of a historic movement by
which a new West was about to emerge and which was to last until 1989.
The entire eastern frontier once again shifted accordingly as the scales of
history tipped more in the direction of the Atlantic with the birth of
'EuroAmerica'. The political nature of the new construct was clear from the
inclusion in it of Athens and Vienna but not Prague and Budapest, the metropolitan cores of the old Danubian *Mitteleuropa*. Even Ankara became a
nominal member of the new Europe.

Europe as a Cold War construct was subordinated to a wider opposition
of West versus East. Europe's eastern frontier shrank back to the Elbe and
eastern Europe became a semi-periphery of the USSR. That it was thinly
veiled politics masquerading as geography is evident in the inclusion of Israel
and Japan in the 'West'. A new historical category was born and to which
Europe was subordinated, the North Atlantic. With its centre anchored somewhere in the depths of the Atlantic Ocean, Europe was reduced to an economic community between the capitalist states and an eastern bulwark against
communism. The old and defunct *Mitteleuropa* disappeared – at least for a
time – and, in the political vacuum created by the vanishing of Central Europe,
western Europe migrated further eastwards to include Vienna, the heart of
the old *Mitteleuropa*.

The term Cold War, with its origins deep in the conflict between medieval
Christendom and Islam, was reinvented by Walter Lipmann shortly after the
end of the Second World War and was widely deployed as an ideological
cover for the new US-led internationalism: the founding of the World Bank,
the International Monetary Union, the Truman Doctrine, the Marshall Plan

and the US Loan to Britain. At stake was not merely an attempt to curb Soviet expansion, which had been exaggerated, but the global hegemony of the United States. As the Second World War was drawing to a close, Roosevelt's war aim was the marginalisation of Europe, which he perceived to be the major source of instability, and the fragmentation of the continent into relatively powerless states. Essential to that task, which was designed to create a permanent superpower alliance with the USSR to ensure world stability, was the disappearance of Germany as a major power (Aga-Rossi, 1993).

The construction of Europe along Cold War lines was not only designed to serve as a bulwark against the Red Army and as a guarantee of US hegemony, but it was also an attempt to prevent a future revival of the Third Reich. The failure of the allies and the Russians to arrive at an agreement on post-war Europe, in the end, led to the division of Germany. Post-war Europe was never only an attempt to suppress German dominance of the continent, but it was the unresolved nature of the German question that sustained the Cold War. The German question had for over a century determined the political identity of Europe and the solution that was found was nothing less than the dismemberment of Germany. It was inevitable that this would also be the division of Europe into two blocs with the centre of gravity lying outside. It was in Germany that the two military blocs found their focus even before the war was over. The two German states and a divided Europe both had emerged out of the failed drive of the German nation to take possession of *Mitteleuropa* upon whose embers the new order was built.

If *Mitteleuropa* lived on in the subterranean consciousness, it did so as nostalgia for the Old Regime of the vanquished Habsburgs and, in its more ominous form, in the ambition of the extreme right to return to the borders of pre-1945. Since Germany had been for long associated with Central Europe as a mega-bloc, it was not surprising that any discussion of Germany's border would raise fundamental questions about the identity of Europe. After the war it was a choice of Germany or Europe. Not surprisingly Europe seemed a more palatable option. But the Europe that emerged out of the upheaval of the war was destined to be a bifurcated one. The bifurcation of Europe and the suppression of the German question placed France at the helm of western Europe. The new reduced western Europe was a French-led Europe, but the fundamental opposition of West and East remained. The only difference this time was that it was part of a greater global order. To an extent, it was also a battle of two civilisations possessing different and incompatible world-views. The defeat of Russia, and with it large chunks of Eastern Europe, enhanced the Christian identity of the West which could be contrasted to the atheist communist world. The new opposition was that of the North Atlantic versus the Soviet Union. This crystallised in the formation of the North Atlantic Treaty Organisation (NATO) in 1949 and the Warsaw Pact Organisation in 1955. Its advent had already been symbolically announced in Churchill's 'Iron Curtain' speech in 1946 and in the announcement of the Truman doctrine the following year with its professed goal of the containment of communism. With Germany divided, the new Europe became an international order whose centre no longer rested in Germany. In 1949 'West Germany' as the Federal Republic of Germany was formally created, having emerged out of the three zones administered by the Allied occupation armies, and 'East Germany', the German Democratic Republic, emerged out of the Soviet zone, both becoming full member states of the UN in 1973. The construction 'West Germany' epitomised the identity of Europe as a Cold War construct. American popular culture had a homogenising influence on Europe, which found a new identity in the culture industry and new middle-class materialism of the post-war decades. The same culture, American in its conception and ethos, could be found from California to Vienna.

But in what way was the identity of Europe shaped by the Cold War? After 1945 two hostile world powers confronted each other ostensibly intent on bringing about each other's destruction. To an extent this was an expression of the irreconcilable conflict of West versus East. However, in the decades after the war a new dimension entered the centuries-old hostility between East and West: the race to gain hegemony over the Third World. It was under these circumstances that the conflict between West and East became not one merely about the Cold War but about the neo-colonial race for the Third World. What then was the Cold War about if it was not a real war with winners and losers? In the view of critics such as E. P. Thompson and Noam Chomsky the Cold War was simply about itself and not merely about capitalism and communism: for both sides it served as an ideological instrument by which the industrial war economies of West as well as East were deployed to exercise hegemony over their respective populations and the tightening of controls. So, while appealing to the threat posed by the Other, each of the superpowers was able to exercise counter-revolutionary violence against radicals and to fragment the labour movement within its own domain. It was this 'isomorphism' that led to the overthrow of Dubcek and Allende and the suppression of radical dissent in the two power blocs (Thompson, 1982, p. 23). There was no essential difference between the suppression of reform in Eastern Europe by the USSR and US intervention in the Third World: both were struggles against non-aligned reform which could not be tolerated. According to Mary Kaldor (1991, p. 35; 1990) the two systems 'were not in conflict but were complementary, tied together by high levels of military spending and a permanent external threat. The existence of each provided a legitimation for the other.' In short it was the internal threat, bolstered by the fiction of an external attack, that provided the framework for the Cold War. While manifestly proclaiming the growth of vast and unprecedented war economies to be in the interest of national security, the effective goal was the act of permanent preparation for a war of 'exterminism'. The Cold War and its rhetoric of political terror served as a political ballast by which West and East constructed hegemonic forms of identity and a legitimation for the production of military waste. The Cold War provided both participants with a fulcrum of stability for the consolidation of counter-revolutionary mega-power blocs. The West found its new identity in the threat of a total destruction in a war and system of technology which could neither be won nor lost. This zero-sum game was the ultimate and most destructive expression of European identity which had become embedded in an adversarial system that had penetrated to the institutional cores of both societies. For the first time in human history the industrial technology of war became an integral part of the superstructure in the formation of a mega-framework of hegemonic control. The very identity of Europe as the Christian-Humanist West became part of the drive towards the industrialisation of war in which two civilisations confronted each other. In this dualism the legacy of two revolutions was brought to bear on systems of state violence, one legitimated by the principles of the French Revolution and the other by the October Revolution. Liberal democracy and its counter-ego communism were thus deployed to mobilise gigantic frameworks of coercion and hegemonic apparatuses which penetrated all dimensions of society and structured political discourse for decades.

Communism also provided a major legitimation of the West in the form of its dissidents who looked to the West for a freedom that was not to be found under communism. Their focus on non-explicitly political issues such as human rights, coupled with the fact that they came in small numbers, served to supply the West with a major legitimation. Throughout the Cold War it was conveniently ignored that four European countries in the 'western' camp were anything but democratic: Spain, Portugal, Greece and Turkey were military dictatorships. The attitude of Western Europe to the failure of the Hungarian revolution in 1956 and the invasion of Prague in 1968 revealed the equation of Europe with the West: the Czechs and Hungarians were supported as an oppressed people but not as Europeans asserting their European identity since this was by definition free from oppression (Finkielkraut, 1985).

THE EUROPE OF THE MARKET

While it was the ideological framework of the Cold War that principally shaped the identity of Europe after the Second World War, one of the most important driving forces was the new wave of economic nationalism. Of course the two were related; anti-communism provided a powerful legitimation of the new materialism that swept western Europe in the boon decades after the war, and capitalism became its own ideology. The ideological vacuum created by the defeat of fascism facilitated the consolidation of a new idea of Europe. The idea of Europe that emerged after the war was one that accommodated itself to the nation-state and was reflected in de Gaulle's belief in a 'Europe of Nation-States', each pursuing its own objectives independently but with the cooperation of each other (Milward et al., 1993). This was also reflected in Churchill's cautious support for a 'kind of Europe' with which Britain could be at least externally associated. Britain preferred the enigma, formulated by Churchill, of being 'with but not of' Europe, but with the rider than when put to the test she would opt for the Atlantic (Radice, 1992). Post-war British national identity found its embodiment in the Commonwealth, which served for Britain a role similar to that served by Europe for the rest of Western Europe.

The new notion of Europe had nothing to do with nostalgia for the Europe of Berlin and Vienna but became an increasingly bureaucratic entity centred in Brussels. Bureaucratic centralism and the ideological consolidation of Western Europe as a trading bloc organised along Cold War lines was seen as the way forward. The emergence of new political institutions helped to shape the new and reduced Europe: the Organisation for European Economic Co-operation (OEEC) in 1948 which became the Organisation for Economic Co-operation and Development (OECD), the Council of Europe in 1949, and in 1957 Euratom. In 1958 the EEC was born. Though it had American support, it reflected France's ambition to assume the political leadership of Europe, with the German economy, unburdened of the need to finance defence, providing the necessary economic muscle. There was nothing new in this – ever since Charlemagne's expansion westwards, Europe had always been characterised by a struggle between France and Germany for hegemony over the rest of the continent.

With the foundation of the EEC, the idea of Europe took on a new dimension. It was no accident that it was an economic community and not a manifestly political one. Politically the identity of Europe was shaped by the mass of prejudice and paranoia that the Cold War was able to generate. Europe was no longer merely about politics but about the 'common market' and the new consumerism of post-war reconstruction. In the post-war period it was generally agreed that Europe as a spiritual and philosophical project was over (Patocka, 1983). The war had discredited European culture as the life of the mind; the new Europe was a materialist one that sought no other legitimation than that which could not be supplied by capitalist modernity. The 'common' market, as one of its critics said, was 'common for those who meet the bill. And that bill is written in power units more than in economic units' (Galtung, 1973, p. 17). In E. P. Thompson's (1980, p. 85) words, 'going into Europe' for the British middle class was 'about the belly. A market is about consumption. The Common Market is conceived of as a distended stomach: a large organ with various traps, digestive chambers and fiscal acids, assimilating a rich diet of consumer goods.'

The new idea of Europe as an economic community was an important focus for the social democratic parties anxious to sever connections with the old and discredited idea of Europe. The ideological exhaustion of nationalism was the perfect opportunity to launch new political programmes. West Germans could identify more easily with a notion of Europe given the division of their country and the carnage that was committed in its name. For the US the project of European unity was a means of solving the problems created by the failed nation-states which had come into existence in 1919. Germany was in a special way an extreme example of a failed nation-state. In order that the catastrophe of the Weimar Republic would never again be repeated, nothing less than the suppression of the old European nation-state was deemed to be the solution.

In order to suppress the German question and, more importantly, to establish a politically stable Europe as a bulwark against communism, the new global order under the leadership of the US encouraged the formation of a federation of European states. But this was never conceived as anything more than a system of cooperation between the European nation-states. A federation on the model of the United States was never a viable alternative to the nation-state, which had, in fact, been rehabilitated. America could never be the model for Europe which is the home of numerous language groups. While, clearly, not all these groups possess nationalist traditions, or are even politically mobilised, they can, nonetheless, be said to exist as cultural entities within a political framework whose dissolution would be an invitation for confrontation. Moreover, the circumstances under which the US system of federation arose were very different from the European historical experience. West Germany was the only country where this system of federation was successfully implanted. But this was an anomaly and the German federal constitution was imposed from the outside after two world wars had been fought. While the example of Switzerland suggests that the idea of federation is not alien to the European experience, there is nothing in the history of modern Europe to indicate that a federal system of government can be imposed above the level of the nation-state in the form of a United States of Europe.

Yet, Europe was more than an organisation of economic cooperation based on autonomous nation-states. It was also a moral-political community, the

EEC becoming in time the EC, and after 1993, the European Union when the myth of community was abandoned. The idea of Europe as a liberal democratic community was essentially a foil for the pursuit of a new programme in political and economic engineering, for economics cannot work without morality and politics. The postulation of community at the end of history is deeply rooted in the European intellectual tradition. Community rather than society, the state or nationality had for long been seen as the goal of history. The idea is integral to Christianity, the utopian ideas of the Renaissance, nationalism and communism.

Most attempts to create a European cultural identity are pathetic exercises in cultural engineering: the Eurovision Song Contest, Euro-Disney, the ECU, the annual European City of Culture and the cultural apparatus of the new institutions was not the stuff out of which new symbolic structures could be built. European culture has generally signified the culture of the past not that of the state. Bureaucratic assimilation and institution-building can therefore only have a reifying effect. It is probably, too, for this reason that the anthem of the European Community – the fourth movement of Beethoven's Ninth Symphony – has a reifying tone to it. Attempts to create an official European culture in the 1980s were doomed to failure as there was little that could be done to reverse the earlier conception of European unity as an economic venture with minimal political unity. Ironically in attempting to move beyond nationalism, the European Community attempted to fashion a European identity using the very tools of nationalism: the flag, anthem, passport, group name and sense of a common history. But, unlike national identity, the politics of European identity sought legitimation in bourgeois high culture, as is exemplified in the choice of anthem and its dedication to 'cities of culture'. National identity, in contrast, has traditionally looked not to the city but the countryside for inspiration, and the culture with which it seeks to define the nation has in general been linguistic. While community is possible at many levels (Gusfield, 1975), the politics of Europeanism proved unable to create a cohesive community identity capable of providing an alternative to national identity. Rather than promoting new kinds of community compatible with modernity, the EC enhanced the new societal structures which reified community.

What then is European culture? According to George Steiner (1992, pp. 43–4) it is best exemplified in the institution of the café, which in his view defines a 'historical space roughly from western Portugal to that line which runs south from Leningrad to Kiev and Odessa' but certainly excludes Moscow. But what sense does this make? The institution of the café is Arabic and is to be found in cities throughout North Africa from Tangier to Alexandria; and while it may be true that the institution is unknown in Moscow, it is also absent from the prosaic culture of the British Isles. For Patocka (1983) European culture is to be found in the philosophical tradition of metaphysical thought inaugurated by Plato. This idea of European culture embracing elite culture is also to be found in Cees Nooteboom's (1993) evocation of a cosmopolitan life-style, but with the notable difference that the Dutch writer emphasises that national identity is itself a melting-pot of cultural influences that transcend nationality and Europeanism consists simply in the recognition of unity in difference. America can be identified as a way of life, but Europe cannot, except perhaps when Europeans travel to the United States and suddenly discover their Europeanness. What I think is the ultimate test is that there is still no European labour movement or even political party that is genuinely European (Papeke, 1992, p. 66). The only notable exception is perhaps the ecological movement, but this does not appeal to unifying myths of integration, seeking instead its identity in a new attitude to nature.

CONCLUSION

In the period after 1945 the nation-state was no longer the reference point for the idea of Europe, which became closely linked to a new reality. This did not, however, mean that Europe became the basis of a new political identity. The idea of the West was the new reference point for Europe which had effectively become America's eastern frontier. Europe's age old ethnoculturalism thus survived in the adversarial politics of the Cold War and the cultural violence it sustained. Until the cessation of the Cold War in 1989, the EC integrated states of Western Europe held a monopoly on the idea of Europe: Europe was Western Europe and its symbol was the Cold War artefact of 'West Germany'. In 1989 this cosy world collapsed and with it Europe as the liberal democratic West.

9 Europe after the Cold War

THEORETICAL PERSPECTIVES

This chapter is principally concerned with the consequences of the ending of the Cold War with regard to the identity of Europe. Five major issues in particular are discussed and which are all linked to the ending of the Cold War: the question of German unification; the rediscovery of *Mitteleuropa*; the problem of the double transition from communism to capitalism and liberal democracy in the former communist world; the movement toward unity in Western Europe; and the rise of nationalism and racism throughout Europe.

The year 1989 was a turning point in the history of Europe and symbolised a break from the age that began with the 1917 communist revolution (Hobsbawm, 1991d). Since the revolutions of 1989 new definitions of Europe have emerged: the old polarities of Eastern Europe and Western Europe are being challenged by the revival of Central Europe as a political programme and ideal. Until 1989 the identity of Europe, as the West, was secured by the supposed communist threat, but since the disappearance of the old imagined enemy there has been a concerted attempt to construct a new bogey with which European identity can reorient itself in a multi-polar world. Instead of the old poles of opposition of West versus East, the new polarity is that of North versus South. In this transformation the 'East' has not disappeared; it has just shifted southwards to include Islam and the Third World. The Islamic Revolution of 1979 was the first sign of the formation of a new adversarial system, which culminated in the Gulf War in 1991. It is in this context of a clash of cultures that 'Fortress Europe' has taken on a renewed significance.

My aim in this chapter is to chart the course in which the idea of Europe in disengaging itself from the bipolar system of the Cold War attached itself to a new politics of legitimation based on the notion of 'Fortress Europe'. It was not until after the revolutions of 1989, which ushered in the end of the Cold War, that the idea of Europe ceased to be a cultural reference model for the 'West'. Although the notion of the 'West' has not been altogether abandoned, there has been an increased emphasis on 'Europe' in the post-Cold War period. This suggests that the idea of Europe should be considered as part of a politics of legitimation and traced to certain structures and interests in contemporary society.

It is apparent, however, that there is little unanimity on what actually constitutes Europe. Given the multifarious and deeply divided nature of Europe in the post-Cold War period, the idea of Europe has lent itself to a wide vari-

ety of identity projects. It is in this context that I should like to locate the
rebirth of the project of *Mitteleuropa*, which can be seen as a kind of 'anti-
Europe', in the sense that it takes for its goal a different notion of Europeanism
to that of the European Union. So in global terms the idea of Europe is linked
to 'Fortress Europe' while within the European context it is the very diversity of national cultures that sustains the idea of Europe. In this way we can
see how a cultural idea becomes instrumentalised once it enters the political
framework and becomes a focus for identity-building projects. I have throughout this book stressed the connection between national and European identity: when regional and traditional identities were superseded by national
identities in the nineteenth century, the uneven and contradictory nature of
modernisation ensured the survival of tradition as neo-tradition, and very
often as identities that had no tradition at all. Similarly with the advent of a
European identity, old national identities, dormant since 1945, have resurfaced in entirely new guises with the result that processes of Europeanism
and nationalism have become implicated in each other's programmes.

There is another dimension to this which should not be ignored. The institutionalisation of a cultural idea such as Europe in a polity organised principally around economic interests can result, given the crisis nature of capitalism,
in a legitimation crisis unless there is a corresponding collective identity based
on a stable system of democratic norms. Much of the new wave of racism is
not really about hostility to foreigners but is indicative of a deeper malaise.
Outbursts of xenophobia and racial violence are, I suggest, symptoms of what
Durkheim called 'anomie', the breakdown in social cohesion and solidarity.
This is a much deeper tendency and is also symptomatic of what Habermas
(1987) has called the 'colonisation of the life world' by impersonal structures
that are no longer under the control of social actors and which have the effect
of eroding value systems. This has a direct bearing on my theme of Europe.
The contemporary experiment in the construction of a new mega-Europe, conceived of as a gigantic exercise in political and economic engineering, will
continue to exert more pressure than ever before on traditional forms of life,
which in turn will find their expression in pathological identities. As this
scenario gradually becomes reality, it is important that 'Social Europe' and
the autonomy of socio-cultural spaces be rescued from neo-liberal style
agendas (Byrant, 1991). Out of the 340 million population of the European
community, some 3 million are reckoned to be homeless and 50 million can
be described as poor, while some 15 million migrants live in marginalised
circumstances. When we add to this the simmering discontent of many
people with the processes of decision-making, in which those who are the
most affected by power have the least voice, the project of Europe risks becoming a potential melting-pot of populist agitation. The core of the problem is

that the idea of Europe has not formed the basis of a collective identity committed to democratic norms and cultural tolerance.

The reason for this failure resides in the fact that the dominant concept of European identity pursued today is that of the state model. The mechanisms of integration that this promotes are based on enhancing bureaucratic control, political centralisation and economic crisis management. Clearly there is a need for a collective identity that is not merely a prop for institution-building. In the absence of such a post-national collective identity, national identity will be strengthened simply because Europeanism is devoid of both tradition and life-world contexts and consequently appeals to populist sentiment, which is reappropriated as a collective identity. Just as nationalism reinvented and reappropriated older cultural and ethnic traditions in the nineteenth century, today Europeanism is reinventing nationalism, which has become a reified European tradition. It is, however, more than this. In the past, as is well documented, nationalists had great difficulty in convincing people that they belonged to 'nations'. The situation is not different today. The main difference is that the 'geographical entity' which is being called Europe is simply too large and abstract to be imagined in any meaningful sense. The crux of the problem is that it has no emotional value. Consequently, Europe is being 'imagined' or 'invented' as a memoryless bureaucratic macrocosm to protect life-worlds organised around patterns of consumption and welfare, and with nationalism providing the necessary emotional substitution for deficits in legitimation (Smith, 1992). Today, then, the European idea has engendered a contradiction: the antinomy of political, economic and militiary integration on the one side, and on the other social and cultural fragmentation.

THE END OF THE COLD WAR CONSENSUS

Until 1989 the question of the eastern border of Europe appeared to have been settled. The Cold War had fixed the territorial limits of Western Europe. With the Iron Curtain firmly drawn between the Baltic and the Adriatic, there was no doubt as to the limits of Western Europe. Confident in its identity as the West, the word 'western' was dropped and Western Europe became simply 'Europe', or the 'European Community'. For forty years the Cold War provided a secure framework for the identity of Western Europe whose professed goal was the recovery of Eastern Europe and the restoration of a supposedly historical Europe. In German foreign policy this was called 'normalisation', the alleged goal of the *Ostpolitik*. Secure in the knowledge that this was impossible, the West, united behind the facade of the Cold War, rested content with the illusion that the burden of historical destiny was on its side.

The collapse of the Cold War and the kind of politics it sustained was not a cause for jubilation in the West. With the fall of the imagined enemy, the West lost its bogey and with it the basis of much of its stability. In order for Europe to remain a dominant ideology, a whole new programme of reconstruction had to be mobilised after the dismantling of the Cold War edifice.

The year 1989 was the turning point particularly for Eastern Europe. The events that began in the late summer of 1989 and reached a climax by Christmas were truly revolutionary and can be compared in their world historical significance to the October Revolution of 1917. It was a revolution, as distinct from a movement for reform, in that it aimed to bring about the overthrow of the existing state, though it was more of a revolution in reverse than a forward-thinking one, for one of its peculiar characteristics, as Habermas (1991) has pointed out, was its total lack of innovating ideas. It was not only an attempt to negate the heritage of 1917 but was also a belated attempted to catch up on the West. Without the reserve power of the USSR to fall back upon, the communist governments of Eastern Europe were, in the final instance, unable to maintain the coercive apparatus of the state in the face of mass opposition. The totalitarian state thus crumbled in the face of opposition from civil society which, for a very brief moment, was triumphant. The ensuing crisis in legitimation was also, at least initially, a triumph for the West. The West seemed to have proved its self-proclaimed moral superiority over communism.

But what was to happen with the disappearance of the old enemy? Was the Cold War really vindicated? The subsequent legitimation crisis in the West had much to do with the old question of the eastern frontier which could now be called the vanishing frontier. I think it is not an exaggeration to speak of what Habermas (1976) earlier defined as a legitimation crisis. Clearly this was less severe in Western Europe than in Eastern Europe. No state collapsed in Western Europe as result of the upheaval of 1989 and 1990, but the deeply embedded assumptions upon which the political system had been erected were suddenly robbed of any meaning. This is evident in the mixed response in the West to the collapse of communism. Within the space of a few years the traditional poles of Right and Left collapsed and a new political vocabulary emerged. The old communist political class in Eastern Europe and the USSR became 'the Right' and the capitalist modernising strata the new 'Left'. In Italy the collapse of the Cold War consensus received its ultimate expression in the disappearance of the Christian Democrats in 1994 and the election to government of a 'post-modernist' party in alliance with neo-fascists.

The collapse of the old poles of antagonism meant that new strategies had to be evolved. The years since 1989 have been uncertain ones with regard to the identity of Europe and it is by no means clear what the outcome will be. However, certain tendencies can be discerned. The upheaval in Eastern Europe that has accompanied the dismantling of the Cold War has witnessed a major restructuring in the identity of Europe. This is particularly apparent in the case of German unification.

Until the fall of the Berlin Wall in 1989 and the unification of Germany the following year, the question of Europe's eastern frontier appeared to have been definitively settled. Until 1989 there was little doubt where the frontiers of Western Europe lay. Few frontiers in history were more visible. 'Asia stands on the Elbe', Adenauer remarked in 1946 (Garton Ash, 1993, p. 50; Weidenfeld, 1976). The post-war division of Germany epitomised the division of Europe into two armed camps with the result that the unification of Germany posed major questions of the identity of Europe itself. The disappearance of 'West Germany' from the map was tantamount to the loss of 'Western' Europe itself. The post-war system, kept in check by the Cold War, was built upon the suppression of the German question. But Germany is one of those things that does not just go away and the unification of Germany inevitably raised the spectre of a new Germanisation of Europe. Though few genuinely believed that this would involve a rekindling of the eastern question in the desire to return to the borders of pre-1945, German unification was nonetheless viewed by many, especially in eastern Europe, with some consternation.

Unlike other Western European nation states, German national identity has historically been closely bound up with the question of its eastern frontier. For many Poles the fact of German unification put into question the very existence of Poland. The phrase 'Silesia remains ours' was frequently to be heard in Germany in the early 1990s. Polish fears were not groundless as there are groups in Germany whose professed ambition is the recovery of territory lost in 1945. Moreover, it was never clear in the discussions relating to German unification whether the new state was to be a 'reunified' Germany or, the more cautious, a 'unified Germany. The ambivalent notion of 'reunification' always carried undertones of the past in the desire for the restoration of the old frontiers. More alarming than the announcements of the extreme right, who constitute less than 5 per cent of the voting population, was the ambivalence displayed by the principal parties of the centre-right to the extreme right as far as the territorial issue was concerned.

It is a different story today, however, when German national identity is more focused on the ability of the export dependent economy to sustain a high standard of living. It is in the prospect of German domination of the finance markets that the real fears lie. Post-war German democracy is one of the most stable in the world and few countries today have a stronger democratic political culture. The circumstances under which German unification occurred in 1990 were very different from 1871 when Bismarck unified the country after wars with Denmark, Austria and France. The initial reaction to German unification revealed that the ending of the Cold War was an ambivalent development, though few reactions were as extreme as that of Conor Cruise O'Brien's (James and Stone, 1992) diatribe in the *Sunday Times* of a fourth Reich on the rise. Yet the Cold War had, after all, arisen and been sustained by the division of Germany, even though, when the state of war against Germany was finally suspended in 1951, Germany ceased to be the focus of the Cold War. Given the symbolic significance of Germany and the memories of two world wars, it was not surprising that the question of German unification would challenge many of the presuppositions of the post-war reconstruction.

Perhaps one of the most significant developments in the restructuring of European identity is the emergence of new conceptions of Europeanism in the former Eastern Europe. While under communism Europeanism was considered an expression of bourgeois decadence, today it has become a major issue on the political agenda of most of the former communist countries. Not without nostalgia for the mystique of the old Europe of the Habsburgs, nations excluded from Europe for four decades can challenge the Cold War identity of Europe as the West. Prague and Budapest are rapidly becoming the new cultural metropoles of Europe and Berlin is no longer the totem of the West. Europe in fact has advanced several hundred miles eastwards, a migration epitomised in the relocation of Berlin as the capital of a unified Germany. With the renaming of Leningrad as St Petersburg, that city sought to regain its lost European identity.

'Europe', however, is as much about creating distances as it is about building bridges. The idea of Europe has become a political football by which groups can distinguish themselves from others. The penchant for Europe has been a significant aspect in the political restructuring of Eastern Europe. The appeal of the idea of Europe today, especially in Eastern Europe, can be compared to the appeal of nationality at the end of the First World War. The great crisis of communism in 1989/90 is similar to the impact of the October Revolution and the collapse of the empires of the Habsburgs, Hohenzollerns, Romanovs and Sultans in 1918. It is not surprising that confused notions of nationality and Europeanism have surfaced in the aftermath of the collapse of the last European empire as an expression of a distorted modernity. According to opinion polls in 1994, some 30 per cent of Russians would like a return to the Romanovs; in Italy the ghost of Mussolini has reappeared.

Eastern Europeans are now seeing themselves as 'Europeans'. But the Europe they aspire to is that of the metropolitan cores of Western Europe. This is of course an idealised kind of Europe and is associated with the western metropolis. The fact is that the majority of 'Europeans' do not live in 'cosmopolitan' cities such as London, Paris and Amsterdam, but in medium sized industrial cities whose relationship to the Europe of the European Union is not always a happy one. Europeanism is today as much associated with the rural periphery as with the metropoles. If Europeanism means enthusiasm for the politics of the European Union, then the west of Ireland is more European than the Home Counties. The penchant for 'Europe' is ambivalent, too, for other reasons.

For the Czech Republic, for instance, the idea of belonging to Europe serves as a means of demarcating itself from Slovakia. The western parts of Czechoslovakia, comprising Bohemia and Moravia, were historically closer to Western Europe as a result of having been under the jurisdiction of Austria, while Slovakia in the east was closer to the Hungarian tradition despite the fact that this was non-Slavic. The Czech Republic, formed after the break-up of Czechoslovakia in 1993, was thus able to lay claim to a tradition of Europeanism in order to alienate the less industrialised Slovakia, which is populated by a potentially troublesome Hungarian minority of some 600,000 (Draper, 1993). Western Europe did not, of course, always see things the same way. Chamberlain famously dismissed Czechoslovakia as a 'far away place of which we know nothing' and a year later Britain went to war on behalf of Poland (Glenny, 1990, p. 70). In 1945 Poland was a lost cause and the West haggled with Stalin for control of Greece. The idea of Europe tends to be selectively applied.

The situation is not significantly different in the former Yugoslavia. Both Slovenia and Croatia had been historically closer to Western European traditions in religion and political culture than Serbia and Montenegro, which had been administered by the Ottoman empire. Europeanism in recent years is thus a strategy of political identification by which Slovenia and Croatia can unburden themselves of the idea of Yugoslavia (Hobsbawm, 1991c). While both Slovenia and Croatia had been a part of Napoleon's Illyric Republic and later provinces of the Austro-Hungarian empire, there are clearly major differences between the two countries. Slovenia can make stronger claims to a tradition of Europeanism than Croatia can, as Slovenia had been a province of Austria while Croatia had been ruled from Budapest. Slovenians are now beginning to be proud that Vienna is closer to Ljubljana than Belgrade. For the Baltic republics, too, membership of Europe is a means of differentiating themselves from Russia. In short, a European identity has its uses. What is stressed is as likely to be the characteristics that separate a group from others than those that they have in common.

In the turmoil that followed the fall of the Berlin Wall in late 1989 new definitions of Europe surfaced with alarming speed. It soon became apparent Europe did not mean the same for everyone. For many, the Central Europe project is potentially a means of 're-Europeanisation' and reintroducing some of the values and aspirations eliminated by the Soviet system (Schöpflin, 1989, p. 27). There the idea of recovering history is strong, while for the Soviet Union under Gorbachev (1987, pp. 194–5), 'Europe is our Common Home' and an ideological legitimation of *perestroika*. While the United Kingdom, Ireland and Scandinavia talked about 'going into Europe', Eastern Europeans talk about 'returning to Europe'. Throughout European history, it was very often in challenges from the periphery and semi-periphery that definitions of Europeanism often arose. In the metropolitan cores, Paris, Milan, Zurich, European identity is relatively secure and does not have to be constantly affirmed – except in opposition to the periphery. But in the peripheries, where political and cultural identities are more fragile and insecure, Europeanism is more contentious. With Eastern Europe struggling to take upon itself the mantle of Europe, it is not surprising that the 1990s have witnessed a reaction against Europeanism in the metropolitan cores of Western Europe. Even traditionally liberal and cosmopolitan countries such as Denmark have reacted strongly against the new vision of a unified Europe while a relatively traditional country such as Ireland has more fully embraced the European package.

The resurfacing of *Mitteleuropa* has added a new dimension to the problem of European identity. Western Europe can no longer be simply contrasted to a Soviet-policed 'Eastern' Europe now that Central Europe has resurfaced. Milan Kundera (1984) spoke of Europe as a 'spiritual unity synonymous with the word "West"' and affirmed that Europe is also the cultural home of the Poles, Czechs and Hungarians, who belong to 'a part of Europe deeply rooted in Roman Christianity'. Proponents of the idea of Central Europe, such as Kundera, declare Russia to be non-European. This raises the thorny question of where exactly eastern Europe can possibly be, given that what used be the called Eastern Europe is now being called Central Europe. Is Russia now eastern Europe? If the periphery did not exist it would have to be invented in order to have a centre.

The idea of Central Europe is not only a utopia for the future, it is also nostalgia for an imagined past. The problem with this project of rekindling the old European spirit of *Mitteleuropa* is that what is being reintroduced is not, in fact, old European culture. That is not only impossible, but also undesirable. The 'project of Central Europe' is a potentially dangerous ambition and is not unconnected with nationalist and obscurantist undercurrents that seek to distort democratic reformism. As a 'utopia' it is also a dangerous idea and suggestive of what Dahrendorf (1990, p. 56) calls a 'total society'. As I have argued earlier, the past is never a historic past but is closely connected with the present, and the project of restoring the past is, at best, a highly ambivalent strategy since it is always a selective past, and which usually has first to pass the litmus test of national chauvinism.

As much of eastern Europe tries to 'return to Europe' via the invention of *Mitteleuropa*, a new wedge has been driven between the two constitutive parts of the former Eastern Europe: south-east Europe and the area now proclaiming itself to be Central Europe. A stronger distinction is emerging today between the periphery and the semi-periphery. The Baltic republics, Poland, the former Czechoslovakia, Hungary and Slovenia have undergone a relatively smooth transition to capitalism and liberal democracy. Given their stronger historical association with the mainstream European traditions, these countries, as semi-peripheries, appear to varying degrees to have attained a greater degree of integration with Western Europe than the more peripheral ones, including Bulgaria, Romania, Albania and the former Yugoslavia, with the possible exception of Slovenia, which can claim to be on the road from the Balkans to *Mitteleuropa*.

We can speak, then, of two historical regions within what used to be called 'Eastern Europe'. The semi-peripheral regions of the central European empires and the semi-peripheral regions of the Ottoman empire. It is a mistake to see these regions as constituting an undifferentiated Eastern Europe. The historical experience of the two regions has been too diverse to make such claims tenable. What has Romania in common with Poland or the Czech Republic? Not much more than Ireland and Greece surely. This may be a lot or a little depending on one's perspective, but it makes nonsense out of attempts to impose comprehensive constructs, based on dubious historical theories, on such diverse entities. It is for this reason that caution should be used in proclaiming the notion of a *Mitteleuropa* programme. The idea of *Mitteleuropa* is as much an invented construct as Western Europe or Eastern Europe. Moreover, enthusiasm for it usually goes with a hostile attitude to Russia and south-eastern Europe (Neumann, 1993). Many countries, Poland, Hungary, the former Czechoslovakia, for instance, see themselves as a European waiting-room for thousands of Ukrainians, Russians and other emigrants from the former USSR (Carter, 1993, p. 477).

Yet *Mitteleuropa* is also a normative idea to distinguish between western consumerist capitalism and Soviet communism (Kumar, 1992). This is what Konrad (1984) calls Central European 'anti-politics'. For others it was a cultural concept based on a revival of civil society (Schögel, 1985). The old idea of *Mitteleuropa* had re-emerged in the period of communist rule, along with the idea of civil society, as an ideology of opposition and was a major blank of liberal reform in the peaceful revolutions of 1989 and 1990 (Glenny, 1990, pp. 185–7). It is highly questionable, however, that these ideas can continue to have the same oppositional significance that they had in the communist period (Kumar, 1993). It is difficult to use the term *Mitteleuropa* in any meaningful way since it has become a political football. In pre-unification Germany, for instance, the term was used by conservative politicians as part of the *Ostpolitik* in the 1980s while for Social Democrats it was a means of pulling away from the US alliance (Garton Ash, 1993, pp. 316–17). Switzerland, for instance, has rarely figured in the *Mitteleuropa* debate, which seems to refer more to the old Habsburg territories.

In the transition from communism to capitalism Eastern Europe has, in fact, been partly absorbed by Western Europe. This is particularly evident in the case of Germany where the five federal states of the former GDR have simply become disadvantaged regions within a national state. The price of unification has often simply been increased regional differences within states. The direct consequence of the revolutions of 1989–1990 was the exacerbation of ethnic and regional tensions. The transition to capitalism and the penetration of western enterprise into Eastern Europe has generated uneven modernisation within these countries. The structural fragmentation that has emerged out of this has led to a situation whereby some regions have been more or less 'westernised' while other areas have been abandoned to an uncertain fate, which is becoming altogether linked with xenophobic nationalism and ethnic and regional conflict. It is this scenario that makes nonsense out of the Fukuyama (1992) thesis of the world-wide victory of liberal democracy. My contention is that what emerged after the collapse of the Cold War consensus was an ideological vacuum in which new ideological struggles emerged and, moreover, that the penetration of neo-liberal late capitalism into the ex-communist world does not amount to a fundamental consensus about the inherent value of Western European norms. If the present is characterised by anything it is uncertainity, and not by the end of ideology.

The break-up of the Soviet Union itself has also raised new questions about the identity of Europe. The old question of the eastern frontier has once again reappeared in the resurfacing of new states. Does the Transcaucasian region belong to Europe? What is the status of the Ukraine and Belarus with regard to Europe? Are these regions to be considered parts of Europe or parts of Russia? The more basic issue underlying these questions is how we are to consider Russia. According to geographical criteria, these peripheral regions, including Russia as far as the Urals, belong to the continent of Europe. But does Europe really extend as far eastwards as the Ural mountains? I believe that the battle for Europe is very much bound up with the formation of semi-peripheries and peripheries with regard to two poles, Western Europe and Russia. While there is a strong case for distinguishing between the peripheral and semi-peripheral regions within what used to be called Eastern Europe, there is also a good case to be made for differentiating even further between the semi-peripheries of Eastern Europe and the peripheries of the USSR. Religion and ethnic identity are the complicating factors in the question of European identity in these frontier regions.

For over a thousand years the identity of Western Europe was shaped by Christianity, while Islam has made the greatest impact in many of the peripheral regions of Europe. During the communist period Islam was mostly suppressed as a political force, but today it is likely to be one of the most potent forces in shaping the twenty-first century. In 1992 the four Asian republics of the CIS, Kirghizistan, Uzbekistan, Tajikistan and Turkmenistan, formed a pan-Islamic trading bloc with Iran, Turkey and Pakistan. The crucial question for the twenty-first century will be whether or not Europe can absorb an Islamic identity. The reality today is that for the first time since the Middle Ages a large Islamic world is forming in the peripheries of Europe. Within the European semi-periphery Azerbaijan is a particularly interesting example. It is the largest of the Transcaucasian republics with its seven million population, and it is predominantly Muslim and closer in its cultural identity to Turkey and Iran. Azerbaijan is also a complicated case since its Muslim population is predominantly Shi'ite and has close links with northern Iran, which, unlike Sunni Turkey, is also Shi'ite. Russia itself contains four Muslim regions: the mid Volga region, the Crimea, the Northern Caucasus and the Muslim Transcaucasia (Bennigsen, 1972).

Belarus, Moldova and the Ukraine also belong geographically to Europe as does Russia itself. But are they European only by virtue of their ability to differentiate themselves from their neighbours further east? The Ukraine is the largest European country and also possesses the fifth largest population (51 million). It cannot be so easily ignored. There is also the resurfacing of Moldova which historically was part of the Ottoman territories that today form Romania and to which it is ethnically closely related.

The revolutions of 1989/90 that swept communism away from Eastern Europe and the collapse of the USSR itself in December 1991 could have provided the basis for a new European identity. But this did not happen and the collapse of communism simply served to enhance western chauvinism. There has been no convergence of values; instead, Eastern Europe has been reduced to being a disadvantaged periphery of the West. The result has been the formation of a kind of 'anti-Europe'. Underlying this development is a pervasive tendency to equate the idea of Europe with modernisation. As a social programme modernisation as far as most of Eastern Europe is concerned has been a failure and there are some who argue that modernisation as a global phenomenon has in fact collapsed in the post-communist world (Kurz, 1991).

EUROPE A LA CARTE

In 1989 two developments collided. First, the end of the Cold War, with the unification of Germany, got underway, followed by the fall of communist governments throughout Eastern Europe and the final collapse of the USSR itself. Second, the process towards integration within the European Community had taken on increased momentum in the period following the break-up of communism. In 1989 there were 34 states in Europe, in 1992 there were 54 in a world of some 170, a development that led to speculations of a 'new medievalism'. The crisis in European society stems from this combination of events: the irony that Eastern Europe was unravelling at a time when Western Europe was undergoing a process of unification. The fact that European integration was in full swing when the Cold War unexpectedly ended led to increased uncertainty as to the identity of Europe. Europe not only found its identity as 'Western Europe' challenged by the disappearance of its alter-ego, 'Eastern Europe', but resistance within the Western European nation-states in the form of populism and neo-nationalism supplied an alternative to Europeanism.

It is important to note, however, that nationalism does not necessarily imply a rejection of Europeanism. An important aspect of the new nationalism is its malleability, its ability to wear many hats. This in itself is nothing new since nationalism was always a protean phenomenon. In the past regional identities survived alongside national identities; today national identities are readjusting to Europeanism, which they are reformulating in their terms.

The full extent of the crisis of 1989 did not become evident until 1992, when three developments became apparent. First, the transition to European integration, with the Maastricht treaty on the agenda of most member states, was accompanied by an upsurge in regional nationalism as well as a stronger resistance from the nation-states themselves. The promotion of 'Euro-nationalism' as a new kind of bureaucratic patriotism by Brussels served only to fan the flames of long-dormant regional and nationalist movements. This was understandable since many feared the consequences of an increased concentration of administrative and fiscal power in the hands of a bureaucratic power bloc at Brussels. Populist movements reflecting a wide spectrum of nationalist and citizen protest movements were able to exploit the deficit in democracy that this was perceived to entail.

Second, there was a perception of a loss of political leadership in most Western European countries. Liberal democracy was at a low ebb. Social democratic parties were undergoing a rapid loss in electoral appeal, the conservative parties were finding it increasingly difficult to solve a major crisis in capitalism, unemployment was reaching an all-time high and recession had set in.

Third, the immediate consequence of the collapse of communism was the threat of full-scale immigration from Eastern Europe, a development that became the subject of public hysteria in West Germany after the initial euphoria of the fall of the Berlin Wall subsided. That this was accompanied by a general increase in world-wide immigration served only to exacerbate the paranoia that quickly set in in Western Europe.

This was the scenario against which new battles emerged. After 1989 Europe was open to new definitions. As in Eastern Europe, the idea of Europe does not signify the same for everybody in the West. The new idea of Europe is a Europe à la carte: Europe as a matter of choice. One can choose various aspects of the menu of a Europe that owes its existence to the so-called common market. This tendency to fashion Europe around the economy as opposed to the state was of course inherent in the EC since its inception. The idea of European unity, as I have already argued, was generally conceived of as a minimal unity for the purpose of the most effective pursuit of national interests: the nation-state was never in question, and was seen to be the basis of the new Europe of peaceful cooperation. The EC was intended only to supply the necessary steering power for the crisis management of late capitalism and a means by which the member states could pursue their mutually exclusive goals. As such it was always part of the sustainability project of the Cold War consensus. The idea of Europe was tolerated in so far as it facilitated the necessary pursuit of national projects. As a cultural idea, it was instrumentalised to serve as a political mechanism for integration and a steering medium for capitalism.

However, when the movement towards enhanced integration took on a new momentum with the Maastricht debate in 1992/93, the consensus on what constitutes Europe collapsed and the nation-state reasserted itself amidst the surfacing of the extreme right. European unity became less popular the more imminent it became: unity may have been attractive as an abstract goal, and as a means of pursuing other projects, but as a reality it was apparently undesirable. The truth is that the Europe of the late twentieth century is nowhere nearer to unity than in 1815 when the Concert of Europe was established after the Congress of Vienna. With the exception of the US, Russian and Ottoman empires, passports were not required to travel in most parts of the world in the nineteenth century. There were no legal restraints on travel in western Europe until after the Great War (Barzini, 1984, p. 23).

The spectacle of an 'integrated' Europe met not only with opposition from the extreme right in the name of national identity, but with reservations that were more rooted in economic and social realities. An 'integrated' Europe was commonly felt not to be a 'unified' Europe simply because as a free-trading bloc it is too small to provide each of its member states with equal access to markets. An integrated Europe would inevitably benefit a privileged select group of states, and within those an even more privileged core, with high unemployment in greatly disadvantaged peripheries.

Many people today also fear the consequences of a concentration of power in the hands of a dehumanised bureaucratic agency whose legitimation is that it speaks in the name of 'Europe'. The rhetoric of Europe provides a legitimation, which otherwise would be lacking, for political strategies that seek to mobilise new kinds of power. One should not be deluded into believing that the Europe of the European Union has come about because of its inherent value. The ideas of elites are promoted for their functional value in maintaining or pursuing a system of power. In the case of the European Union this is a matter of securing the optimal conditions for the accumulation and free flow of capital and to make Western European capitalism competitive on a global level. The idea of Europe is today increasingly becoming an expression of the homogenisation of society, the tendency of capitalism to impose economic uniformity and social cohesion by means of the market and the dynamics of capital accumulation. Linked to this is the growth of new structures of informal decision-making which lie behind the formal and ostensibily democratic institutions and could become the basis of an authoritarian state apparatus (Bunyan, 1991).

The idea of Europe is not another word for internationalism or pan-European unity. In the 1990s Europeanism is just as likely to be an ideological strategy to express hostility and chauvinism. This is because Europe has different meanings for different people in different contexts. Europeanism is not a fixed set of ideas and ideals which can be unilaterally aspired to as an alternative to national chauvinism and xenophobia. It is a strategy of discourse and is constituted by constantly shifting terms of reference. When we look beneath the surface of the rhetoric of internationalism, we invariably find thinly disguised discourses of power. It is not too difficult to find some illustrative examples.

In Italy, where enthusiasm for Europe has generally been quite strong, Europeanism has its uses. For the League of the North, the north of Italy belongs to Europe while the south belongs to Africa. In the north of Italy nostalgia for *Mitteleuropa* has become popular. Metternich's famous remark that Italy is only a 'geographical expression' has been taken too literally by the nascent nationalism in the north, a development which has brought into question the very notion of Italy as a unified political entity. The rediscovery of the Habsburg heritage and the mystique of *Mitteleuropa* is a powerful ideological instrument which can be used against Rome and the south of Italy.

In the 1970s and 1980s the ideal of Europe meant for Greece, Spain and Portugal a means of recovery from dictatorships and a transition to democracy. For Greece, Europe had the additional appeal of being a convenient instrument of opposition to Turkey. Greece could lay claim to a selective tradition of Europeanism while Turkey could be portrayed as a semi-Oriental despotism. In Spain Europeanisation had earlier been a means of articulating a Spanish identity based on the principle 'Europe will save us from foreigners' (Del Corral, 1959, p. 64). This is not unlike the Japanese use of the idea of Europe which can be used to distance Japan from Asia (Kishida, 1992).

France has continued to be in favour of Europeanism, generally understood by successive French governments to be synonymous with French ambitions. So long as Europe meant French aspirations it would be acceptable. One of the overriding commitments to Europe, especially for Britain and France, remained the desire to contain Germany. The Germans, for their part, are the least afraid of Europe, since they now occupy an enlarged share of its territory. Within Britain, Europeanism served a variety of political strategies. In the 1980s it was generally understood as a political statement against Thatcherism and the imperialist jingoism of the Falklands campaign. In Scotland and Wales a commitment to Europeanism expresses a strong attitude of hostility to England, and is especially directed against the Tory oligarchy in London. A major plank in the Scottish Nationalist Party is 'A free Scotland in a unified Europe'. In this sense, then, Europeanism can be compatible with nationalism. In Ireland Europeanism generally indicates opposition to traditional Catholic and nationalist populism while for many Europe is often seen as disguised militarism and a threat to the country's official military neutrality (Maguire and Noonan, 1993). Anti-Europeanism can also be a subtle neo-nationalist strategy to articulate a new nationalist identity that seeks to unburden itself of the problem of Northern Ireland. This idea of anti-militarism was also an essential part of 'Nordic identity', which was based on a notion of an anti-militaristic society that was superior to Western Europe: Nordic identity was defined in opposition to European identity which was pervceived as being divided and highly armed (Waever, 1992).

Europeanism can also be compatible with social democracy (Dankert, 1989). Building on the tradition of Eurocommunism in the 1970s, the left has generally been the most enthusiastic supporter of the European ideal. Europeanism is often seen as an alternative to the neo-liberal style of politics that have characterised the 1980s; and, since 1989 with the rise of nationalism and the growing electoral success of the extreme right, Europeanism suggests an alternative to the nascent nationalism. But if this is true, Europeanism is also increasingly becoming a substitute for the traditional polarity of right/left. It is also connected to the nascent new middle class and the new managerial elites for whom the idea of Europe has become a means of access to power and wealth. For the Vatican, too, Europe has its uses: the collapse of communism and the enlargement of Europe holds out the prospect of a new 'Christian Europe' modelled on the hegemonic project of Roman Catholicism (Chenaux, 1990; Kettle, 1990).

Europe can mean whatever one intends it to mean. It is a discursive strategy (Chilton and Ilym, 1993). At no time in history have people talked more about 'Europe' than today. Few phrases come quicker to the lips of the political class. Hugh Duncan (1972, p. 33) has written about the power of names, those symbolic forms that legitimate power: 'whoever creates or controls these names controls our lives.' His notion of a 'sociodrama' explains the way in which symbolic discourses have the power of creating reality through a process of identification and legitimation: one participates in a discourse which reaches its greatest power when it becomes its own legitimation. Europe is one of these symbolic names that evokes a transcendent point of unity beyond the nation-state. As such it has the power of social integration; it conveys a sense of spatial mystique as well as a philosophical myth of history. Power attains its greatest legitimation in the evocation of a resonating name that needs no other legitimation than itself. Today the idea of Europe is taking on the character of such a transcendent and ultimate entity which requires only an act of belief in its legitimacy. One is admonished to be either 'for Europe' or 'against' it and it is in the name of this rather obscure historical category that the great questions of the day are being debated. This suggests that the idea of Europe can be seen as the attempt to invent a new principle of political sovereignty with which to legitimate the new kinds of power that are emerging in late capitalism.

In this context it can be seen as a new form of obscurity which seeks to attain the status of a dominant ideology in a radical departure from the social democratic project. From another perspective, the political struggles of the new social movements are finding in the new hegemon a fulcrum of opposition. This is possible because for the first time in history Europe has been institutionalised in the political and economic framework of the polity of western nation-states. For many Europe is becoming the symbol of the EU and the outward arm of the OECD, a symbol of unrestrained economic growth and the epitome of a form of life based on consumption which no longer bears any relation to human needs. In this scenario the idea of Europe is part of a massive onslaught on nature, the final expression of what Adorno and Horkheimer (1979) called the 'dialectic of Enlightenment': the domination of nature in the name of civilisation. The idea of Europe has today become detached from the cultural apparatus of the bourgeoisie and is becoming the ideology of international finance capitalism and a political focus for new strata of elites who are replacing the bourgeois elite. It is a pseudo-internationalism and is ultimately the internationalism of capitalism and not of human beings. Not surprisingly many of the new social movements are resisting the techno-cosmopolitanism of the new 'Europe'. In particular feminism has little affinity with the idea of Europe whose values are those of male identity projects.

THE GEO-POLITICS OF EUROPEANISM

In Western Europe, it is a commonplace observation that in most countries there is a strong regional difference between north and south. Without elaborating on this at length, it will suffice to enumerate a number of instructive examples. Italy is the most obvious example of an industrially advanced north and a relatively underdeveloped south; its northernmost region is closely linked to Austrian Central Europe whilst, at the other extremity of its peninsula, Sicily is a short stepping-stone between Europe and Africa. England has its great divide between a north laden with the discarded structures of old industries and a prosperous south based on finance capitalism. The legacy of the Reformation in many countries created an enduring schism between a Protestant north and a Catholic south: the Netherlands, Germany and Ireland are obvious examples, the exception being Scotland with a Protestant south and Catholic north. Finally the linguistic dispute in Belgium between the Flemish population in the north and the Walloons in the south must be mentioned. In many ways these divisions reflect the more general north–south divide within Western Europe. The Mediterranean, it must not be forgotten, has always been a greater frontier than the Iron Curtain for Western Europe.

It is instructive to contrast the geo-political divide in Western Europe to that in Eastern Europe. It will be immediately observed that the principal divide is not north–south, but east–west. I have already commented on how this was epitomised in the divorce of the Czech Republic from Slovakia. In most countries it was the traditional hostility to Russia that precipitated a westward turn. In many countries, however, it is the ethnic issue that is crucial in shaping the regional divide. This is because Eastern Europe is less ethnically homogeneous than Western Europe and the ethnic groups cut across many states. It will be recalled from earlier chapters how these identities were formed by frontier conditions.

In Romania the province of Transylvania represents a major point of conflict with Hungary and contains about two million ethnic Hungarians, who are a potential source of unrest. Until 1918 the province, which had a large Romanian population, had formed part of Hungary but was awarded, against the wishes of the majority, to Romania after the war. Despite attempts to become more integrated into Western Europe after the overthrow of Ceausescu, powerful forces within Romania are still reluctant to break the country's link with Russia. While Bulgaria does not have a noted regional divide, the national identity of the country tends to be shaped by an attitude of hostility to its south-east neighbour, Turkey. In 1989 the problem of the Turkish minority, who represent 10 per cent of the population, came to a crisis point when the policy of forced assimilation failed and over 300,000 Bulgarian Turks crossed the border to Turkey, which as a result was forced to close its borders. While Poland is relatively homogeneous, there is a also a strong divide between the western and south-eastern parts. In the present context mention must be made once again of the former Yugoslavia where the regional divide is very clearly between East, represented by Serbia, and West, represented by Croatia, with Bosnia as the tragic zone of transition. The Ukraine, which means 'borderland', is divided into a relatively advanced eastern region, which had been more integrated into the industrial economy of the USSR than the western parts. This divide is also reflected in religion, with the west being predominantly Catholic Uniate and the east Orthodox. The only Eastern European country that has a significant north–south divide is Albania with its two ethnic groups: the northern Gegs and the southern Tosks. It was the southern frontier to Greece that was the most significant in its isolationist policy, particularly given that Greece was making territorial claims on southern Albania where there was a Greek Orthodox minority. Yet, the eastern frontier was also of particular significance since a considerable proportion of ethnic Albanians were isolated in the Serbian region of Kossovo.

A general conclusion can be drawn. While the regional divisions in Western Europe were determined in a north–south line by the Reformation and the uneven development of capitalism, Eastern Europe was more significantly divided by a greater economic, political and cultural cleavage, a creation of frontier conditions between Western Europe and Russia and, earlier, the Ottoman-Byzantine heritage. Given this scenario of diversity, what, then, is the meaning of the idea of Europe as a unitary and homogenous ideal?

On the surface it would appear that the only homogeneous culture which is really capable of cutting across such divided societies is that of popular culture: western style consumerism, advertising, TV and the entertainment industry. To an extent this really is the integrating cultural mechanism in Eastern Europe today and not western political culture in the traditional sense of the word. Only on the level of popular culture is there a convergence of values. This is ambivalent, however. Western Europe had been exposed to the culture industry in its formative period for over forty years before it was suddenly exported to the captive societies in Eastern Europe. The result has been a greater cultural dislocation in eastern Europe which has been forced to find its identity in the new and finished products of the West. With Europe being reinvented in the image of the market, it is not surprising that many Eastern Europeans, who have experienced only the severity of a capitalist modernity fashioned by neo-liberalism, are seeking their identity in the politics of neo-nationalism (Hockenos, 1993).

In this context we can speak of a clash of two political cultures: the technical political cultures of the Western European core, symbolised by the European Union, and a moral-political culture associated with the disadvantaged regions (Lepenies, 1992, p. 54). The end of the Cold War has not brought Western and Eastern Europe significantly closer. My argument throughout this book has been that the idea of Europe is a cultural frame of reference that turns divisive once it becomes part of the political framework in a politics of legitimation. The politicisation of the idea of Europe can then amount to a 'de-differentiation' of European culture and the consequent loss of intellectual critique (Lepenies, 1992, p. 54). I believe that it is important to ensure that this does not happen and that the idea of Europe be detached from the hegemony of economic and political considerations over social and cultural matters. This will involve seriously questioning the prevailing definitions of what constitutes Europe. These can be summarised as follows .

First, Europe as the West. In this Europe is merely a part of the Atlantic order and subordinate to the US. As I have argued this vision of a 'little' Europe is becoming increasingly irrelevant. Second, the idea of Europe associated with the peace movement of the 1980s (Hyde-Price, 1993, p. 21). This was basically Western Europe which stopped at the Iron Curtain. It was an anti-West notion of Europe designed to disengage Europe from the dictates of US military objectives. Third, Europe as the European Union. This is the dominant idea of Europe and the model that much of the former Eastern Europe aspires to. Fourth, an extended notion of Europe including European Russia. This concept of Europe was popular in post-war France and was particularly associated with de Gaulle's vision of Europe extending 'from the Atlantic to the Urals'. This enlarged notion of Europe was designed to exclude the US. More recently it has been the essence of Gorbachev's idea of a 'common European home'. Fifth, the idea of a European security area including the US and Russia as well the countries of the former USSR. Finally, the idea of Central Europe as an alternative to Western Europe.

It can be seen from this how the idea of Europe is bound up with a politics of legitimation (Garcia, 1993). Underlying the struggle for legitimacy is a more fundamental question of cultural identity. The European Union is unrepresentative of Slavic Europe; indeed, with the exception of Greece, it is almost entirely a bastion of Latin Christendom and contains one of the greatest concentrations of monarchies in the world. Not surprisingly we find many attempts today to promote new cultural identities, such as the grandiose 1991 exhibition in Venice on Celtic civilisation, which was a powerful statement on a unifying cultural heritage on a European scale (Lorenz, 1994, p. 2). The year 1992 was not only the year of European 'unification' but was also the 500th anniversary of 1492, the year of Europe's 'discovery' of America. The imposing 50th aniversary of the D-Day landings in 1994 also revealed the attempt to promote a European identity. This event in fact served only to alienate Eastern Europeans, especially the Russians, who justifiably felt that the war was in fact won in the eastern front, which had cost the lives of some 27 million Russians.

In what follows I should like to concentrate on the attempt in the post-Cold War era to create a hegemonic idea of Europe. By this I mean the substitution of 'Fortress Europe' for the older notion of the 'West'. Although this takes a diffuse form and the idea of Europe is more contentious than ever, certain tendencies can nevertheless be discerned.

FORTRESS EUROPE

While the idea of Europe may be a political football between the competing nationalities, there is a sense in which it is possible to speak of Europe as the basis of a new kind of legitimacy (Garcia, 1993; Waever et al, 1993). This involves looking at the idea of Europe in the global context. Today the idea of Europe is as much about setting limits against the Third World as it is an ideal of unity. This is the most ominous development in recent times, though it was always an integral part of the politics of the Cold War. The old questions of race and national identity have re-emerged in Europe and the idea of European unity has taken on a renewed significance with the spectre of mass emigration from Eastern Europe and, above all, from the Third World, which is encroaching upon the developed world. 'Unification for Europe', according to Lyotard (1993, p. 159), 'also means the unification of its hatreds', among which are racism and anti-semitism.

It is not unlikely that within the next two decades Europe will become a region of immigration, rather as the United States had been in the nineteenth century. For the first time a commitment to Europe means a closing of Europe amidst fears of over-population. The Iron Curtain had protected Western Europe, especially Germany, from immigrants coming from Eastern Europe. With over 90 per cent of world population growth in the Third World, the trend for the future will inevitably be increased migration in the direction of the OECD countries. Given that world population presently stands at about 5400 million and is expected to reach 7000 million by 2010 and 8000 by 2020, the kinds of political ideologies that have hitherto prevailed in the developed West will find themselves with entirely new kinds of challenges. It is, however, important to point out that this is often an exaggerated scenario. The greatest migration in Europe since the fall of the Roman Empire occurred in the aftermath of the Second World War when almost 50 million people became refugees. The number of refugees within Western Europe at the end of the Second World War was far in excess of contemporary figures (Miles, 1993, p. 21). Internal migration is itself an integral part of European history. Europeans are neither racially nor ethnically homogeneous, despite what they like to think of themselves (Huxley and Haddon, 1935).

With the fall of Soviet communism, Western European identity can no longer be constructed along Cold War lines. Unable to invoke the threat of communism, the developed West has found a new bogey again in Islam. One of the images the leader of the French National Front, Le Pen, paints is that of a future in which the French will be forced to beg outside a mosque. This xenophobic spectre of not only a Muslim dominated world but an 'Islamisation of Europe', the enemy outside the gates, is capable of appealing to a deep European hostility to the East, a hostility that, as we have seen, has a long history. An image of Islam is being shaped which emphasises its cultural homogeneity and threatening otherness: 'it is represented as a repellent exoticism by mass psychological mechanisms very like those involved in anti-semitism' (Al-Azmeh, 1993, p. 4). According to Zizek (1993, p. 234), this was exemplified in the reporting on the Gulf War and the war in Bosnia (see also Mestrovic, 1994 and Ahmed, 1992).

The old questions of Europe's historical frontiers are now finding a new context in the ideological vacuum that has emerged with the ending of the Cold War and are crystallising in the invention of a post-communist bogey. With Islam as the focus of hostility, the West has simply transferred the image of totalitarianism from the communist bloc to the Muslim East (Diner, 1991). The East, then, still remains the focus of European hostility, the only difference being that it has been pushed further southwards. It is not surprising that the collapse of Soviet communism was immediately followed by a united western war against Iraq. Economically, of course, the Muslim world is no serious challenge to Europe – the main challenger to the economic supremacy of Western Europe and the US is Japan and south-east Asia – for whom it serves as a moral threat. The problem of Eastern Europe and the neo-fascist spectre of a 'Muslim Europe' are not unconnected: a leading member of the Italian Northern League has suggested that 'civilised' Europe, the West, should take advantage of the growing atavistic nationalism of 'barbarian' Europe, the East, as a 'frontier guard to block the Muslim invasion' (Judt, 1994, p. 44). It is in this sense that Europe is becoming a fortress with the Straits of Gibraltar and the Bosporos as moats and the Third World being held at arm's length while still being used as convenient dumping zones, captive markets and sources of cheap and optional labour (Nederveen Pieterse, 1991, p. 6). Instead of a military struggle, what is coming into focus is a cultural contest based on a pernicious ideology of cultural incompatibility.

At the same time the military dictatorships throughout the Muslim world continue to purchase arms from the West, thus securing the conditions for their continued denouncement as a threat to the West. In this tacit *complot* many of these obedient client states are fulfilling the role played by the USSR in the Cold War game. The new hero of the West is no longer Solzhenitsyn, who has been rehabilitated in Russia, but Salman Rushdie, who epitomises the new clash of civilisations. Like the dissidents of the Cold War era who sought their political norms in a freedom supposedly inherent in western capitalism, Rushdie symbolises a similar legitimation of western liberal democracy and many support him as the champion of a liberty that the developed West allegedly stands for.

The West had failed to stem the rising tide of Arab nationalism in the 1950s, which witnessed the defection of Egypt, Syria and Iran. As a result of the withdrawal of the French from Algeria in 1962, the collapse of the Libyan monarchy in 1969, the victory of the Iranian revolution in 1979 and the failure of the US to depose Saddam Hussein after the Gulf War in 1991, there has been a steady increase in Arab power. What we are witnessing in the 1990s, in fact, is the gradual widening of a divide between the North-West and the South and East. It is this that is replacing the Cold War divide between Western and Eastern Europe. What has become an issue today is not merely the question of Europe's eastern frontier, but the question of frontiers in general.

It is in this context of the break-up of the bipolar world that visions of the new Europe are being shaped. According to Keohane (1984; Wallerstein, 1993) one of the principal trends today is the disintegration of American hegemony. From about 1985, when the US ceased to be the world's largest creditor nation and became the world's largest debtor nation and one dependent on debt-financed growth, new centres of power have arisen in what is becoming a global economy. The new centres are Japan, south-east Asia and Western Europe. In this transformation the US is only one centre of power amidst a global economy. The political vacuum created by the ending of the Cold War in 1989 has led to new definitions of Europe once again resurfacing. The old bogey of communism has disappeared and the Iron Curtain, the last frontier between West and East, has vanished, at least in its overtly political form. One of the great ironies of the late twentieth century is that neo-liberal market economics is being practised in the former communist states, while the European Union has carried out one of the most succcessful experiments in price control with the CAP. The fact that the tremendous impact of the revolutions in Eastern Europe and the collapse of communism in the Soviet Union coincided with the decline of the world hegemony of the United States meant that European identity no longer had to be based on the post-war consensus. It is, then, not surprising that we can detect a shift in European identity since 1989. What is being rediscovered is the idea of a Europe which is disengaging itself from the broader notion of the West which held sway since the October Revolution. Europe is no longer the eastern frontier of the United States but is becoming, in a multi-polar world, a new mega-power. What we are in fact witnessing with the break-up of the Cold War system is the abandonment of the entire post-war system of social and economic reconstruction. This is accompanied by the break-up of the political culture of the twentieth century which was very much based on the right–left polarity. What is coming to an end is not ideology as such, but the end of a specific political tradition formed around the nexus of social democracy and liberal conservatism. It is possible that the political scenario of the twenty-first century will be characterised by entirely new political ideas. Religious nationalism is likely to be the context for a new cold war (Juergensmeyer, 1993). The old war psychosis has not come to an end, it has simply taken new forms (Hedetoft, 1993).

Europe, no longer the lackey of the US, is the real winner of the Cold War. Though over-burdened by Eastern European reconstruction, Western Europe, which controls more than one third of world trade, will probably overshadow the US in the twenty-first century as an economic and political power bloc (Kennedy, 1993, p. 260). This will be enhanced, in Paul Kennedy's (1993, p. 127) view, by new developments in the post-Cold War global economy in which military rivalries and arms races will be replaced by economic rivalries, technology races and various forms of commercial warfare.

The year 1989 was a turning-point in the history of the twentieth century and is comparable to the great revolutionary years in European history: 1789, 1848 and 1917. One striking feature of these revolutionary upheavals was the transformation of universal revolution into counter-revolutionary reaction. It was a revolutionary overthrow of the established political order in the name of liberal democracy and at the same time a belated attempt by Eastern Europe to catch up on the West. In taking over the culture of the West, Eastern Europe was also taking on board more than the fantasy world of Euro-America. What in fact it had to contend with was neo-liberalism. The revolutions in Eastern Europe struck at precisely that moment when the West was abandoning social democracy. The ending of the Cold War in 1989 under revolutionary conditions in Eastern Europe not surprisingly then set into motion a renewed interest in nationalism and religion and the debate on the meaning of Europe took on a new momentum.

The identity of Europe has always been greatly shaped by revolutions (Tilly, 1993), in the twentieth century in particular by four great revolutionary events: the French Revolution of 1789, the October Revolution of 1917, the Islamic Revolution of 1979 and the revolutions in Eastern Europe in 1989/90. The revolution of 1989 was ideologically conceived as a rejection of the 1917 revolution and an attempt to re-embrace the heritage of 1789, while, on the other hand, the Islamic Revolution in 1979, which brought to an end the Pahlavi dynasty in Iran, was conceived as a rupture with the entire western revolutionary tradition. It is likely that for a long time to come the identity of Europe will be shaped by the consequences of the revolutions of 1979 and 1989: the one an affirmation of Europe, the other a denial of it.

Within Europe itself the events surrounding the process of reconstruction since 1989 have crystallised in the formation of a reinforced populist identity. The identity of Europe has always been closely bound up with the generic idea of 'the people'. There are three conflicting political identities which are all based on the notion of 'the people'. First, from the French Revolution the idea of 'the people' became the basis of radical demands for democracy and civil liberties. This notion of 'the people' was essentially defined in opposition to the absolutist state. 'The people' represented civil society which emerged in opposition to the state. Second, the October Revolution of 1917 established the idea of the people as the basis of mass proletarian revolution. In this 'the people' referred less to civil society than to the notion of permanent proletarian or class revolution against capitalist power. Third, the tradition of European cultural nationalism from about the mid-nineteenth century onwards led to the formation of populist national consciousness. In this context 'the people' referred to the historic community of the national state. Unlike other notions of 'the people', this formulation constituted the sovereignty of 'the people' *vis-à-vis* other states. 'The people' were defined not in opposition to the state, but in opposition to other national communities. This definition of the people has been effectively exploited as a means of defining Europe. Margaret Thatcher, though an entrenched opponent of the European Union, praised the European achievement when it was other cultures, and not Anglo-Saxonism, that it was being contrasted to: 'Too often the history of Europe is described as a series of interminable wars and quarrels. Yet from our perspective today surely what strikes us most is our common experience. For instance, the story of how Europeans explored and colonised and – yes without apology – civilised much of the world is an extraordinary tale of talent, skill, and courage!' (Paul, 1991, p. 53).

Political identity has predominantly been based on this idea of 'the people', as an undifferentiated mass and focused on the nation-state. In Germany this subtle reversal can be observed in the substitution of *Wir sind das Volk*,

'We are the People', which represented popular opposition against the former communist government, by *Wir sind ein Volk*, 'We are a single people', the nationalist slogan that became current after German unification. This perfectly encapsulated the transformation of notions of democratic popular sovereignty into authoritarian and obscurantist ideas of national chauvinism.

It is this populist ideology of 'the people' that has become the basis of political identity in Europe today. This can be seen in three manifestations. First, public opposition to European integration, as was revealed during the Maastricht debates of 1992/93, was principally conducted in the name of citizen protest movements. These have largely taken the character of proto-populist movements generally operating outside the parliamentary sphere of politics. Though essentially anti-bureaucratic, they are closely related to nationalism. Bureaucracy and the transnational state is seen as encroaching upon the national community as the guarantor of the middle-class style of life. A second manifestation of 'the people' is the rise of neo-fascism and the extreme right. Though as yet marginalised, the neo-nationalism promoted by these movements is based on a particularly strong sense of the people as an undifferentiated mass. Xenophobia is directed against foreigners in general, but more specifically against non-Europeans. Third, the most significant development has been the growth of white middle-class nationalism. Avoiding the overt racism of the extreme right, the mainstream parties in Western Europe have found a new voice in 'the people'. Race and nationality have become the dominant themes of politics in the post-Cold War.

In the absence of communists the imagined enemy is the immigrant, the outsider, the Other. It is populism flavoured by a new racism that is becoming the main characteristic of the new politics of the end of the twentieth century. It is the racism of the wealthy and speaks in the name of preserving welfare, jobs, prosperity and the cultural norms associated with the so-called western life-style. Welfare needs racism to restrict rights and wealth for the privileged who have rediscovered the uses of nationalism. The only difference between this racism, which has been revitalised by the new right, and the old racism, is that it does not make appeals to history and resort to direct violence. It is based not so much on ideas of racial superiority that have their foundation in blood as on more subtle defences of cultural differences (Taguieff, 1990; Balibar, 1991b; Phillips, 1993; Solomos and Back, 1994). The new soft racism crystallises on the question of the inassimilability of non-European immigrants and speaks in the name, not of race as such, but of national identity and cultural boundaries. As such it can disguise itself as an anti-racism. It is a diffuse racism than can speak in the name both of a national identity and Europeanism. What we are witnessing today is the revival of the idea of Europe as part of a process of political identity building that seeks to associate the idea of Europe with a defence of cultural differences and life styles based upon welfarism and consumption. The idea of Europe is thus becoming more focused on culture than on the state. It is, once again, that attempt to invent a collective identity for the legitimation of politics and is closely connected with social fragmentation as a result of economic upheaval.

CONCLUSION

European identity is rapidly becoming a white bourgeois populism defined in opposition to the Muslim world and the Third World. As European states are cautiously approaching the delicate matter of a European federation of states, the crucial question is whether the European idea is capable of integrating the diverse nationalities by offering a stable system of norms. Since there is little within the national traditions capable of uniting the continent, the point of unity is found outside Europe. Hostility to the less developed countries and the Muslim world have provided new bogeys to a dispirited Europe. The collapse of communism in 1989/90 was the test case of the ability of Europe to evolve a new collective learning process. This did not happen and European identity became tied to an adversarial framework.

10 Conclusion: Towards Post-National Citizenship

The aim of this book has not been to demonstrate that the idea of Europe is an idea with negative implications. I do not wish to suggest that it should be abandoned as a cultural concept. It is in many senses a collective concept for unclear ideas, not all of which should be rejected. The general thrust of the argument has been that there are many 'Europes' and that the one that has become predominant today is very much one of exclusion and not inclusion. I have stressed the importance of looking at the idea of Europe from a global point of view. The idea of Europe that I have attempted to deconstruct is one that is focused on the notion of unity and one for which modernisation is the model. After surveying the idea of Europe through the centuries it is not difficult to conclude that there is little new in the world that is emerging today: the Europe of our time is not one that has relinquished the age-old pursuit of enemies. The 'little' Europe of the Cold War era is over and so are the illusions and luxuries it afforded. It is no longer exclusively a question of West versus East but of North versus South. A new and greater Europe is being born in what is becoming a major confrontation between Europe and the rest of the world amidst the rise of a racist malaise of xenophobic nationalism. White bourgeois nationalism has found new outlets in populist political rhetoric.

On a positive note, however, it must be recognised that, since the old Europe developed within the context of the Cold War the restrictions it imposed are now absent: high military spending is now no longer necessary and there is no reason why the new Europe cannot devote itself to new goals determined by social and environmental demands (Freeman et al, 1991). The discourse of Europe can be seen as the space in which new demands can be articulated. So simple-minded opposition to Europe can also be undemocratic. As Alain Touraine argues: 'European construction offers us the chance to live simultaneously at various levels of political and social organization; if we don't use it, we will be torn between universalism and particularism or close ourselves into a desperado nationalism' (Touraine, 1994 p. 22).

I have also attempted to demonstrate that the ideal of European unity has not, in fact, been an alternative to the nation-state, either in theory or in practice. To briefly restate one of the central theses of this book, when the idea of Europe became differentiated from the Christian world-view after the Renaissance it became closely associated with the emerging ideal of the nation-state and ever since, aside from a number of anomalous utopian ideas, the dominant understanding of the idea of Europe has been that of a Europe of nation-states. Europe is not, then, an alternative to nationalism but a confirmation of the hegemony of the nation-state. In fact Europe is a function of the nation-state, which has also fostered the nationalism of the region. As a strategy of discourse it is a protean notion by which the ugly aspects of the nation-state can be rejected while its basic ideology is retained. To suppose that the Europe of the European unity refers to a cosmopolitan ideal beyond the particularism of the nation-state is, quite simply, an act of delusion. As a concrete entity Europe is meaningless without the nation-state. In fact the movement towards European unity has possibly led to a strengthening of the nation-state since there has been a transfer of major mechanisms of economic and political integration to the EU onto which the burden of legitimation has been shifted. Europe emerged out of the disunity among nation-states, but ultimately reinforced them. I have tried to demonstrate that, even for conservative-populist opposition to the ideal of Europe the issue is not, strictly speaking, Europe. It is rather that Europe, as a discursive strategy, is the focus for articulating a variety of political standpoints which are increasingly tending to coalesce in opposition to immigrants. In the discourse of Europe mutually opposed groups can find in the single entity a focal point for the pursuit of their projects. The very concept of a European union makes little sense if something is not going to be excluded.

What I hope to have demonstrated is that an unreflected idea of Europe is a dangerous idea. The idea of Europe embodies prejudices that lie deep in the history of Europe. The ideas that have given Europe its identity, the ideals of the Christian humanist West and liberal democracy, have failed to unite Europe; at least we are less likely to believe in such ideas as the civilising power of European modernity. The idea of Europe cannot be disengaged from the atrocities committed in its name. Walter Benjamin (1973, p. 258) wrote under conditions which are real for many people today: 'There is no document of civilization which is not at the same time a document of barbarism.' There is a direct continuity in the idea of Europe from the crusading genocides of medieval Christendom to the systematic extermination of other civilisations by European imperialism to the gas chambers of the Nazis and the pogroms of ethnic cleansing of the new nationalisms in the post-Cold War period. European history does not lead from culture to civilisation, from diversity to unity; these are the terms of an old debate which we can no longer accept. In the wake of the ending of the Cold War we are witnessing today the reconstruction of borderlands, some new, some old. The frontier zones of the old empires dissolved after the First World War are now making a violent return in the form of ethnic nationalism. The almost fifty years of peace that Western

Europe has enjoyed since the end of the Second World War – when war was effectively transported to the Third World – are now over with the reappearance of the old fissures. History, in short, has returned today in the formation of a new dichotomy of Self and Other. It is in the shadow of the two world wars that many of the conflicts in the Balkans and Transcaucasia have been fought. The developments in European history in the present decade have turned Europeans in upon themselves and have led to the reappropriation of the past. But it is a past with which Europeans have not come to terms. Just as Europe took over the world-view of Christendom in the early modern period, it has also taken over the culture of nineteenth century imperialism, and European fascism has been rehabilitated today in various strategies of 'cleansing', be it ethnic or ideological. The lesson is clear: Europe must be judged by its failures as much as by its lofty ideals.

When we survey the scene of destruction in Eastern Europe and the violent return of history that the end of the Cold War has unleashed, it is difficult not to conclude that Europe as a programmatic ideal has been a failure. The dismemberment of Bosnia under the most violent of conditions is the ultimate expression of the failure of Europe as a multi-cultural polity. Bosnia posed a fundamental question about the identity of Europe. This was the question of whether or not Muslims and Christians, both Orthodox and Roman, can live together in a single multi-ethnic state. Europe's answer was no. This decision was the completion of the process begun with the reconquest of Spain. The division of Bosnia gives expression in an extreme form to the failure of Europe and crystallises the war psychosis that has been the basis of European identity for centuries. In particular the tragedy of Sarajevo encapsulates the failure of Europe as a multi-cultural civilisation. Sarajevo had been the home of four religions – Roman Catholics, Orthodox Christians, Muslims and Jews (there had been a large Jewish population since the fifteenth century, when they had been expelled from most parts of Europe) had lived there for centuries – and was renowned for its tolerance and cosmopolitanism. Moreover, it is hardly necessary to add that the failure of the European Union to act in concert to save Bosnia from its horrible fate by the dark forces of Christendom is yet another serious demonstration of the failure of Europeanism to link itself with a notion of collective responsibility and solidarity. The tendency in the European Union, with its monopoly on the idea of Europe, was to define Bosnia as non-European and thereby justify non-action (Ali and Lifschulz, 1993). Muslim Bosnians believed they were being judged by many Europeans as Muslims. One cannot help speculating about the consequences of a Muslim attack on a Christian enclave in the periphery of Europe. Many western pundits spoke of the undesirability of a Muslim state in Europe. But it must also be said that the inability of the

European Union and the United Nations to intervene in the war in Bosnia also disillusioned many Europeans with their international agencies and European identity was severely shaken.

Is there anything in the discourse of Europe that provides a point of departure for a politics of collective responsibility? Is it possible to speak of 'learning processes' in history? (Eder, 1985; Wehler, 1988). Can anything be rescued from the idea of Europe? I should like to bring this essay to a conclusion with a brief excursus on this issue.

The thesis I wish advocate is that unless the idea of Europe can be linked to multi-culturalism and post-national citizenship, it is best regarded with scepticism as a political notion. Europe must be judged by how it treats its minorities as well as its attitude to the non-European world, and not merely by the chauvinistic norms of the nation-state. With the break-up of traditional political identities, there is a need today for an alternative collective identity that is not based on the counter-factualism that is inherent in national identity. I remain doubtful that the idea of Europe can achieve this but I do not wish to preclude the possibility that it can provide a space for overcoming resurgent nationalism and new populist kinds of racism. In order to achieve this it is, I believe, crucial to separate the ethno-cultural idea of Europe from citizenship. This distinction hangs on the difference between universalisable norms and cultural values, which are relativistic. Citizenship is a normative concept while Europe is a cultural idea. Citizenship should not be any more conflated with the idea of an 'essentialist' Europe than with the principle of nationality. I hope to have demonstrated in this book that Europe's claim to universally valid norms is at best highly contentious if not downright false. The idea of Europe is essentially a cultural idea based on a geo-political entity and its politicisation as a political identity inevitably results in a distorted and regressive adversarial value system. The only way out of this dilemma is to break the connection between the idea of Europe and the ethno-culturalism that it has until now been based upon.

The idea of Europe, in contrast to the idea of the nation, is not yet a monolithic notion with regressive tendencies, but is characterised by tensions and contradictions which can be exploited for a new politics of autonomy. If the idea of Europe can be aligned with the progressive forces in European history it may be of emancipatory interest. Of particular relevance in this is the secular and pluralist traditions of European cities and the earlier traditions of citizenship associated with them. The ideal of citizenship is very much bound up with the ideal of the autonomy of the city resisting the tyranny of centralised power (Benevolo, 1993). It is possible that a revival of the memory of the diversified tradition of civil societies could offer an ideal strong enough to combat the tribalism of the new nationalism and the existing norms of European identity. This is not an unlikely prospect since the more the nation-state is undermined, the more the city will come to the fore (Castells, 1994). While there has been considerable discussion of the new nationalism of the regions, little attention is being given to the potentiality of the city as a source of cultural renewal.

One of the most important issues raised by the question of European unity and the conflicts in south-east Europe is that of citizenship. The problem for the twenty-first century is exactly how we are to conceive of citizenship. Throughout the nineteenth and twentieth centuries the predominant idea of citizenship has been linked to the nation-state. Citizenship was seen in terms of the relationship of the individual to a territorial entity, the modern state. Citizenship thus came to be enshrined in the constitutions of the liberal democracies and monarchies. This view of citizenship has given rise to the belief that constitutional and civil rights can only be guaranteed within the limits of the nation-state. The crucial question for the future is whether it is possible to create a post-national kind of citizenship (Andrews, 1991; Habermas, 1992; Meehan 1993a, 1993b; Vogel, 1991; Welsh, 1993). Society has always existed as a legal and moral order, but since this has always been tied to the nation-state, at least in modern times, the undermining of the sovereignty of the nation-state by European unity results in a legitimation crisis unless new principles of legitimation can be found which substitute the old idea of society as a moral and legal order with a notion of universal community based on citizenship.

If we look more closely at the old idea of citizenship as it emerged during the French Revolution, it can be seen that the revolutionary understanding of citizenship was closely linked to ideas of radical democracy and popular sovereignty. The idea of self-determination lay at the core of the early conceptions of citizenship. The individual was conceived first and foremost as a citizen of a democratic polity rather than as a subject of a monarch or church. But with the transformation of citizenship into nationality, the original and radical idea of popular sovereignty was lost. This loss of sovereignty was connected to the idea of negative liberty: the idea that liberty consists in freedom from coercion. Citizenship circumscribes a public sphere in which the autonomy of the individual is guaranteed from the arbitrary intrusion of the state. This is what is widely regarded as a civil liberty or civil rights and forms part of a broader notion of human rights. But the idea of citizenship also includes an active component, a political or public liberty. This is related to the sphere of public discourse and the principle of free association: the citizen as a political actor. We can also distinguish a third liberty, the right to welfare. This involves the idea that the role of the state is to serve society and to be the basis of the social welfare state. This is to follow T. H. Marshall's (1992) well-known classification of citizenship into three types, the civil, the political and the social. According to Marshall the three kinds of citizenship became differentiated from each other from the twelfth century onwards and it is possible to associate each with a specific century: civil rights with the eighteenth century, political with the nineteenth and social with the twentieth.

I should like to argue that the dominant understanding of citizenship in modern times has, in fact, been shaped by conceptions of nationality, which in turn have been linked to purely political notions of citizenship. This is an aspect of citizenship that is rarely discussed. The nation-state has been the framework for the institutionalisation of citizenship. This is because the genesis of the notion of citizenship has been closely tied to the idea of freedom, which itself has been very much linked to the principle of nationality. In this transformation the political identity of the individual is shaped less by his or her relation to the state, as an apparatus of power, than to the nation as a moral community. Citizenship, reduced to nationality, thus becomes a means by which the political identity of the individual is shaped in the drawing of borders between nationalities. In this model there is no clear distinction between citizenship and national patriotism: the citizen is transformed into the patriot. This is in direct opposition to the original conception of citizenship that emerged with the French Revolution when citizenship was considered to be opposed to the coercive state. Notwithstanding the contradictions of the revolutionary concept of citizenship, there was not a close identification between citizenship and nationality in the original formulation of citizenship (Sewell, 1988). The constitutions of modern states do not make clear distinctions between citizenship and nationality. The basic criterion in most cases for citizenship is nationality, which in the original revolutionary conception was incidental to citizenship. In the final instance, this is reduced to the privilege of birth – and in some cases, such as in modern Germany, to blood (Brubaker, 1990). In the course of the nineteenth century, as the Old Order adapted itself to the conditions of capitalist modernity, the model of citizenship became a reflection of the property relations of bourgeois society: the citizen was an economic agent based on property ownership within a patriarchal system of power. With the emergence of universal franchise the notion of citizenship was subordinated to democracy. Notions of democracy that reduce, or subordinate, citizenship to a secondary consideration must be rejected for their narrowness: citizenship is not a mere extension of democracy which itself can exist only on the basis of active citizenship. In any case the reduction of citizenship to the principle of nationality was never the sole feature of citizenship throughout history (Heather, 1990; McNeil, 1986).

This narrow concept of citizenship as nationality is becoming increasingly irrelevant to Europe as the twenty-first century approaches. The liberal constitutional idea of citizenship has become an instrument by which Europe, in the name of democracy and nationality, can close and tighten its borders (Brubaker, 1989). This kind of citizenship is no longer appropriate to the requirements of the late twentieth century. In 1970 the UNHCR estimated that there were 2.5 million refugees, and 8 million in 1980; and by 1992 the number had risen to 18 million refugees world-wide, while Amnesty International estimates that there were 35 million displaced persons. It is not surprising, then, that the Western European states are imposing new restrictions on immigration and that disillusionment with democracy is finding a new voice in racism and xenophobic nationalism. This is also a problem within Greater Europe. For instance, since the collapse of the USSR over twenty-five million Russians have been stranded in non-Russian states without clear rights to citizenship. Citizenship is being disengaged from universal rights and is being subordinated to the particularism of nationality. Citizenship should not be a means by which Europe defines its identity as a white bourgeois nationalism. This is the danger today, that citizenship is being reduced to the national chauvinism of the advanced nations. In this regression, 'Europeans' are consumers, recipients of welfare, tourists.

The connection between national identity and citizenship is growing stronger today in the face of the threat of mass immigration. Instead of being a means for protecting minorities, refugees, asylum seekers, ethnic minorities and stateless persons, it is becoming a means for protecting the majority from the outsider. Citizenship has become a synonym for nationality and a legitimation of nationalist xenophobia. It has become a means by which minorities can be deprived of their rights rather than being a means of solidarity and a basis of democracy. The effect of most policies of the European Union has been to restrict citizenship by limiting the rights of refugees to enter the member states (Fernhout, 1993). The dominant concept of unity in the EU is an instrumentalist-technocratic one which does not question the nation-state as the basis of citizenship. Its principal failure is that it does not recognise that membership of a state does not mean membership of the national community, which the state is supposed to be based upon.

Post-national citizenship is an alternative to the restrictive notion of nationality. The essence of post-national citizenship is that citizenship is determined neither by birth nor nationality but by residence. Unlike nationality, citizenship should not be embodied in the national culture of the state. Citizenship is international and transcends the particularist assumptions of culture and nationality. It is also more than a mere political-legal principle but involves recognition of social rights. It is crucial to break the connection between citizenship and nationality, both intellectually and constitutionally. The only way Europe can overcome its political ambiguity is in the redefinition of the basic political unit and notions of sovereignty (Tassin, 1992).

European identity remains trapped in a racial myth of origins which has found its expression today in a new nationalism of materialist chauvinism. Immigration laws are the crux of European identity, for these are the instruments Europe uses to restrict democracy and civil rights which are reserved for the privileged. Alongside new laws on immigration, what is also required is a fundamental questioning of the prevailing European forms of identity. European identity and the possibility of a post-national citizenship are very closely linked to the question of immigration laws (Lorenz, 1994, p. 14). So long as citizenship remains linked to nationality, the conviction will remain that citizenship laws exist in order to protect the unity and cohesion of the dominant culture from foreign cultures. The only adequate idea of Europe is one that is connected to anti-racism and stands unequivocally for post-national citizenship.

Post-national citizenship is not to be understood merely as a formal constitutional right. It also embraces a substantive dimension, which empowers citizens with the right to participation in the democratic polity. In this sense it is fundamentally different from national citizenship, which is purely formal. Purely formal notions of citizenship are dangerous since they leave open the possibility for their contents to be filled by populist ideology. Citizenship should be the ultimate basis of legitimation for institution-building, not ambiguous cultural identities. It is important that it be linked to participation in the new political institutions that are being created.

The crucial issue here is the institutionalisation of pluralism. Citizenship does not merely entail a liberalisation of laws on immigration but also pertains to the right to cultural autonomy. This also involves creating the space in which minorities can define themselves rather than having their identity defined for them by the dominant ideology. Post-national citizenship is inextricably linked to cultural pluralism, which recognises the rights of ethnic minorities to their cultural autonomy without being forced to integrate into the dominant culture, which in most cases is the national culture. This involves a rejection of the prevailing ideas of assimilation which have now been widely recognised to be a failure. A post-national identity would therefore involve a commitment to cultural pluralism based on post-national citizenship which would be relevant to Muslims as well as Christians and other world religions, atheists, east and west Europeans, black and white, women as well as men.

Bibliography

Abaza, M. and Smith, G. (1988) 'Occidental Reason, Rationalism, Islamic Fundamentalism: A Critique', *International Journal of Sociology*, 3, 4, 343–64.

Abu-Lughod, I. (1963) *Arab Discovery of Europe: A Study in Cultural Encounters* (Princeton: Princeton University Press).

Abu-Lughod, J. L. (1989) *Before European Hegemony: The World-System AD 1250–1350* (New York: Oxford University Press).

Adorno, T. and Horkheimer, M. (1979) *Dialectic of Enlightenment* (London: Verso).

Aga-Rossi, E. (1993) 'Roosevelt's European Policy and the Origins of the Cold War: A Reevaluation', *Telos*, 96, 65–85.

Agnelli, A. (1973) *La Genesi Dell'Idea di Mitteleuropa* (Milan: Giuffre).

Ahmad, F. (1993) *The Making of Modern Turkey* (London: Routledge).

Ahmed, A. (1992) *Postmodernism and Islam* (London: Routledge).

Al-Azmeh, A. (1992) 'Barbarians in Arab Eyes', *Past and Present*, 134, 3–18.

Al-Azmeh, A. (1993) *Islam and Modernities* (London: Verso).

Albrecht-Carre, R. (1965) *The Unity of Europe: An Historical Survey* (London: Secker & Warburg).

Ali, R. and Lifschulz, L. (eds) (1993) *Why Bosnia? Writings on the Balkan War* (Stony Creek, Conn.: Pamphleteer's Press).

Alloula, M. (1986) *The Colonial Harem* (Manchester: Manchester University Press).

Alting von Gerusau, F. (1975) *European Perspectives on World Order* (Leyden: Sijthoff).

Amin, S. (1989) *Eurocentrism* (New York: Monthly Review Press).

Anderson, B. (1984) *Imaginary Communities: Reflections on the Origin and Spread of Nationalism* (London: Verso).

Anderson, M. S. (1988) *War and Society in Europe of the Old Regime 1618–1789* (London: Fontana).

Anderson, P. (1974a) *Passages from Antiquity to Feudalism* (London: Verso).

Anderson, P. (1974b) *Lineages of the Absolute State* (London: Verso).

Andrews, G. (ed.) (1991) *Citizenship* (London: Lawrence & Wishart).

Annoni, A. (1959) *L'europa nel pensiero italiano del settecento* (Milan: Marzorati).

Arendt, H. (1968) *The Origins of Totalitarianism* (New York: Meridian).

Arens, W. (1979) *The Man-Eating Myth* (Oxford: Oxford University Press).

Aristotle (1962) *The Politics* (London: Penguin).

Armstrong, J. A. (1982) *The Nation State before Nationalism* (Chapel Hill: University of North Carolina Press).

Athearn, R. (1986) *The Mythic West in Twentieth-Century America* (Lawrence, Kansas: University Press of Kansas).

Baechler, J. et al. (eds) (1988) *Europe and the Rise of Capitalism* (Oxford: Blackwell).

Baldry, H. C. (1965) *The Unity of Mankind in Greek Thought* (Cambridge: Cambridge University Press).

Balibar, E. (1991a) *'Es gibt Keinen Staat in Europa:* Racism and Politics in Europe Today', *New Left Review*, 186, 5–19.

Balibar, E. (1991b) 'Is there a Neo-Racism?', in Balibar and Wallerstein, op. cit.

Balibar, E. and Wallerstein, I. (1991) *Race, Nation, Class: Ambigious Identities* (London: Verso).

Balzaretti, R. (1992) 'The Creation of Europe', *History Workshop Journal*, 33, 181–96.

Banton, M. (1987) *Racial Theories* (Cambridge: Cambridge University Press).

Barker, F. et al. (eds) (1985) *Europe and its Others*, vols I & II (Colchester: University of Essex).

Barraclough, G. (1955) *History in a Changing World* (Oxford: Blackwell).

Barraclough, G. (1963) *European Unity in Thought and Practice* (Oxford: Blackwell).

Barraclough, G. (1976) *The Crucible of Europe: The Ninth and Tenth Centuries in European History* (Berkeley: University of California Press).

Bartlett, R. (1993) *The Making of Europe: Conquest, Colonization, and Cultural Change 950–1350* (London: Allen Lane).

Barzini, L. (1984) *The Europeans* (London: Penguin).

Bassin, M. (1991) 'Russia between Europe and Asia: The Ideological Construction of Geographical Space', *Slavic Review*, 50, 1–17.

Baudet, H. (1976) *Paradise on Earth: Some Thoughts on European Images of Non-European Man* (Westport, Conn.: Greenwood Press).

Baudrillard, J. (1988) *America* (London: Verso).

Bauman, Z. (1985) 'On the Origins of Civilisation: A Historical Note', *Theory, Culture and Society*, 2, 7–14.

Bauman, Z. (1989) *Modernity and the Holocaust* (Cambridge: Polity Press).

Bearce, G. D. (1961) *British Attitudes towards India 1784–1858* (London: Oxford University Press).

Beck, B. H. (1987) *From the Rising Sun: English Images of the Ottoman Empire to 1715* (New York: Lang).

Becker, M. B. (1988) *Civility and Society in Western Europe 1300–1600* (Bloomington: Indiana University Press).

Beloff, M. (1957) *Europe and the Europeans* (London: Chatto & Windus).

Belloc, H. (1973) *The Crisis of Civilization* (Westport, Conn.: Greenwood Press).

Benevolo, L. (1993) *The European City* (Oxford: Blackwell).

Benjamin, W. (1973) 'Theses on the Philosophy of History', in *Illuminations* (London: Fontana/Collins).

Bennigsen, A. (1972) 'The Muslims of European Russia and the Caucasus', in Vucinich, op. cit.

Berge, D. E. (1983) 'Manifest Destiny and the Historians' in Malone, M. P. (ed.) *Historians and the American West* (Lincoln: University of Nebraska Press).

Berger, P. and Luckmann, T. (1984) *The Social Construction of Reality* (London: Penguin).

Bernal, M. (1987) *Black Athena: The Afroasiatic Roots of Classical Civilization.* Vol. 1. *The Fabrication of Ancient Greece 1785–1985* (New Brunswick: Rutgers University Press).

Best, G. (1986) 'One World or Several: Reflections on the Modern History of International Law and Human Rights', *Historical Research*, 61, 212–16.

Betz, H.-G. (1990) 'Mitteleuropa and Post-Modern European Identity', *New German Critique*, 50, 173–92.

Bianchini, S. (1993) *Sarajevo le radici dell'odio* (Rome: Edizioni).

Billington, R. A. (1949) *Westward Expansion: A History of the American Frontier* (New York: Macmillan).

Bitterli, U. (1993) *Cultures in Conflict: Encounters between European and Non-European Cultures 1492–1800* (Cambridge: Polity Press).

Black, A. (1993) 'Classical Islam and Medieval Europe: A Comparison of Political Philosophies and Cultures', *Political Studies*, XLI, 58–69.

Blackburn, R. (ed.) (1991) *After the Fall: The Failure of Communism and the Future of Socialism* (London: Verso).

Bloch, M. (1962) *Feudal Society* (London: Routledge & Kegan Paul).

Bloomfield, J. (1993) 'The New Europe: A New Agenda for Research', in Fulbrook, M. (ed.) *National Histories and European History* (London: UCL Press).

Bohnstedt, J. W. (1968) 'The Infidel Scourge of God: the Turkish Menace as Seen by the German Pamphleteers of the Reformation Era', *Transactions of the American Philosophical Society*, 58, 9.

Boorstin, D. (1976) *America and the Image of Europe: Reflections on American Thought* (Gloucester, Mass.: Peter Smith).

Bowle, J. (1952) *The Unity of European History* (Oxford: Oxford University Press).

Bozeman, A. B. (1960) *Politics and Culture in International History* (Princeton: Princeton University Press).

Braudel, F. (1974) *Capitalism and Material Life 1400–1800* (London: Fontana).

Braudel, F. (1979) *Afterthoughts on Material Civilization and Capitalism* (Baltimore: Johns Hopkins University Press).

Braudel, F. (1980) 'The History of Civilization: The Past Explores the Present', in *On History* (Chicago: Chiacago University Press).

Braudel, F. (1990 & 1987) *The Mediterranean and the Mediterranean World in the Age of Philip II*, vols. 1 and 2 (London: Fontana).

Briffault, R. (1936) *Europa: A Novel in the Age of Ignorance* (London: Hale).

Briffault, R. (1937) *Europa in Limbo* (London: Hale).

Brubaker, W. R. (ed.) (1989) *Immigration and the Politics of Citizenship in Europe and North America* (New York: Lanham).

Brubaker, W. R (1990) 'Immigration, Citizenship and the Nation-State in France and Germany: A Comparative Historical Analysis', *International Journal of Sociology*, 5, 4, 379–407.

Buehler, W. (1968) *Europa – Ein Überblick über die Zeugnisse des Mythos in der Antiken Literatur und Kunst* (Munich: Wilhelm Fink).

Bull, H. and Watson, A. (eds) (1984) *The Expansion of International Society* (Oxford: Clarendon Press).

Bunyan, T. (1991) 'Towards an Authoritarian European State', *Race and Class*, 32, 3, 19–27.

Burke, E. (1967) *Reflections on the Revolution in France* (London: Dent).

Burke, P. (1980) 'Did Europe Exist before 1700', *History of European Ideas*, 1, 21–9.

Burke, P. (1985) 'European Views of World History from Giovio to Vico', *History of European Ideas*, 6, 3, 237–51.

Burns, C. D. (1947) *The First Europeans: A Study of the Establishment of Medieval Christendom AD 400–800* (London: Allen Lane).

Cahnman, W. (1952) 'Frontiers between East and West', *Geographical Review*, 49, 605–24.

Cairns, H. A. C. (1965) *Prelude to Imperialism: British Reactions to Central African Society 1840–1890* (London: Routledge & Kegan Paul).

Callincos, A. (1991) *The Revenge of History: Marxism and the East European Revolutions* (Cambridge: Polity Press).

Carr, E. H. (1945) *Nationalism and After* (London: Macmillan).

Carr, E. H. (1964) *What is History?* (London: Penguin).

Carr, E. H. (1979) *The Russian Revolution from Lenin to Stalin 1917–1929* (London: Macmillan).

Carter, F. W. et al. (1993) 'International Migration between East and West', *Ethnic and Racial Studies*, 16, 467–91.

Castells, M. (1994) 'European Cities, the Informational Society, and the Global Economy', *New Left Review*, 204, 18–32.

Castles, S. (1984) *Here for Good: Western Europe's New Ethnic Minorities* (London: Pluto).

Castoriadis, C. (1987) *The Imaginary Institution of Society* (Cambridge: Polity Press).

Castoriadis, C. (1992) 'Reflections on Racism', *Thesis Eleven*, 32, 1–13.

Cerutti, F. (1992) 'Can there be a Supranational Identity?', *Philosophy and Social Criticism*, 18, 2, 147–62.

Chabod, F. (1961) *Storia dell'idea europa* (Bari: Editori Laterza).

Chadwick, H. (1990) *The Early Church* (London: Penguin).

Chadwick, O. (1993) *The Secularization of the European Mind in the Nineteenth Century* (Cambridge: Cambridge University Press).

Chenaux, P. (1990) *Une Europe Vaticane?* (Brussels: Ciaco).

Chiapelli, F. (ed.) (1976) *First Images of America*, vols. I & II (Berkeley: University of California Press).

Chilton, P. and Ilyin, M. (1993) 'Metaphor in Political Discourse: the Case of the "Common European House" ', *Discourse and Society*, 4, 7–31.

Chirot, D. (1985) 'The Rise of the West', *American Sociological Review*, 50, 181–95.

Christiansen, E. (1980) *The Northern Crusades: The Baltic and the Catholic Frontier, 1100–1525* (London: Macmillan).

Cohen, N. (1993) *Europe's Inner Demons: The Demonization of Christians in Medieval Christendom* (London: Pimlico).

Cole, R. (1972) 'Sixteenth-Century Travel Books as a Source of European Attitudes toward Non-White and Non-Western Culture', *Proceedings of the American Philosophical Society*, 116, 1, 59–67.

Coles, P. (1968) *The Ottoman Impact on Europe* (London: Thames & Hudson).

Compagnon, A. and Seebacher, J. (eds) (1993) *'L'Espirit de l'Europe*, 3 vols (Paris: Flammarion).

Conze, W. (1992) *Ostmitteleuropa von der Spätantike bis zum 18. Jahrhundert* (Munich: Beck).

Cornish, V. (1936) *Borderlands of Language in Europe and their Relation to the Historic Frontier of Christendom* (London: Sifton Praed).

Couloubaritsis, L. et al. (1993) The Origins of European Identity (Brussels: European Interuniversity Press).

Crankshaw, E. (1982) *Bismarck* (London: Macmillan).

Croan, M. (1989) 'Lands In-Between: The Politics of Cultural Identity in Contemporary Eastern Europe', *Eastern European Politics and Society*, 3, 176–97.

Crouch, C. and Marquand, D. (eds) (1992) *Towards Greater Europe? A Continent without an Iron Curtain* (Oxford: Blackwell).

Curio, C. (1958) *Europa: storia di un'idea,* vols I & II (Florence: Vallecchi).

Curtain, P. D. (1964) *The Image of Africa: British Ideas and Action, 1780–1850* (Madison: University of Winconsin Press).

Dahrendorf, R. (1990) *Reflections on the Revolution in Europe* (London: Chatto & Windus).

Daniel, N. (1960) *Islam and the West: The Making of an Image* (Edinburgh: Edinburgh University Press).

Daniel, N. (1966) *Islam, Europe and Empire* (Edinburgh: Edinburgh University Press).

Daniel, N. (1975a) *The Cultural Barrier: Problems in the Exchange of Ideas* (Edinburgh: Edinburgh University Press).

Daniel, N. (1975b) *The Arabs and Medieval Europe* (London: Longman).

Dankert, P. (ed.) (1989) *Europe without Frontiers* (London: Mansell).

Dann, O. (1993) *Nation und Nationalismus in Deutschland 1770–1990* (Munich: Beck).

Dann, O. and Dinwiddy, J. (eds) (1988) *Nationalism and the French Revolution* (London: Hambledon Press).

Davies, W. (1983) 'China, the Confucian Ideal, and the European Age of Enlightenment', *Journal of the History of Ideas*, XLIV, 523–48.

Davis, R. H. C. (1988) *A History of Medieval Europe*, 2nd edn (London: Longman).

Dawson, C. (1932) *The Making of Europe* (London: Sheed & Ward).

Del Corral, L. (1959) *The Rape of Europe* (London: Allen & Unwin).

Diment, G. and Slezkine, Y. (eds) (1993) *Between Heaven and Hell: The Myth of Siberia in Russian Culture* (New York: St. Martin's Press).

Diner, D. (1991) *Der Krieg der Erinnerungen und die Ordnung der Welt* (Berlin: Rotbuch).

Dionisotti, C. (1971) *Europe in Sixteenth-Century Italian Literature* (Oxford: Clarendon Press).

Djait, H. (1985) *Europe and Islam* (Berkeley: University of California Press).

Domenach, J.-M. (1990) Europe: Le Défi culturel (Paris: Découverte).

Draper, T. (1993) 'The End of Czechoslovakia', *New York Review of Books*, 28 January, 20–6.

Drieu La Rochelle, P. (1927) *Le Jeune Européen* (Paris: Gallimard).

Droz, J. (1960) *L'Europe Centrale: evolution de l'idée de 'Mitteleuropa'* (Paris: Payot).

Droz, J. (1985) *Europe Between Revolutions 1815–1848* (London: Fontana).

Dubs, H. (1944) 'The Concept of Unity in China', in Pargellis, S. (ed.) *The Quest for Political Unity in World History* (American Historical Association).

Dudley, D. (1975) *Roman Society* (London: Penguin).

Dudley, E. and Novak, M. (eds) (1972) *The Wild Man Within: An Image in Western Thought from the Renaissance to Romanticism* (Pittsburgh: University of Pittsburgh Press).

Dukes, P. (ed.) (1991) *Russia and Europe* (London: Collins & Brown).

Duncan, H. (1972) *Symbols in Society* (Oxford: Oxford University Press).

Duroselle, J.-B. (1965) *L'Idée d'Europe dans l'histoire* (Paris: Denoel).

Dyson, K. (1980) *The State Tradition in Western Europe* (Oxford: Robertson).

Edelman, M. (1964) *The Symbolic Uses of Politics* (Urbana: University of Illinois Press).

Eder, K. (1985) *Geschichte als Lernprozess? Zur Pathogenese politischer Modernität in Deutschland* (Frankfurt: Suhrkamp).

Elias, N. (1978) *The History of Manners*, vol I. *The Process of Civilization* (Oxford: Blackwell).

Elias, N. (1982) *Power and Civility: The Civilizing Process* vol. II (New York: Pantheon Books).

Elliot, J. H. (1970) *The Old World and the New, 1492–1650* (Cambridge: Cambridge University Press).

Elliot, J. H. (1992) 'A Europe of Composite Monarchies', *Past and Present*, 137, 48–71.

Eliot, T. S. (1946) *Die Einheit der Europäischen Kultur* (Berlin: Habel Verlagbuchhandlung).

Eliot, T. S. (1962) 'Virgil and the Christian World', in *On Poetry and Poets* (London: Faber & Faber).

Eliot, T. S. (1978) 'The Classics and the Man of Letters', in *To Criticize the Critic* (London: Faber & Faber).

Enzenberger, H. M. (1989) *Europe, Europe: Forays into the Continent* (New York: Pantheon Books).

Epstein, F. T. (1973) 'East Central Europe as a Power Vacuum between East and West during the German Empire', in *Germany and the East: Selected Essays* (Bloomington: Indiana University Press).

Faber, R. (1979) *Abendland: Ein 'politischer Kampfbegriff'* (Hildesheim: Gerstenberg).

Fabian, J. (1983) *Time and the Other* (New York: Columbia University Press).

Fairbank, J. F. (ed.) (1968) *The Chinese World Order* (Cambridge, Mass.: Harvard University Press).

Fernhout, R. (1993) '"Europe 1993" and its Refugees', *Ethnic and Racial Studies*, 16, 493–506.

Finkielkraut, A. (1985) 'What is Europe?', *New York Review of Books*, 15 December.

Fischer, J. (1957) *Oriens-Occidens-Europa: Begriff und Gedanke 'Europa' in der Späten Antike und im Frühen Mittelalter* (Wiesbaden: Franz Steiner).

Fleming, D. F. (1961) *The Cold War and its Origins, 1917–1960*, vols I & II (London: Allen & Unwin).

Foerster, R. M. (1967) *Europa: Geschichte einer politischen Idee* (Munich: Nymphenburger).

Foucault, M. (1980a) *The Order of Things* (London, Tavistock).

Foucault, M. (1980b) *Power/Knowledge: Selected Interviews and Other Writing 1972–1977* (New York: Pantheon).

Fouracre, P. (1992) 'Cultural Conformity and Social Conservatism in Early Modern Europe', in *History Workshop*, 33, 152–61.

Frank, A. G. (1992) 'Economic Ironies in Europe: A World Economic Interpretation of East–West European Politics', *International Social Science Journal*, 44, 41–56.

Freeman, C. et al. (eds) (1991) *Technology and the Future of Europe* (London: Pinter).

Friedmann, J. B. (1981) *The Monstrous Races in Medieval Art and Thought* (Cambridge, Mass.: Harvard University Press).

Fritzemeyer, W. (1931) *Christenheit und Europa* (Munich: Oldenbourg).

Fuhrmann, M. (1981) *Europa – zur Geschichte einer kulturellen und politischen Idee* (Constance: Universitätsverlag).

Fukuyama, F. (1992) *The End of History and the Last Man* (London: Penguin).

Galtung, J. (1973) *The European Community: A Superpower in the Making* (London: Allen & Unwin).

Galtung, J. (1990) 'Cultural Violence', *Journal of Peace Research*, 27, 291–305.

Garcia, S. (ed.) (1993) *European Identity and the Search for Legitimacy,* (London: Pinter).

Garcia, S. (1993) 'Europe's Fragmented Identities and the Frontiers of Citizenship', in Garcia, op. cit.

Garton Ash, T. (1993) *In Europe's Name: Germany and the Divided Continent* (New York: Random House).

Gellner, E. (1983) *Nations and Nationalism* (Oxford: Blackwell).

Gerhard, D. (1958) 'The Frontier in Comparative View', *Studies in Comparative History and Society*, 1, 205–29.

Ghanoonparvar, M. R. (1993) *In a Persian Mirror: Images of the West and Westerners in Iranian Fiction* (Austin: University of Texas Press).

Giddens, A. (1985) *The Nation-State and Violence* (Berkeley: University of California Press).

Giesen, B. (1993) *Die Intellektuelen und die Nation* (Frankfurt: Suhrkamp).

Gillard, D. (1980) *The Struggle for Asia, 1828–1914: A Study in British and Russian Imperialism* (London: Methuen).

Gilley, S. (1981) 'Christianity and the Enlightenment: An Historical Survey', *History of European Ideas*, 1, 2, 103–21.

Gilman, S. L. (1985) *Difference and Pathology: Stereotypes of Sexuality, Race, and Madness* (Ithaca: Cornell University Press).

Gilpin, R. (1987) *The Political Economy of International Relations* (Princeton: Princeton University Press).

Gilroy, P. (1987) *There Ain't No Black in the Union Jack: The Cultural Politics of Race and Nation* (London: Hutchinson).

Glenny, M. (1990) *The Rebirth of History: Eastern Europe in the Age of Democracy* (London: Penguin).

Göcek, F. M. (1987) *East Encounters West: France and the Ottoman Empire in the Eighteenth Century* (Oxford: Oxford University Press).

Goldammer, K. (1962) *Der Mythos von Ost und West* (Munich: Reinhardt).

Gollwitzer, H. (1951) 'Zur Wortgeschichte und Sinndeutung von Europa', *Saeculum*, 2, 161–71.

Gollwitzer, H. (1964) *Europabild und Europagedanke: Beiträge zur deutschen Geistesgeschichte des 18. und 19. Jahrhundert* (Munich: Beck)

Gong, G. W. (1984) *The Standard of 'Civilization' in International Society* (Oxford: Clarendon Press).

Gorbachev, M. (1987) *Perestroika* (London: Collins).

Grahl, J. and Teague, P. (1989) 'The Cost of Neo-Liberal Europe', *New Left Review*, 174, 33–50.

Gramsci, A. (1971) *Selections from Prison Notebooks* (London: Lawrence and Wishart).

Greenberger, A. J. (1969) *The British Image of India* (London: Oxford University Press).

Greenhalgh, P. (1988) *Ephemeral Vistas: The Expositions Universelles, Great Exhibitions and World Fairs, 1851–1939* (Manchester: Manchester University Press).

Groh, D. (1961) *Russland und das Selbstverständnis Europas* (Neuwied: Luchterhand).

Gusfield, J. (1975) *Community: A Critical Response* (Oxford: Blackwell).

Habermas, J. (1976) *Legitimation Crisis* (London: Heinemann).

Habermas, J. (1984) *The Theory of Communicative Action*, vol. I (London: Heinemann).

Habermas, J. (1987) *The Theory of Communicative Action*, vol. II (Cambridge: Polity Press).

Habermas, J. (1991) 'What Does Socialism Mean Today?', in Blackbourn, op. cit.

Habermas, J. (1992) 'Citizenship and National Identity: Some Reflections on the Future of Europe', *Praxis International*, 12, 1,1–19.

Habermas, J. (1993) 'Die Festung Europa und das neue Deutschland', *Die Zeit*, May 28.

Hale, J. (1993) 'The Renaissance Idea of Europe', in Garcia, op. cit.

Halecki, O. (1950) *The Limits and Divisions of European History* (New York: Sheed & Ward).

Hall, S. (1992) 'The West and the Rest of Us', in Hall, S. and Gieben, B. (eds), *Formations of Modernity* (Cambridge: Polity Press).

Haller, M. (1990) 'The Challenge for Comparative Sociology in the Transformation of Europe', *International Social Science Journal*, 5, 183–204.

Hamm, B. (1992) 'Europe – a Challenge to the Social Sciences', *International Social Science Journal*, 44, 3–22.

Hammond, D. and Jablow, A. (1977) *The Myth of Africa* (New York: The Library of Social Science).

Hampson, N. (1984) *The Enlightenment* (London: Penguin).

Harbsmeier, M. (1985) 'Early Travels to Europe: Some Remarks on the Magic of Writing', in Barker, vol. I, op. cit.

Hargreaves, A. G. (1982) 'European Identity and the Colonial Frontier', *Journal of European Studies*, 12, 66–79.

Harle, V. (1990) 'European Roots of Dualism and its Alternatives in International Relations', in Harle, V. (ed.) *European Values in International Relations* (London: Pinter).

Hartley, J. M. (1992) 'Is Russia Part of Europe? Russian Perceptions of Europe in the Reign of Alexander I', *Cahiers du Monde russe et sovietique*, 33, 369–86.

Hauner, M. (1990) *What is Asia to Us?* (Boston: Unwin Hyman).

Hay, D. (1957) *Europe: The Emergence of an Idea* (Edinburgh: Edinburgh University Press).

Hay, D. (1980) 'Europe Revisited: 1979', *History of European Ideas*, 1, 1–6.

Hay, D. (1988) 'Italy and Barbarian Europe', in *Renaissance Essays* (London: Hambledon Press).

Hays, C. (1946) 'The American Frontier – Frontier of What?', *American Historical Review*, 51, 2, 199–216.

Hazard, P. (1990) *The European Mind: The Critical Years, 1680–1715* (New York: Fordham University Press).

Heather, D. (1990) *Citizenship: The Civic Ideal in World History, Politics and Education* (London: Longman).

Heather, D. (1992) *The Idea of European Unity* (London: Leicester University Press).

Hegel, G. W. F. (1956) *The Philosophy of History* (New York: Dover).

Hedetoft, U. (1993) 'National Identity and Mentalities of War in Three EC Countries', *Journal of Peace Research*, 30, 3, 281–99.

Heller, A. and Fehler, F. (1988) *The Postmodern Political Condition* (Cambridge: Polity Press).

Heller, A. (1991) 'The European Cornucopia', *The Irish Review*, 10, 81–90.

Herrin, J. (1987) *The Formation of Christianity* (Princeton: Princeton University Press).

Hess, A. (1978) *The Forgotten Frontier: A History of the Sixteenth Century Ibero-African Frontier* (Chicago: University of Chicago Press).

Hobsbawm, E. (1983) 'The Invention of Tradition', in Hobsbawm, E. and Ranger, T. (eds), *The Invention of Tradition* (Cambridge: Cambridge University Press).

Hobsbawm, E. (1991a) *The Age of Empire 1848–1875* (London: Cardinal).

Hobsbawm, E. (1991b) *Nations and Nationalism since 1780* (Cambridge: Cambridge University Press).

Hobsbawm, E. (1991c) 'The Return of *Mitteleuropa*', *The Guardian* (International Edition), 11 October.

Hobsbawm, E. (1991d) 'Goodbye to all that', in Blackburn, op. cit.

172   *Bibliography*

Hobsbawm, E. (1992a) 'Nationalism: Whose Fault-Line is it Anyway?', *New Statesman and Society*, 24 April, 23–6.

Hobsbawm, E. (1992b) 'The Crisis of Today's Ideologies', *New Left Review*, 192, 55–64.

Hobsbawm, E. (1992c) 'Ethnicity and Nationalism in Europe Today', *Anthropology Today*, 8, 1, 3–8.

Hobsbawm, E. (1993) 'The New Threat to History', *New York Review of Books*, 16 December, 62–4.

Hockenos, P. (1993) *Free to Hate: The Right in Post-Communist Eastern Europe* (London: Routledge).

Hodgen, M. (1964) *Early Anthropology in the Sixteenth and Seventeenth Centuries* (Philadelphia: University of Pennsylvania Press).

Hodgson, M. (1962/3) 'The Interrelations of Societies in History', *Comparative Studies in Society and History*, 5, 227–50.

Hofman, H. and Kramer, D. (eds) (1992) *Das verunsicherte Europa* (Frankfurt: Anton Hain).

Holborn, H. (1951) *The Political Collapse of Europe* (New York: Knopf).

Honour, H. (1976) *The New Golden Age: European Images of America from the Discoveries to the Present Time* (London: Allen Lane).

Horne, D. (1984) *The Great Museum* (London: Pluto).

Horsman, R. (1981) *Race and Manifest Destiny: The Origins of American Racial Anglo-Saxonism* (Cambridge, Mass.: Harvard University Press).

Hourani, A. (1980) *Europeans and the Middle East* (London: Macmillan).

Hourani, A. (1991) *Islam in European Thought* (Cambridge: Cambridge University Press).

Hulme, P. (1986) *Colonial Encounters: Europe and the Native Caribbean, 1492–1797* (London: Methuen).

Husbands, C. (1988) 'The Dynamics of Racial Exclusion and Expulsion: Racist Politics in Western Europe', *European Journal of Political Research*, 16, 701–20.

Husserl, E. (1965) 'Philosophy and the Crisis of European Man'', in *Phenomenology and the Crisis of Philosophy* (New York: Harper & Row).

Huttenback, R. A. (1976) *Racism and Empire* (Ithaca: Cornell University Press).

Huxley, J. and Haddon, A. C. (1935) *We Europeans: A Survey of 'Racial' Problems* (London: Jonathan Cape).

Hyde-Price, A. G. V. (1993) 'The System Level: The Changing Topology of Europe', in G. Wyn Rees (ed.) *International Politics in Europe* (London: Routledge)

Israel, J. (1985) *European Jewry in the Age of Mercantilism 1550–1750* (Oxford: Oxford University Press)

James, H. (1989) *A German Identity 1770–1990* (New York: Routledge).

James, H. and Stone, M. (eds) (1992) *When the Wall Came Down: Reactions to German Unification* (Routledge: London).

Jaspers, K. (1947) *Vom Europäischen Geist* (Munich: Piper).

Jennings, F. (1975) *The Invasion of America: Indians, Colonialism, and the Cant of Conquest* (Chapel Hill: University of North Carolina Press).

Johnson, P. (1993) *A History of the Jews* (London: Orion).

Joll, J. (1980) 'Europe – An Historian's View', *History of European Ideas*, 1, 7–19.

Jones, A. H. (1971) 'The Search for a Usable American Past in the New Deal Era', *American Quarterly*, 25, 710–24.

Jones, E. L. (1987) *The European Miracle*, 2nd edn (Cambridge: University Press).

Jones, W. R. (1971) 'The Image of the Barbarian in Medieval Europe', *Comparative Studies in Society and History*, 13, 1, 376–407.

Judt, T. (1994) 'The New Old Nationalism', *New York Review of Books*, 26 May, 44–51.

Juergensmeyer, M. (1993) *The New Cold War* (Berkeley: University of California Press).

Kabbani, R. (1988) *Europe's Myths of Orient* (London: Pandora Press).

Kaldor, M. (1990) *The Imaginary War: Understanding the East–West Conflict* (Oxford: Blackwell).

Kaldor, M. (1991) 'After the Cold War', in Kaldor, M. (ed.) (1991) *Europe from Below: An East–West Dialogue* (London: Verso).

Kant, I. (1957) *Perpetual Peace* (Indianapolis: Bobbs-Merrill).

Katz, J. (1980) *From Prejudice to Destruction: Anti-Semitism, 1700–1933* (Cambridge, Mass.: Harvard University Press).

Keane, J. (ed.) (1988) *Civil Society and the State* (London: Verso).

Kearney, R (ed.) (1992) *Visions of Europe* (Dublin: Wolfhound Press).

Keen, S. (1986) *Faces of the Enemy* (San Francisco: Harper & Row).

Keene, D. (1969) *The Japanese Discovery of Europe, 1720–1830*, rev. edn. (Stanford: Stanford University Press).

Kennedy, P. (1989) *The Rise and Fall of the Great Powers: Economic Change and Military Conflict from 1500–2000* (London: Fontana).

Kennedy, P. (1993) *Preparing for the Twentieth-First Century* (New York: Random House).

Keohane, R. O. (1984) *After Hegemony: Co-operation and Discord in the World Economy* (Princeton: Princeton University Press).

Kepal, G. (1994) *The Revenge of God: The Resurgence of Islam, Christianity and Judaism in the Modern World* (Cambridge: Polity Press).

Kettle, M. (1990) 'John Paul's Grand Design for Europe', *The Guardian*, 27 April.

Kiernan, V. G. (1969) *The Lords of Humankind: European Attitudes towards the Outside World in the Imperial Age* (London: Weidenfeld & Nicolson).

Kiernan, V. G. (1980) 'Europe in the Colonial Mirror', *History of European Ideas*, 1, 39–61.

Kishida, T. (1992) 'Europe and Japan', in Nelson, op. cit.

Koessler, R. and Melber, H. (1993) *Chancen internationaler Zivilgesellschaft* (Frankfurt: Suhrkamp).

Konrad, G. (1984) *Antipolitics* (New York: Harcourt Brace Jovanovich).

Kortepeter, C. M. (1973) *Ottoman Imperialism during the Reformation: Europe and the Caucasus* (London: University of London Press).

Kramer, J. (1980) *Unsettling Europe* (New York: Random House).

Kramer, J. (1988) *Europeans* (New York: Farrar, Straus & Giroux).

Kristof, L. (1968) 'The Russian Image of Europe', in Fischer, C. (ed.) *Essays in Political Geography* (London: Methuen).

Kumar, K. (1992) 'The 1989 Revolutions and the Idea of Europe', *Political Studies*, XL, 439–61.

Kumar, K. (1993) 'Civil Society: an Inquiry into the Usefulness of an Historical Term', *British Journal of Sociology*, 44, 3, 376–95.

Kundera, M. (1984) 'The Tragedy of Central Europe', *New York Review of Books*, 26 April, 33–8.

Kurz, R. (1991) *Der Kollaps der Modernisierung* (Frankfurt: Eichborn).

Kuzmics, H. (1988) 'The Civilizational Process', in Keane, op. cit.

Lach, D. F. (1965, 1977) *Asia in the Making of Europe*, vols. 1, & 2 (Chicago: University of Chicago Press).

Lambropoulos, V. (1993) *The Rise of Eurocentrism* (Princeton: Princeton University Press).

Larrain, J. (1994) *Ideology and Cultural Identity* (Cambridge, Polity).

Lash, S. and Urry, J. (1987) *The End of Organized Capitalism* (Cambridge: Polity Press).

Leibfried, S. and Pierson, P. (1992) 'Prospects for Social Europe', *Politics and Society*, 20, 3, 333–66.

Lemberg, H. (1985) 'Zur Entstehung des Osteuropabegriffs im Jahrhundert vom "Norden" zum "Osten" Europas', *Jahrbuch für Osteuropas*, 33, 48–9.

Lepenies, W. (1993) *Aufstieg und Fall der Intellektuellen in Europa* (Frankfurt: Campus Verlag).

Lewis, B. et al. (eds) (1985/6) *As Others See Us: Mutual Perceptions, East and West* (New York: *Comparative Civilization Review*, 13 & 14).

Lewis, B. (1993a) 'Europe and Islam', in *Islam and the West* (Oxford: Oxford University Press).

Lewis, B. (1993b) *The Arabs in History* (Oxford: Oxford University Press).

Lewis, (1993c) *Islam in History* 2nd edn, (Chicago: Open Court).

Leyser, K. (1992) 'Concepts of Europe in the Early and High Middle Ages', *Past and Present*, 137, 25–47.

Livey, J. (1981) 'The Europe of the Enlightenment', *History of European Ideas*, 1, 91–102.

Lomax, D. W. (1978) *The Reconquest of Spain* (London: Longman).

Lopez, R. S. (1980) *La Nascita dell'Europa Secoli V-XIV* (Turin: Giulo Einaudi)

Lorenz, W. (1994) *Social Work in a Changing Europe* (London: Routledge).

Louis, H. (ed.) (1954) 'Über den geographischen Europabegriff', *Mitteilungen der geographischen Gesellschaft in München*, 39, 73–93.

Lowenthal, D. (1990) *The Past is a Foreign Country* (Cambridge: Cambridge University Press).

Lucas, C. (ed.) (1988) *The French Revolution and the Creation of Modern Political Culture*, vol. 2, *The Political Culture of the French Revolution* (Oxford: Pergamon Press.

Luhmann, N. (1982) *The Differentiation of Society* (New York: Columbia University Press).

Lyons, F. S. L. (1963) *Internationalism in Europe, 1815–1914* (Leyden: Sythoff).

Lyotard, J.-F. (1984) *The Postmodern Condition* (Minneapolis: University of Minnesota Press).

Lyotard, J.-F. (1993) 'Europe, the Jews, and the Book', in *Political Writings* (London: UCL Press).

Macdonald, S. (ed.) (1993) *Inside European Identities* (Oxford: Berg).

MacKay, A. (1977) *Spain in the Middle Ages: From Frontier to Empire, 1000–1500* (London: Macmillan).

McNeil, W. H. (1963) *The Rise of the West* (Chicago: Chicago University Press).

McNeil, W. H. (1964) *Europe's Steppe Frontier, 1500–1800* (Chicago: University of Chicago Press).

McNeil, W. H. (1974) *The Shape of European History* (New York: Oxford University Press).

McNeil, W. H. (1986) *Poly-ethnicity and National Unity in World History* (Toronto: University of Toronto Press).

Magris, C. (1989) *Danube* (New York: Farrar, Straus & Giroux).

Maguire, J. and Noonan, J. (1992) *Ireland and Neutrality* (Cork: People First).

Malcolm, N. (1994) *Bosnia: A Short History* (London: Macmillan).

Mangone, G. J. (1954) *A Short History of International Society* (New York: McGraw-Hill).

Mann, M. (1988) 'European Development Approaching a Historical Explanation', in Baechler, op. cit.

Mann, M. (1986) *The Sources of Social Power, vol. I, A History of Power from the Beginning to AD 1760* (Cambridge: Cambridge University Press).

Mann, M. (1993) *The Sources of Social Power, vol. II, The Rise of Classes and Nation-States, 1740–1914* (Cambridge: Cambridge University Press).

Mannheim, K. (1979) *Ideology and Utopia* (London: Routledge & Kegan Paul).

Marcu, E. D. (1976) *Sixteenth Century Nationalism* (New York: Abaris).

Marcus, J. T. (1961) 'Time and the Sense of History: West and East', *Comparative Studies in Society and History*, 3, 123–39.

Marshall, P. J. and Williams, G. (1982) *The Great Map of Mankind: British Perceptions of the World in the Age of the Enlightenment* (London: Dent).

Marshall, T. H. and Bottomore, T. (1992) *Citizenship and Social Class* (London: Pluto).

Marguand, D. (1994) 'Reinventing Federalism; Europe and the Left', *New Left Review*, 203, 17– 26.

Massarella, D. (1990) *A World Elsewhere: Europe's Encounter with Japan in the Sixteenth and Seventeenth Centuries* (New Haven: Yale University Press).

Mayer, A. (1966) 'Post-War Nationalism', *Past and Present*, 34, 114–26.

Mayer, A. (1968) *Politics and Diplomacy of Peace Keeping: Containment and Counterrevolution at Versailles 1918/19* (London: Weidenfeld & Nicolson).

Mayer, A. (1981) *The Persistence of the Old Regime* (London: Croom Helm).

Mayer, A. (1988) *Why the Heavens did not Darken? The "Final Solution" in History* (New York: Pantheon Books).

Mayne, R. (1972) *The Europeans* (London: Weidenfeld & Nicolson).

Meehan, E. (1993a) 'Citizenship and Community', *Political Quarterly*, 64, 2, 172–86.

Meehan, E. (1993b) *Citizenship and the European Community* (London: Sage).

Meinecke, F. (1970) *Cosmopolitanism and the National State* (Princeton: Princeton University Press).

Mennell, S. (1989) *Norbert Elias: Civilization and the Human Self-Image* (Oxford: Blackwell).

Mestrovic, S. (1994) *The Balkanization of the West* (London: Routledge).

Metlitzki, D. (1977) *The Matter of Araby in Medieval England* (New Haven: Yale University Press).

Meyer, H. C. (1955) *Mitteleuropa in German Thought and Practice 1815–1945* (The Hague: Martinus Nijhoff).

Meyer, J. W. (1989) 'Conceptions of Christendom: Notes on the Distinctiveness of the West', in Kohn, M. (ed.) *Cross National Research in Sociology* (London: Sage).

Miles, R. (1989) *Racism* (London: Routledge).

Miles, R. (1993) 'Introduction–Europe 1993: the Significance of Changing Patterns of Migration', *Ethnic and Racial Studies*, 16, 460–6.

Milward, A. et al. (1993) *The Frontier of National Sovereignty* (London: Routledge).
Mollat du Jourdin, M. (1993) *Europe and the Sea* (Oxford: Blackwell).
Mommsen, W. J. (ed.) (1992) *Der Lange Weg nach Europa* (Berlin: edition q).
Moore, R. I. (1987) *The Formation of a Persecuting Society: Power and Deviance in Western Europe 950–1250* (Oxford: Blackwell).
Morin, E. (1987) *Penser l'Europe* (Paris: Gallimard).
Moscovici, S. (1981) 'On Social Representations', in Forgas, J. (ed.) *Social Cognition* (London: Academic Press).
Moscovici, S. (1984) 'The Phenomenon of Social Representations', in Farr, R. and Moscovici, S. (eds) *Social Representations* (Cambridge: Cambridge University Press).
Mosher, M. (1993) 'Nationalism and the Idea of Europe: How Nationalists Betray the National State', *History of European Ideas*, 16, 891–7.
Mosse, G. L. (1978) *Toward the Final Solution: A History of European Racism* (New York: Fertig).
Mudimbe, V. Y. (1988) *The Invention of Africa* (Bloomington: Indiana University Press).
Mumford, L. (1991) *The City in History* (London: Penguin).
Münch, R. (1993) *Das Projekt Europa* (Frankfurt: Suhrkamp).
Münkler, H. (1991) 'Europa als politische Idee', *Leviathan*, 19, 4, 520–41.
Naumann, F. (1915) *Mitteleuropa* (Berlin: Georg Reimer).
Najam, E, W. (1956) 'Europe, Richelieu's Blueprint for Unity and Peace', *Studies in Philology*, 53, 25–34.
Nasir, S. J. (1976) *The Arabs and the English* (London: Longman).
Nederveen Pieterse, J. (1991) 'Fictions of Europe', *Race and Class*, 32, 3, 3–10.
Nederveen Pieterse, J. (1992) *White on Black: Images of Africa and Blacks in Western Popular Culture* (New Haven: Yale University Press).
Needham, J. (1961) *Science and Civilization in China*, vol. 1 (Cambridge: Cambridge University Press).
Nelson, B. et al. (eds) (1992) *The Idea of Europe* (New York: Berg).
Neumann, F. (1942) *Behemoth: The Structure and Practice of National Socialism* (London: Gollancz).
Neumann, I. B. (1992) 'Review Essay: Identity and Security', *Journal of Peace Research*, 29, 2, 221–6.
Neumann, I. B. (1993) 'Russia as Central Europe's Constituting Other', *East European Politics and Societies*, 7, 348–69.
Neumann, I. B. and Welsh, J. M. (1991) 'The Other in European Self-Definition: An Addendum to the Literature on International Society', *Review of International Studies*, 17, 327–48.
Neulen, H. W. (1987) *Europa und das 3. Reich* (Munich: Universitas Verlag).
Nolte, H.-H. (1992) 'Europe in Global Society to the Twentieth Century', *International Social Science Journal*, 44, 23–39.
Nooteboom, C. (1993) *Wie wird man Europäer?* (Frankfurt: Suhrkamp).
Novalis (1967) 'Christenheit oder Europa', in *Schriften*, vol. 3 (Darmstadt: Wissenschaftliche Buchgesellschaft).
Obolensky, D. (1971) *The Byzantine Commonwealth: Eastern Europe 500–1453* (London: Weidenfeld & Nicolson).
Okey, R. (1986) *Eastern Europe 1740–1985*, 2nd edn (London: Unwin Hyman).
Okey, R. (1992) 'Central Europe/Eastern Europe: Behind the Definitions', *Past and Present*, 137, 102–33.

Ortega y Gasset, J. (1972) *The Revolt of the Masses* (London: Unwin).

Palmer, A. (1970) *The Lands Between: A History of East-Central Europe since the Congress of Vienna* (London: Weidenfeld & Nicolson).

Panikkar, K. M. (1953) *Asia and Western Dominance* (London: Allen & Unwin).

Papeke, S. (1992) 'Who Needs European Identity and What Could it Be?', in Nelson, op. cit.

Parker, W. H. (1960) 'Europe How Far?', *Geographical Journal*, 126, 278–97.

Parry, B. (1974) *Delusions and Discoveries: Studies in India in the British Imagination 1880–1930* (Berkeley: University of California Press).

Patnaik, E. (1990) 'Europe's Middle East: History or Invention?', *American Journal of Islamic Studies*, 7, 335–56.

Patocka, J. (1983) *Platon et l'Europe* (Lagrasse: Verdier).

Patocka, J. (1991) *L'Idée de l'Europe en Bohême* (Grenoble: Millon).

Paul, R. (1991) 'Black and Third World Peoples' Citizenship and 1992', *Critical Social Policy*, 11, 2, 52–64.

Pearce, R. H. (1953) *The Savages of America: A Study of the Indian and the Idea of Civilization* (Baltimore: Johns Hopkins Press).

Pegg, C. H. (1983) *Evolution of the European Idea 1914–1945* (Chapel Hill: University of North Carolina Press).

Pesonen, P. (1991) 'The Image of Europe in Russia Literature and Culture', *History of European Ideas*, 13, 4, 399–409.

Petrovich, M. B. (1976) *A History of Modern Serbia,* vols. 1 & 2 (New York: Harcourt Brace Jovanovich).

Phillips, C. (1987) *The European Tribe* (London: Faber & Faber).

Phillips, J. R. S. (1988) *The Medieval Expansion of Europe* (Oxford: Oxford University Press).

Pillorget, R. (1988) 'The European Tradition in Movements of Insurrection', in Baechler, op. cit.

Plato (1974) *The Republic* (London: Penguin).

Poliakov, L. (1974) *The Aryan Myth: A History of Racist and Nationalist Ideas in Europe* (New York: Basic Books).

Policar, A. (1990) 'Racism and its Mirror Images', *Telos*, 83, 99–108.

Pomian, K. (1990) *Europa und seine Nationen* (Berlin: Wagenback).

Postan, M. M. (1970) 'Economic Relations between Eastern and Western Europe', in Barraclough, G. (ed.) *Eastern and Western Europe in the Middle Ages* (London: Thames & Hudson).

Puzzo, D. A. (1964) 'Racism and the Western Tradition', *Journal of the History of Ideas*, 25, 579–86.

Rabasa, J. (1985) 'Allegories of the "Atlas" ', in Barker, vol II, op. cit.

Rabb, T. K. (1975) *The Struggle for Stability in Early Modern Europe* (Oxford: Oxford University Press).

Radice, G. (1992) *Offshore: Britain and the European Idea* (London: Tauris).

Rahimieh, N. (1990) *Oriental Responses to the West* (Leiden: Brill).

Raychaudhuri, T. (1988) *Europe Reconsidered: Perceptions of Europe in Nineteenth Century Bengal* (Delhi: Oxford University Press).

Raychaudhuri, T. (1992) 'Europe in India's Xenology: The Nineteenth Century Record', *Past and Present*, 137, 156–82.

Reuter, T. (1992) 'Medieval Ideas on Europe and their Modern Historians', *History Workshop Journal*, 33, 176–80.

Reynolds, S. (1984) *Kingdoms and Communities in Western Europe, 900–1300* (Oxford: Clarendon Press).

Riasanovsky, N. (1972) 'Asia through Russian Eyes', in Vucinich, op. cit.

Rijksbaron, A. et al. (eds), (1987) *Europe from a Cultural Perspective* (The Hague: UPR).

Robbins, R. (1991) 'The Mirror of Unreason', *Marxism Today*, March.

Roberts, J. M. (1978) *Europe, 1880–1945* (London: Longman).

Rodison, M. (1974) 'The Western Image and Studies of Islam', in Schlacht, op. cit.

Rodison, M. (1987) *Europe and the Mystique of Islam* (Seattle: University of Washington).

Rothenberg, G. E. (1966) *The Military Border in Croatia 1740–1881* (Chicago: University of Chicago Press).

Rootes, C. and Davis, H. (eds) (1994) *A New Europe? Social Change and Political Transformation* (London: UCL Press).

de Rougement, D. (1966) *The Idea of Europe* (New York: Macmillan).

de Rougement, D. (1983) *Love in the Western World* (Princeton: Princeton University Press).

de Rougement, D. (1980) 'L'Europe, Invention Culturelle', *History of European Ideas*, 1, 31–8.

Rousseau, G. S. and Porter, R. (eds) (1990) *Exoticism in the Enlightenment* (Manchester: Manchester University Press).

Rubin, M. (1992) 'The Culture of Europe in the Later Middle Ages', *History Workshop Journal*, 33, 162–75.

Saberwal, S. (1986) *India: The Roots of Crisis* (Oxford: Oxford University Press).

Saberwal, S. (1992) 'On the Making of Europe: Reflections from Delhi', *History Workshop Journal*, 33, 145–51.

Said, E. (1979) *Orientalism* (New York: Vintage).

Said, E. (1994) *Culture and Imperialism* (New York: Vintage).

Saitta, A. (1948) *Respublica Christiana agli stati uniti di Europa* (Roma: Edizioni di Storia e Letteratura).

Sale, K. (1991) *The Conquest of Paradise: Christopher Columbus and the Columbian Legacy* (London: Hodder & Stoughton).

Salecl, R. (1993) 'The Fantasy Structure of Nationalist Discourse', *Praxis International*, 13, 3, 213–23.

Salvatorelli, L. (1964) *Miti e storia* (Turin: Giulio Einaudi).

Sarkisyanz, E. (1954) 'Russian Attitudes toward Asia', *Russian Review*, 13, 245–54.

Sartre, J.-P. (1978) *What is Literature?* (London: Methuen).

Sattler, R.-J. (1971) *Europa: Geschichte und Aktualität des Begriffes* (Braunschweig: Albert Limbach).

Schieder, T. (1962) 'Bismarck und Europa', in *Begegnungen mit der Geschichte* (Göttingen: Vandenhoeck & Ruprecht).

Schlacht, J. (ed.) (1974) *The Legacy of Islam*, 2nd edn (Oxford: Oxford University Press).

Schlereth, T. J. (1977) *The Cosmopolitan Ideal of Enlightenment Thought* (Notre Dame: University of Notre Dame).

Schlögel, K. (1986) *Die Mitte liegt Ostwärts: Die Deutschen, der verlorene Osten und Mitteleuropa* (Berlin: Siedler).

Schlorske, C. E. (1980) *Fin-de-siècle Vienna: Politics and Culture* (New York: Knopf).

Schluchter, W. (1981) *The Rise of Western Rationalism: Max Weber's Developmental History* (Berkeley: University of California Press).

Schmidt, H. D. (1966) 'The Establishment of "Europe" as a Political Expression', *Historical Journal*, 9, 172–8.

Schmitt, C. (1990) 'The Plight of European Jurisprudence', *Telos,* 83, 35–122.

Schöpflin, G. (1989) 'Central Europe: Definitions New and Old', in Schöpflin and Wood, op. cit.

Schöpflin, G. and Wood, N. (eds) (1989) *In Search of Central Europe* (Totowa, New Jersey: Barnes & Noble)

Schulin, E. (1985) 'European Expansion in Early Modern Times: Changing Views on Colonial History', *History of European Ideas*, 6, 3, 253–65.

Schwoebel, R. (1967) *The Shadow of the Crescent: The Renaissance Image of the Turk, 1453–1517* (Nieuwkoop: de Graaf).

Scüzs, J. (1988) 'Three Historical Regions of Europe', in Keane, op. cit.

Sertina, I. V. (1992) 'The Moor in Africa and Antiquity: Origins and Definition', in Sertina, I. V. (ed.) *Golden Age of the Moor* (London: Transaction).

Seton-Watson, H. (1977) *Nations and States* (Boulder, Colorado: Westview Press).

Seton-Watson, H. (1989) 'What is Europe, Where is Europe? From Mystique to Politique', in Schöpflin and Wood, op. cit.

Shavit, Y. (1992) 'The "Glorious Century" or the "Cursed Century": *Fin-de-siècle* Europe and the Emergence of Modern Jewish Nationalism', in Reinharz, J. and Mosse, G. L. (eds) *The Impact of Western Nationalism* (London: Sage).

Sievernich, G. and Budde, H. (eds) (1989) *Europa und der Orient 800–1900* (Berlin: Bertelsmann).

Sinnhuber, K. A. (1954) 'Central Europe, Mitteleuropa, Europe Centrale', *Transactions of the Institute of British Geographers*, 20, 15–39.

Sitwell, W. H. (1988) 'Le Citoyen/La Citoyenne: Activity, Passivity, and the Revolutionary Concept of Citizenship', in Lucas. C. (ed.) *The French Revolution and the Creation of Modern Political Culture*, vol. II (Oxford: Pergamon Press).

Smith, A. (1992) 'National Identity and the Idea of Europe', *International Affairs*, 68, 1, 55–76.

Smith, A. (1993) 'A Europe of Nations – or the Nation of Europe', *Journal of Peace Research*, 30, 2, 129–35.

Smith, B. (1985) *European Vision and the South Pacific* (New Haven: Yale University Press).

Smith, H. N. (1950) *Virgin Land: The American West as Symbol and Myth* (Cambridge, Mass.: Harvard University Press).

Smith, M. C. and Stirk. P. M. R. (eds) (1990) *Making the New Europe: European Unity and the Second World War* (London: Pinter).

Solomos, J. and Back. L. (1994) 'Conceptualising Racism: Social Theory, Politics, and Research', *Sociology*, 28, 1, 143–61.

Soueleyman, E. (1941) *The Vision of World Peace in Seventeenth Century France* (New York: Putnam).

Southern, R. W. (1962) *Western Views on Islam in the Middle Ages* (Cambridge, Mass.: Harvard University Press).

Southgate, B. C. (1993) ' "Scattered over Europe" Transcending National Frontiers in the Seventeeth Century', *History of European Ideas*, 16, 131–7.

Spengler, O. (1971) *The Decline of the West* (London: Allen & Unwin).

Springborg, P. (1992) *Western Republicanism and the Oriental Prince* (Austin: University of Texas Press).

Steadman, J. M. (1969) The Myth of Asia (New York: Simon & Schuster).

Steiner, G. (1992) 'Culture – the Price you Pay', in Kearney, op. cit.

Stökl, G. (1965) *Das Bild des Abendlandes in den altrussischen Chroniken* (Cologne: Westdeutscher).

Strout, C. (1963) *The American Image of the Old World* (New York: Harper & Row).

Strydom, P. (1992) 'On the Concept of Europe: A Sociological Analysis of its Cultural Foundations', *Working Paper* (Cork: Centre for European Social Research, University College).

Sugar, P. F. (1977) *Southeastern Europe under Ottoman Rule 1354–1804* (Seattle: University Press).

Szamuely, T. (1988) *The Russian Tradition* (London: Fontana).

Szporluk, R. (1990) 'The Eurasia House: Problems of Identity in Russia and Eastern Europe', *Cross Currents: A Yearbook of Central European Culture*, 9, 3–15.

Taguieff, P.-A. (1990) 'The New Cultural Racism in France', *Telos*, 83, 109–22.

Talmor, E. (1980) 'Reflections on the Rise and Development of the Idea of Europe', *History of European Ideas*, 1, 63–6.

Tanner, M. (1993) *The Last Descendants of Aeneas: The Hapsburgs and the Mythic Image of the Emperor* (New Haven: Yale University Press).

Tassin, E. (1992) 'Europe: A Political Community?', in Mouffe, C. (ed.) *Dimensions of Radical Democracy* (London: Verso).

Taylor, A. J. P. (1942) *The Habsburg Empire 1815–1918* (London: Hamish Hamilton).

Taylor, A. J. P. (1988) *The Course of German History* (London: Routledge).

Tazbir, J. (1977) 'Poland and the Concept of Europe in the Sixteenth–Eighteenth Centuries', *European Studies Review*, 7, 29–45.

Tazbir, J. (1986) 'European Consciousness in Modern Times', *Hemispheres*, 5, 5–24.

Thaden, E. C. (1984) *Russia's Western Borderlands, 1710–1870* (Princeton, New Jersey: Princeton University Press).

Thapar, R. (1971) 'The Image of the Barbarian in Early India', *Comparative Studies in Society and History*, 13, 408–36.

Thompson, E. P. (1980) 'Going into Europe', in *Writing by Candlelight* (London: Merlin Press).

Thompson, E. P. (1982) 'Notes on Exterminism: The Last Stage of Civilization', in *Exterminism and Cold War*, edited by *New Left Review* (London: Verso).

Tilly, C. (1990) *Coercion, Capital, and the European States AD 990–1990* (Oxford: Blackwell).

Tilly, C. (1993) *European Revolutions 1492–1992* (Oxford: Blackwell).

de Tocqueville, A. (1948) *Democracy in America*, vols 1 & 2 (New York: Knopf)

Todd, E. (1990) *L'Invention de l'Europe* (Paris: Seuil).

Todorov, T. (1993) *On Human Diversity: Nationalism, Racism and Exoticism in French Thought* (Cambridge Mass.: Harvard University Press).

Touraine, A. 'European Countries in a Post-National Era', in Rootes and Davis, op. cit.

Toynbee, A. (1954) '"Asia" and "Europe": Facts and Fantasies', in *A Study of History*, vol. 8 (London: Oxford University Press).

Toynbee, A. (1949) *Civilization on Trial* (London: Oxford University Press).

Toynbee, A. (1953a) 'Islam and the West', in *The World and the West* (London: Oxford University Press).

Toynbee, A. (1953b) 'Russia and the West', in *The World and the West* (London: Oxford University Press).

Toynbee, A. (1962) *The Present-Day Experiment in Western Civilization* (London: Oxford University Press).

Treverton, G. F. (1992) *America, Germany, and the Future of Europe* (Princeton: Princeton University Press).

Trevor-Roper, H. R. (1953) *Hitler's Table Talk, 1941–44* (London: Weidenfeld & Nicolson).

Trotsky, L. (1971) *Europe and America: Two Speeches on Imperialism* (New York: Pathfinder Press).

Troeltsch, E. (1977) 'Der Europäismus', in *Gesammelte Schriften*, vol. 3 (Tübingen: Scienta Verlag Aalen).

Truettner, W. H (ed.) (1991) *The West as America: Reinterpreting Images of the Frontier, 1820–1920* (London: Smithsonian Institute Press).

Turner, F. J. (1921) *The Frontier in American History* (New York: Holt).

Ullmann, W. (1969) *The Carolingian Renaissance and the Idea of Kingship* (London: Methuen).

Umar, M. (1988) 'The Role of European Imperialism in Muslim Countries', *Islamic Quarterly*, 32, 2, 77–100.

Vajda, M. (1988) 'East-Central European Perspectives', in Keane, op. cit.

Valery, P. (1973) *Regards sur le monde actuel* (Paris: Vialetay).

Vaughan, D. M. (1954) *Europe and the Turk: A Pattern of Alliances 1350–1700* (Liverpool: University Press).

Vogel, U. (ed.) (1991) *The Frontiers of Citizenship* (London: Macmillan).

Voyenne, B. (1964) *Histoire de l'idée Européene* (Paris: Payot).

Vucinich, W. (ed.) (1972) *Russia and Asia* (Stanford: Hoover Institution Press).

Waever, O. (1992) 'Nordic Nostalgia: Northern Europe after the Cold War', *International Affairs*, 68, 1, 77–102.

Waever, O. et al. (1993) *Identity, Migration and the New Security Agenda in Europe* (London: Pinter).

Wallace, W. (1990) *The Transformation of Western Europe* (London: Royal Institute of International Affairs).

Wallace-Hadrill, J. M. (1985) *The Barbarian West 400–1000* (Oxford: Blackwell).

Wallach, R. (1972) *Das Abendländische Gemeinschaftsbewusstsein im Mittelalter* (Hildesheim: Gerstenberg).

Wallerstein, I. (1974) *The Modern World System* (New York: Academic Press).

Wallerstein, I. (1980) *The World System II* (New York: Academic Press).

Wallerstein, I. (1993) 'The World-System after the Cold War', *Journal of Peace Research*, 30, 1, 1–6.

Walvin, J. (1973) *Black and White: The Negro and English Society, 1555–1945* (London: Allen Lane).

Webb, W. P. (1952) *The Great Frontier* (Boston: Houghton Mifflin).

Weber, M. (1958) *The City* (New York: Free Press).

Wehler, H.-U. (1988) *Aus der Geschichte lernen?* (Munich: Beck).

Weidenfeld, W. (1976) *Konrad Adenauer und Europe* (Bonn: Europa-Union Verlag).

Weidenfeld, W. (ed.) (1985) *Die Identität Europas* (Bonn: Bundeszentrale für politische Bildung).

Weinberg, G. (1964) 'Hitler's Image of the United States', *American Historical Review*, 4, 1006–21.

Welsh, J. M. (1993) 'A Peoples' Europe: European Citizenship and European Identity' (Florence: Working Papers, European University Institute).

Wieczynski, J. L. (1976) *The Russian Frontiers: The Impact of Borderlands upon the Course of Early Russian History* (Charlottesville: University Press of Virginia).

Williams, R. (1976) 'Civilization' in *Keywords: A Vocabulary of Culture and Society* (London: Fontana).

Winkler, H. and Kaelble, H. (eds) (1993) *Nationalismus, Nationalitäten, Supranationalität: Europa nach 1945* (Stuttgart: Cotta).

Wirsling, G. (1932) *Zwischeneuropa und die deutsche Zukunft* (Jena: Eugen Diederichs).

Wittfogel, K. A. (1957) *Oriental Despotism* (New Haven: Yale University Press).

Wittkower, R. (1977) *Allegory and the Migration of Symbols* (London: Thames & Hudson).

Wittram, R. (1973) *Russia and Europe* (London: Thames & Hudson).

Wolf, E. (1982) *Europe and the People without History* (Berkeley: University of California Press).

Wolff, P. (1968) *The Awakening of Europe* (London: Penguin).

Woolf, S. (1989) 'French Civilization and Ethnicity in the Napoleonic Empire', *Past and Present*, 124, 96–120.

Woolf, S. (1991) *Napoleon's Integration of Europe* (London: Routledge).

Woolf, S. (1992) 'The Construction of a European World-View in the Revolutionary-Napoleonic Years', *Past and Present*, 137, 72–101.

Wyrwa, T. (1987) L'Idée Européenne dans la Résistance à travers la presse clandestine en France et en Pologne 1939–1945 (Paris: Nouvelles Editions Latines).

Yapp, M. E. (1992) 'Europe in the Turkish Mirror', *Past and Present*, 137, 134–55.

Young, R. (1990) *White Mythologies: Writing History and the West* (London: Routledge).

Zijderveld, A. (1972) *The Abstract Society* (London: Allen Lane).

Zizek, S. (1993) 'Caught in Another's Dream in Bosnia', in Ali and Lifschulz, op. cit.

Index